Why the American People Must Fight Back!

- Our tax laws are destroying the middle class.

- The welfare program is a national disgrace.

- Money totally corrupts the election system.

- Scores of federal agencies are useless and should be closed.

- Too many politicians have developed the habit of lying.

- The federal budget purposely fudges to fool the people.

- Because of Washington, state governments are out of control.

- The two parties have become a powerful and privileged oligarchy.

- Lobbyists falsely manipulate the democratic process.

- Government bureaucracies are too large and too pampered.

- Our Social Security and Medicare funds are stolen by Washington.

FOR A PENETRATING DIAGNOSIS OF *ALL* THAT'S ROTTEN IN WASHINGTON—AND HOW TO FIX IT— READ ON. . . .

A CALL FOR REVOLUTION

HOW GOVERNMENT IS STRANGLING AMERICA —AND HOW TO STOP IT

MARTIN L. GROSS

Ballantine Books • New York

To my wife

Copyright © 1993 by Martin Gross

All rights reserved under International
and Pan-American Copyright Conventions. Published
in the United States by Ballantine Books, a division of Random
House, Inc., New York, and simultaneously in Canada
by Random House of Canada Limited, Toronto.

Library of Congress Catalog Card Number: 93-73731

ISBN: 0-345-38773-2

Cover design by Richard Hasselberger

Manufactured in the United States of America

First Edition: November 1993

10 9 8 7 6 5 4 3 2 1

"Were we directed from Washington when to sow and when to reap, we should soon want for bread."

THOMAS JEFFERSON

CONTENTS

Chapter One

The Coming Revolt

"The federal government has grown stale, wasteful, inefficient, bureaucratic, and is failing the American people. Rock 'em, sock 'em, shake 'em-up changes are what the American people want."

Who said this? Some mustached wild anarchist? Some angry proponent of small government? Someone like Martin L. Gross, author of *The Government Racket: Washington Waste from A to Z?*

No. Give up? It was Al Gore, Vice President of the United States, an exemplar of the Washington Establishment, who spent sixteen years in the U.S. Congress doing more than his fair share of taxing and spending. The occasion was the

day before the release of the "National Performance Review,"
his much-awaited report on "reinventing government."

Why the sudden conversion, the abrupt realization that
Washington is the core reason for American discontent?

For years, Washington has been in a state of denial, refus-
ing to admit that the federal government is irrational and the
cause of much of the nation's struggle and confusion, let alone
acknowledging its $4.3 trillion debt and a yearly deficit that ap-
proaches $300 billion—$400 billion if the truth be known.

Then why 'fess up now?

Because the antigovernment forces, once considered
"crackpots" with a mad Jeffersonian delusion, have been
making their mark indelibly on the national consciousness.

The Perot movement, my book, other works, numerous
television exposures of waste following publication of my
work, ferocious talk-show hosts and their super-verbal listen-
ers, plus the heightened activity of the Citizens Against Government Waste, the National Taxpayers Union, and other
public interest groups, have all fused into what I call "THE
MOVEMENT," a coalition to save America from itself.

The stirrings of revolution are afoot in the land.

No one ever said that Bill Clinton's absent father sired a
fool. And despite Al Gore's robotic reputation, he's a good
student and an accomplished politician. The new team could
hear the rumblings of a testy, insecure public. In a 1993 *Washington Post*/ABC opinion poll, 80 percent of the public confirmed that the "country needs to make major changes in the
way government works."

The discontent, even anger, is deeper than Washington
believes. One poll which has measured response to the question: "Do you expect the federal government to do the right
thing?" has dropped from a 76 percent "yes" in the 1960s to
only a 20 percent approval today. And the average American
now thinks that forty-eight cents on every tax dollar is

wasted—an accurate, if understated, belief. The vox populi is
sorely vexed.

But things are different now, right? Finally, the critics
and the Establishment ostensibly agree. At least according to
Mr. Gore, the White House is in the same corner as the
"crackpots." Those in power seem to concur that the federal
government is the pits—fiscally, managerially, in size, respon-
siveness, and otherwise (fill in your own insult). Now that the
Vice President and President are aboard the revolution, the
diagnosis has surely been made and we have only to await
the cure. Right?

Wrong. And don't hold your breath.

The White House could see the obvious political gain of
tapping this discontent. But Washington, the thief of our national treasure, cannot be rehabilitated by tinkering. To pull
off a true solution, they would have to make *massive* cuts of
hundreds of billions of dollars per year in unneeded spending.

Instead of that, the administration spent six months an-
alyzing, projecting, and promising. Anticipation was high and
great fanfare sounded throughout the land about a miracle
that would truly change government as we know it and control the out-of-control operation. The result was the "National
Performance Review."

And does it live up to its expectations?

Hardly. In fact, it's not unlike the amateur violinist who
stands on the stage and apes the facial expressions of Jascha
Heifetz. But when his bow moves, all that comes out is
scratchy, discordant squeaks.

How much money does the Gore plan save? If *all* the
suggestions are implemented, the entire "reinvention" will
save $108 billion in five years, only 1.3 percent of all govern-
ment spending. That's less than $22 billion a year, a feeble
goal that this author could accomplish with Mr. Clinton before his morning jog. (I will *walk* alongside.) Some $8 billion
of the total are actually new user fees. In the real world, $75

billion in savings over five years is more likely—*if* the plan
works. That's $15 billion a year, much less than the increased
spending of the administration, which is estimated at $32 bil-
lion a year.

The reduction is petty cash for a government in which
the yearly overhead—not salaries, pensions, benefits, entitlements, and programs, just paperclips to limousines—is now
$356 *billion*, more than the entire budget of France, a nation
replete with programs for the working and middle classes.

Why so miserly a remedy from Washington? We're dealing with smart people, but the White House *falsely* sold the
program to a good-news-hungry nation. As Elaine Kamarek,
Gore's spokesman said, "This is not an exercise in budget cutting."

Nor, it seems, is it primarily a waste watch or a waste
cutter. Nor is it a policy adviser that declares that too much
money is being spent on a particular program or department.
Instead, states the Gore report, it is "focused primarily on
how government should work, not on *what* it should do. Our
job was to improve performance in areas where policymakers
had already decided government should play a role."

Their caveat doesn't make the shallow cuts any more
palatable. On the fiasco of job training, for example, the report says the "system is fundamentally broken." One would
think so. As I and now the Vice President have explained,
there are *150* different training and employment programs operating out of *fourteen* agencies. According to the Inspector
General of Labor, the cost is $17 billion a year. Yet 70 percent
of the jobs obtained are for $5 an hour or less—positions that
need no training.

What does the Gore report do about eliminating these
wasteful programs and replacing them with a single effective
one, such as the heralded German apprentice system? The report's proposal is quite unradical. It advocates combining the
Food Stamp Training Program with the Veteran's Employment

and Training Service. Savings? Sixty-six *million* dollars over five years. A nice token for a "broken" system that now expects to spend $85 *billion* in the same period.

Fourteen agencies just for job training? You bet. In fact, some government functions are now handled by twenty different federal bureaus simultaneously. Unfortunately, Overlap and Duplication is not the name of a prestigious Washington law firm.

Gore's report does suggest eliminating a few programs, such as the now-infamous wool and honey subsidies. But the only telling reduction is in manpower—152,000 more than the announced 100,000 over five years, mainly through attrition.

Because 160,000 government employees leave, die, or retire each year, I had originally recommended a 650,000 reduction. But the federal government felt it could only manage 100,000. Now they have raised the ceiling in response to public impatience.

Actually, as we shall see in Chapter 12, we can eliminate over 725,000 federal employees—about one third the work staff—through attrition, with assurance that the public will never miss them or even know they're gone.

The Gore report does deserve credit for making this small, first hesitant step to slow down the Mammoth. But if not a cost-cutter, what is it? It should have been advertised as what it truly is: a management study, with many suggestions on how to make the big, bad government work somewhat better—much like helping a blind, crippled old bull elephant traverse the savanna. But once there, the animal is still incapable of operating in the real world.

The Vice President seeks a "customer-friendly" government with the service and politeness found at an elegant, overly expensive boutique. A nice thought, but the taxpayer-customer might find it friendlier if the price were right. Walmart is infinitely more popular than Henri Bendel.

If the report is just a way of co-opting the Movement, as

some fear, then it is a grave disservice to the nation. However, if it's the beginning of a series of large bipartisan cuts to reduce the size of government, then it's worth at least a touch of the hoopla. We shall look more closely at some of the Vice President's suggestions in our chapters on waste and the Cabinet.

Big Time Crisis

Meanwhile, whether the administration is sincere or not, America, the land of big government, is in crisis, big time.

Citizen grumblings are rising. Where, people are asking, is the boom politicians were so sure was coming? Everything was supposed to be in place. Low interest rates and low inflation, achieved at the end of the Bush era, were going to be the springboard for the "traditional" big burst in the economy.

But unemployment still hovers near 7 percent, which is itself a fake statistic engineered to pacify the population. It doesn't include a multitude of part-timers, does not count the millions of adults on full-time welfare, and excludes those who've given up looking for jobs and are scrounging out a living in catch-as-catch-can enterprises.

It's becoming increasingly clear that this is not a transitory crisis, one that can be solved by a quick fix on the boom side of the business cycle or the loose talk of Keynesian economics—priming the pump of a dry well. This time the failure is all encompassing, economically and philosophically.

We have put up several scapegoats: Japan, changeover from the Cold War, poor education. All are surely contributors, but the main villain is so close, once so respected, and so intimately tied with our lives and history, that it's difficult to point the finger of blame.

Yet the charge is inescapable. Simply stated: the main cause of our continuing pain is none other than the United States government—in Washington, the state houses, and town halls.

The root failure stems from the mother of all governments, Washington, D.C. That center of waste and irresponsibility is not only bankrupting the nation, but over the last thirty years has turned its back on those who fed it: the overtaxed, overworked, neglected middle class. There's no doubt that America is suffering from a thirty-year infection of the pocketbook and soul, one that is crippling a once-healthy nation.

Government at all levels has emerged as our number one growth industry. Sadly, we are becoming a nation of apparatchiks instead of productive workers. In fact, for the first time in American history—even in the history of the Western industrialized world—there are more people working for government at all levels (18.7 million) than in manufacturing (18.1 million).

Since manufacturing jobs *make* money while government jobs *take* money, this has become an equation for economic disaster. The crossover took place in 1992 and is continuing. In just one decade, the 5 million edge of manufacturing over government has disappeared.

The cost of all this is staggering. We've heard about the 24 percent bite of the Gross Domestic Product (GDP) taken by Washington, which is three times larger, in real dollars, than FDR's so-called big government at the height of the Depression.

But the total fiscal damage also includes the cost of running the states and the crazy quilt of local governments. In addition to Washington and the fifty states, the nation boasts 86,000 governmental units, including 3,043 counties, over 19,000 municipalities, and untold towns and villages, ad infinitum. The cost has been setting records for the past four decades. In FDR's days, some seventeen cents on the dollar went to government at all levels. By the time of Harry Truman, it was still a sensible twenty-two cents. Under John F. Kennedy, it reached the thirty-cent level, the precipitous beginnings of what we are now witnessing, and suffering through.

And today? Let's do the math together. Of the $6.15 trillion GDP, $2.55 trillion nonduplicated dollars goes to government at all levels—more than 41 percent of the GDP! With the new taxes and expenditures, the figure will pass the 42 percent level in 1994, a recipe for disaster. *America's prime goal should be to return the cost of government to the thirty-cent level, a cut of thirty percent!*

Bipartisan Blame

This is not just partisan excess. Though the wasteful ideas were mainly developed by Democrats, the opposition Republican party long ago learned to first accept, then embrace, big government. Today, the distinction between Jimmy Carter and George Bush has become blurred. Having signed on, both parties have done equally well in spending our national treasure.

The result? An American government that is now a model of bipartisan excess, even stupidity. Who's to blame? The Congress? The presidency? Or the people?

Both branches of government are at fault. As far as Congress goes, people are beginning to suspect the awful truth: Representative government in the United States no longer works. And the Presidents, of both parties, have been the overseers of excessive growth of the Executive Branch, including scores of programs that cost billions and fail to produce.

What about the people? Isn't there a maxim that says *we get the government we deserve*? Yes, but it's simply not true. The American people deserve much better, but they haven't had the education or ammunition to fight the shrewd political class for their own protection.

One thing they do know. They can no longer afford their politicians or their government, and neither can the economy. After taxes and monies borrowed by government, there's not enough left over to run a vibrant private sector. This is especially true of middle-class workers, who earn from $30,000 to $80,000, pay most of the taxes, and receive the least in return from the bloated enterprise.

In my prior book, I estimated the waste in the federal government at $300 billion a year, or about 25 percent of the non–Social Security outlays. I have since raised the possibility of savings to an estimated $325 billion. But if we look at the entire $2.55 trillion government bill, we find that as Washington drags the states into a fiscal morass, the total waste of government, nationwide, is closer to $600 billion annually, and possibly more.

Some of it is the fault of the states and localities who have fallen into the trap of acting like "little Washingtons," replete with excess staffs and too-large budgets.

But much of it is not their fault. As programs expand in Washington, they force states to pay their share of "mandates" for welfare, roads, education, pollution control—money local taxpayers can no longer afford.

Washington dictates but the locals pay. In addition to such partially funded mandates as Medicaid, states and localities are increasingly burdened by hundreds of "unfunded mandates," the newest of the government rackets. Just last year, seven new bills passed by Congress required states to spend an additional $1.68 billion of their own money to satisfy the capital's insatiable requirements.

Little wonder that since 1960, the cost of state and local government in the United States has risen some 350 percent in *real dollars* and has now passed the milestone trillion-dollar mark. That number, which represents $15,000 a year for each family of four, is in addition to the $23,000 per family that the federal government now spends. The total—$38,000 of government cost per each such family—is too overwhelming to even contemplate.

Washington sets a poor example for everyone. Regardless of which party has been in power in the White House, the cost of supporting the federal government has gone up 10 percent a year compounded for almost all the last twenty years. As every schoolchild knows (or should know), compounding costs at that rate is a formula for self-destruction.

From a $200 billion budget in 1973, federal spending has skyrocketed to $1.5 trillion in 1993, more than a sevenfold increase. If the cost had just followed inflation like others, the government today would be only *half* its present gargantuan size.

The money being spent is not just printed by Washington. It is drained from the private sector, which is starving for capital. But Washington is there first. In a recent year, according to the Bureau of the Public Debt (yes, there is one!), Treasury securities traded to the tune of $1.7 trillion, eating up an enormous slice of all credit available to the nation.

Madison's Prophecy
Two hundred years ago, James Madison warned about the danger of an overcentralized, overexpensive government. If we weren't careful, he said, our democracy would turn into an oligarchy run by politicians in Washington. America, circa 1994, is proof of the soundness of his prophecy.

Why, I am often asked, do we put up with it?

For many reasons, including the government's skill at propaganda and obfuscation, which hides their failures. And as a trusting, well-intentioned people, Americans ascribe the same virtue to others, sometimes falsely. Lastly, voters are diverted from examining the truth by the entertaining theatrics of government, part of Washington's pageant of bread and circuses.

We're regularly treated to the soap opera of politics, from White House televangelism to the hype surrounding the capital's real life goings-on. Recently, we've been titillated by such personalities and situations as Lani Guinier, Zoë Baird,

Kimba Wood and Nannygate, Travelgate, and homosexuals in the military, among others.

Of course, this is nothing new. We've wept at or cheered Anita Hill and Clarence Thomas, Gennifer Flowers, Irangate, Watergate, and even going back as far as Senator Joe McCarthy and Nixon's Checkers speech. We've also heard the noise of continual ideological sparring. Conservatives wail at perversions of the mass media and the loss of authority and standards. Liberals counter by caterwauling about the twelve years of Republican indifference to the poor, the minorities, and the environment.

But while the pyrotechnics have been going on, innocent Americans have had their pockets picked—by experts. Citizens of every tribe and stripe have become the victims of America's manipulators. Their identity is no secret: the "political class," the army of politicians, bureaucrats, lobbyists, ideologues, and assorted hangers-on of both parties who run the inefficient, unresponsive, wasteful, poorly organized, expensive anti-intellectual federal government in Washington.

Without fear of reasonable contradiction, we can state that the U.S. government, circa 1994, has evolved over three decades into the worst in the history of the Republic. And it's costing us more than two seats on the aisle, both in cash and damage to the national fiber.

No longer is politics a charming spectator sport, as it was thirty years ago. If not a matter of life and death, it is surely one of security and attainment of the American dream. Each year, our politicians use fresh pseudologic to convince us to part with more of our money for services we do not want, do not truly understand, and generally never receive. The result is that the apocalypse of the U.S. government comes nearer every day as the critical mass of taxes, debt, and expenditures becomes impossible to sustain.

Does the mood of the people reflect any of this? It's beginning to. For years, Americans drew on their confidence in government, built up over centuries. Busy at their labors, they felt it was safe to leave the work of politics to politicians.

That has proven to be a grave mistake, and there are now signs that the citizens are awakening to the truth in increasing numbers. For the first time in American history, government is seen as an *enemy* rather than a friend, a truly sad commentary.

People, for example, have overwhelmingly expressed their opinion, by a two-thirds majority in polls and at the ballot box, about three vital instruments needed to reform modern democracy: *the line-item veto, term limits, and the balanced budget amendment.*

But their representatives in Congress have turned their backs on all three, indifferent to the people's will and arrogant about their superior knowledge of government—little of which actually exists. The result? Never before have so many people paid so much and received so little in return, both materially and spiritually, from those in control of their nation.

According to a recent Gallup poll, 65 percent of Americans disapprove of Congress and believe that the nation is "headed in the wrong direction." Voters rank Congressmen's honesty twenty-fourth in a field of twenty-five occupations, perhaps a reflection on car salesmen in the basement of the list.

An Awakened Public

But no longer is it mere grumblings on the supermarket line. Americans are finally finding their voice and expressing their opinions in letters to the editor, on radio and television call-in shows, and in voluminous mail and phone protests to Congress. The White House itself receives 65,000 phone calls, telegrams, and faxes a day, much of it less than salutary.

And for the first time, the once-silent middle class is organizing into voter movements, from local taxpayer groups to

the Citizens Against Government Waste to the National Taxpayers Union to Ross Perot's United We Stand.

The Government Racket: Washington Waste from A to Z,
first published in June 1992, helped to ignite that fire. I've testified before the U.S. Senate and shared my findings with
staffers of the House Budget Committee. From the White
House, I've personally heard that my research has been included in the Vice President's Performance Review. (One deserved kudo for my readers: The White House received so
many copies of the book that they "could open up a used
bookstore," as they put it.)

Voters are beginning to realize that politicians are masters of the art of deception. On television talk shows and at
press conferences they speak in a jargon all their own, with
buzzwords meant to both mollify and falsely inspire the people at the same time.

Politicians have always been somewhat deceptive, but
the corruption of words is reaching new heights. Taxes become spending cuts. Spending becomes investment. Budget
arithmetic is manipulated. Hidden agendas proliferate. It's
even possible that we're no longer witnessing traditional political hype. More and more, the lying seems pathological—
the mouthings of untruths almost by reflex, a dangerous new
precedent.

In the world of budgets, as we shall see, the government
obfuscates heavily, using fake accounting to cover its blun-
ders. The interest on the $4.3 trillion debt is announced at be-
ing some $200 billion a year when it is actually more like $300
billion. The deficit numbers are another Washington cover-up.
Estimated at $275 billion for 1993, the *unmassaged* truth is
that it's closer to $375 billion!

Overblown, deceptive rhetoric leads to false theories,
expensive programs, and poor performance. In a fervent attempt to eliminate poverty in America, a myriad of seventy-
eight welfare programs operating out of six different agencies

end up *increasing poverty* faster than any government can either alleviate or pay for it (see Chapter 5).

There is no limit to the shamelessness. The Social Security "trust fund," which does not actually exist, is officially labeled by Washington as "solvent." But there's not a penny in the till as the government takes the entire giant surplus each year to pay the cost of inefficient government.

Politicians prevaricate when the spirit moves them. They also like to substitute money for brains, which can be in short supply in the political store. Needed social programs, as in support of Indians, for instance, are operated haphazardly and hidden from the nation's purview. In this case, *twelve* different federal agencies spend $5 billion a year, or $20,000 on each Indian family of four—who have income less than one-third that amount.

The combination of government waste and inefficiency can lead to citizen paranoia. If we listen to the underground rumbles, we can even hear whispers that it's all a careful conspiracy, a debacle arranged by politicians, bureaucrats, lobbyists, lawyers, and various rogues of the Left and Right.

Is there such an organized conspiracy? No, there isn't. If there were, the solution would be simple. We'd uncover it and cut off its head. No, the present failure of government is based on ignorance and lack of common sense. It's compounded by the hubris of politicians and bureaucrats who know very little about the government they run, and have lost touch with the majority of the American people—if they ever had it.

But if there were such a conspiracy aimed at destroying the American nation, they could do no better than to slavishly imitate the present operation of Washington, D.C.

The Government Racket exposed hundreds of wasteful practices, all symptoms of irresponsible government. This book intends to follow up by uncovering the root causes of those symptoms and showing how to correct them. We'll try to lay out the diagnosis, then offer a plan on how to down-size, reform, and reorganize the government so that it once again serves the broad mass of the American people. This will be much deeper and more potentially effective than anything ever proposed by our national leaders.

To begin that overhaul, we first need a bill of particulars of flaws that can be rectified. Some are obvious, many are obscure. But together, these errors of judgment and organization, of misplaced emphasis and expenditure, make up a pattern that must be addressed if America is to survive intact.

To put it in melodramatic terms: Either the American people will defeat the oppressive excesses of Washington, or Washington will defeat us, ending the story of the most successful nation in history.

No minor reform will do the job. First, there must be new citizen awareness, followed by a program to clean up all that has gone wrong. We are not witnessing a self-mending illness. Our government has thrown the natural rhythm of economics into disarray. Nor is this a temporary cold in the body politic that can be cured by still more platitudes, additional spending, false bookkeeping, extra taxes, and childish political jargon, from whatever source.

What is needed is a *Citizen's Revolution*, one organized by an educated populace with an agenda for real change.

Bill of Indictment

The charges are not minor. They have been put together here as a Bill of Indictment. Many will be detailed in individual chapters, which will not only dissect the fault but offer a detailed plan to correct what is wrong. Together, it will hopefully serve as a handbook for that Citizen's Revolution designed to save the nation.

Naturally, this must all be done peacefully. But it cannot be accomplished without grassroots agitation, even anger. Until the people reach a true state of exasperation, little will happen. Hitler was defeated by the righteous hatred of Americans, as was the totalitarianism of the Soviet Union. Nothing less is needed to defeat our new enemy—expensive and inefficient American government.

Here then, is the first step, a thirty-three-point Bill of Indictment:

Article 1:   Our tax laws are destroying the middle class.

Article 2:   The federal budget is purposely obfuscated to fool the people.

Article 3:   Despite small reforms, money totally corrupts our election system.

Article 4:   The welfare program is a national disgrace.

Article 5:   There is no sound theory sustaining the present federal operation.

Article 6:   The cabinet system is archaic and must be reshaped.

Article 7:   Lying by our elected officials is becoming commonplace.

Article 8:   The bureaucracy in Washington, and in the states, is too large, overpaid, and overprotected.

Article 9:   The two-party system has become a privileged oligarchy.

Article 10:   The oversight of government operations is weak and ineffective.

Article 11:   Government agencies knowingly duplicate the work of others.

Article 12:   Social Security and Medicare funds are being falsely taken by the government, cheating both the aged and the young who pay.

Article 13:   There are too many unneeded layers in American government.

Article 14:   The states and cities are being bankrupted by federal mandates, and by their own waste and overreaching.

Article 15: Uncontrolled illegal immigration is costing us billions and lowering the pay scale of American workers.

Article 16: Scores of federal agencies are useless and should be closed.

Article 17: Government management is overstaffed and inefficient.

Article 18: Politicians have become a special class with selfish interests.

Article 19: Most voters are denied the "Initiative," the right to directly express themselves at the ballot box.

Article 20: Most Americans have no "referendum" approval of legislation.

Article 21: The electoral system must be changed to ensure majority rule.

Article 22: Former public officials are part of a destructive lobbying system.

Article 23: The decline of American industry has been hastened by our government.

Article 24: Bureaucrats have no incentive to save money.

Article 25: The presidency needs reform, and must have real veto power.

Article 26: Perks at all levels are a debilitating force.

Article 27: The expensive feast of congressional pork must be stopped.

Article 28: Subsidies, to farms and other interests, are self-defeating.

Article 29: Uncle Sam is the world's largest, least efficient banker.

Article 30: "Sunset laws" must be used to stop failed schemes.

Article 31: Congress is too overgrown and philosophically corrupt to properly do its job.

Article 32: Government as a growth industry is a threat to America.

Article 33: Several new constitutional amendments are needed to protect our democracy.

The indictment seems harsh, especially to those who say, "Hasn't it always been this way?" Isn't "government inefficiency" an oxymoron?

Not true. Nostalgia aside, things used to be much better.

Until 1913, when the Sixteenth Amendment repealed the Founding Fathers' prohibition against any "capitation" or "direct" tax, Americans neither filed nor paid any income tax. Even after that, few paid taxes until the start of World War II, when only one in seven people even filed.

The first real strain on government began with deficit financing during the Great Depression. But that was done with a sharp pencil. In 1938, FDR spent less than 8 percent of the GDP on the "big government" of the New Deal, even while feeding millions.

During Harry Truman's postwar administration, the government was still relatively small and the people strong. The interest on the long bond was then 3 percent. Taxes were low, leaving people's pockets full and their spirits high.

From 1947 through 1952, the government paid for the GI Bill of Rights, the most far-reaching and successful piece of social legislation in history. Truman spent billions on the Marshall Plan to rebuild Europe, and America fought the Korean War. Despite that, HST brought in a budget *surplus* of $16 billion, or some $200 billion in today's money.

By 1960, when Dwight Eisenhower was winding down his two-term administration, the nation was still healthy. The long bond was 4 percent, fixed mortgages were around 5 percent, Americans had the highest hourly wages in the world, and the national debt was lower in real dollars than it had been at the end of World War II.

We had, by any measure of performance, a Good Society, one headed by inexpensive and beneficent government.

What happened?

Government expansion began psychologically with the Kennedy administration, but JFK had little time to implement his ideas. That was followed by the aggressive Lyndon Baines Johnson period, with an experiment in big government that dwarfed FDR's. The *Good Society* no longer seemed sufficient, and the political class began to seek out the *Perfect Society*. The federal government was chosen as the vehicle and money as the fuel.

Though begun by Democrats, Republican Presidents signed on despite their antigovernment rhetoric. After Johnson, from Nixon through Ford, we saw the fiscal excesses of Democrat Carter and Republican Bush. Any hope for modesty in government ceased. It was, and is, a bipartisan fiasco.

Courtesy of the political class, the Good Society no longer exists, nor does the sought-after Perfect Society. In seeking one, without reason, we lost the other. In its place is a confused, wounded nation seeking some way back to the internal peace and affluence of a generation ago.

"But why worry?" the political class responds. "After all, we're the richest country in the world and we can afford anything."

No, we're not. This myth of wealth is one of the reasons we stumble so badly in assessing what we can and cannot afford. It was true in the 1950s and 1960s, when we controlled world markets and had relatively inexpensive government.

But no longer. In 1975, the hourly wage for American workers was still a respectable (for the time) $5.30 an hour, which was topped by only some Scandinavian countries. But it soon started on its way down as we began to lose our wealth in the 1970s.

What about today? While we've stood still, others have pulled ahead during the last twenty years. Our hourly manufacturing wage is now $12.50. That's not only topped by Japan and Canada, but by *nine* countries in Europe, including Bel-

gium and Austria. Workers in the western part of Germany receive a true living wage: $18 an hour, or 40 percent more than
we do.

The earnings of American workers have actually been
going *backwards*. In 1973, the average hourly wage of non-
managers was $145 a week. Today, adjusted for inflation, that
would be $465. But do today's workers get that much? No. As
of the spring of 1993, the weekly wage was only $370—a loss
of almost $100.

The broad middle class has been a major victim of
our thirty-year government binge. When we look at most
Americans—including workers, managers, and professionals—the people who pay the bulk of the $515 billion fed-
eral income taxes, we see the damage. They've been going
nowhere, fast.

American families have a combined income of less than
$36,000, before taxes. How does that compare with twenty
years ago? Since 1973, there has been no advance in real family income. And when taxes are counted in, the slim paychecks are actually slimmer, and getting thinner every day.

The tax code was one of the vehicles that hit, then ran
over, the middle class. Eventually, it may be responsible for
its death. As the tax laws keep getting "reformed," the middle
class takes the brunt of the blow, as we shall graphically see,
with no reasonable hope of returning to the ease of the era of
golden oldies.

Can We Survive Our Politicians?

Government has been the cause of the pain, financially and
morally. The money drained from the economy to run massive, untested, unproductive government programs—from
Washington to the cities—is, I am convinced, the main cause
of the nation's economic ills. In fact, some skeptical Americans are beginning to doubt our ability to survive our politicians.

In prior decades, critics of government were dismissed as "crackpots" by politicians and the press. Today, that insult can be justifiably turned around. Washington, it can be said without fear of intelligent criticism, has become a crackpot organization, operating without theory or restraint.

But we're ahead of everyone in one area. We're the land of special interests, from rich doctors to unwed mothers, from lawyers to farmers, from illegal immigrants to utilities, from bureaucrats to ranchers. Yet we unerringly miss those who should be the true target of our largesse, the increasingly hard-pressed, working middle-class Americans who support everyone else.

We have lost our way, but there is a way forward. To remake America, we must understand that it will not happen without citizen intervention. To expect the political class to commit suicide by overseeing the needed reform and downsizing of government is naive, "reinvented government" or otherwise. They are a clever and resilient bunch and reluctant to submit to the needed change of *de-inventing government*—downsizing the entire operation to one we can afford.

If we expect to create a "velvet revolution"—and I am convinced that nothing less will do—Americans need to have as much knowledge about their government as the people they will confront.

I hope this volume, buttressed by investigative reporting, detailed research, and an attempt at logical analysis, will provide the ammunition to make that peaceful citizen revolution possible. And in the process, help to save our nation.

And now, onward to the middle-class barricades. Then forward into the bowels of the enemy—the Washington Establishment.

Chapter Two

More Pork,
More Waste

DOESN'T ANYBODY CARE?

Who would ever think Americans would be fascinated by the fact that Uncle Sam spent $107,000 studying the sex life of the Japanese quail?

Or a half million dollars building a replica of the Great Pyramid of Egypt in *Indiana*?

Or that federal funds were used to study why people are rude on tennis courts and smile on bowling alleys?

In *Government Racket*, I collected scores of pieces of "pork," examples of the callousness with which Congressmen treat the taxpayers' money. The American public took the list to heart—or, more accurately, to the heartburn it caused when they thought of the unrewarding fate of their money.

My favorite was $315,000 to memorialize the South Carolina home of Charles Pinckney, a signer of the U.S. Constitution. Surely worthwhile, except for one small oversight: Mr. Pinckney died before the house was ever built.

These goodies for the folks back home (a kind of campaign reelection fund that we all pay for) are not only symbolic of congressional irresponsibility, but they can add up into the billions. One bill, the Intermodal Surface Transportation Efficiency Act of 1991, whose money is now being spent on highways, had $6.8 billion in pork buried within, including $287 million just from one Pennsylvania Congressman on the committee.

Since the publication of my last book I have gone back to the salt mines of research and developed another list of pork—silly appropriations, wasteful and fraudulent spending for the titillation, and aggravation, of taxpayers. I believe this list comprises the nation's longest compendium of porkage and stupidity.

It's important to understand that when Washington is in the throes of giving away our money, the government makes no distinction between federal projects, state and local governments, nonprofit organizations, private individuals and businesses in America, and foreign governments and companies. They'll give your money away to anybody—except possibly thou and me.

It's also vital to remember that this is *all* borrowed money. Each dollar will have to be paid back with $2 or $3.

Hold onto your pocketbook.

• $23 million spent by the Post Office on a consultant to find out how long it takes for the mail to be delivered. (I could save them the money.)

• $5 million to renovate buildings and finish an aircraft hangar at Wurtswirth Air Force Base in Michigan—after it had been decided to close the base.

• $7 million to study air pollution in Mexico City.

• $995,000 for a performing arts center in North Miami Beach.

• $2.3 million to bring seven hundred workers to San Diego from all over America, as far away as Alaska, to photocopy records of a defunct savings and loan.

• $500,000 to memorialize Cordell Hull, Secretary of State under Franklin Roosevelt.

• Funds for a team of seventy Census Department workers to count the population of Bangladesh and 225 other countries—something not mentioned when the Constitution set up the Dicennial Census.

• $5 million for a new Parliament building for the Solomon Islands in the Pacific. One problem: The island is part of the British Commonwealth.

• $170,000 in cash bonuses for twelve outgoing employees of the Interior Department, one of the worst-run agencies of the federal government.

• $35,000 for "Flow City," an artistic tourist attraction based on a waste station.

• A $378,000 Small Business Administration loan for a businessman with a net worth of $6.4 million.

• A projected $18 million mall on Biscayne Boulevard in the upper income area of Miami Beach.

• $1 million for a Utah study on how to cross the street safely.

• $100,000 to find out why people don't like beets.

• $90,000 to study the social life of vegetarians.

• $46,000 to find out how long it takes to cook eggs. (Burnt or regular?)

• $1.9 million for an Irish genealogy project, one of the going-away presents for former Speaker Tip O'Neill.

• $140,000 for a count of Samoans in Orange County, California. (It's feared the recipient went back to Samoa.)

• $384,948 for a Department of Labor census of the dogs and cats in Ventura County, California.

• $119 million a year for newspapers and periodicals for the Pentagon.

• $491,607 for a bash to honor nine hundred employees of the Department of Agriculture. Don't fret, they say. The year before they spent $667,000.

• $3 million for a new deck on a Los Angeles County parking garage.

• $1.2 million to replace the lobby marble (plus $600,000 for Italian-designed desks) of the European Bank for Reconstruction and Development, which gets $70 million a year from U.S. taxpayers.

• $2.5 million for a parking garage in Burlington, Iowa.

• $192,000 for the Beluga Whale Committee.

• $109 million in new federal loans to students who had already defaulted on their old loans.

• $824,000 paid by the Department of Energy to cover the fines and lawyer's bill of a contractor who broke the law.

• $1 million in government gold and silver used by a private contractor to make jewelry presents for federal employees.

• $10,000 for a Potomac River cruise.

• Rolex watches for contractor employees, paid for by the Environmental Protection Agency.

• $5 million in federal "antipoverty" funds given to Sears Roebuck as an interest-free loan.

• $29 million in vehicles and other equipment that the Bureau of Indian Affairs can't find.

• Millions spent by the Agency for International Development in Miami and New York to convince American businesses to move out of the U.S. to Latin America.

• $20,000 for three marble elevator floors in Congress.

• Fifteen limos and drivers for the Department of Education, which doesn't educate a single American child.

- $37,000 to study "the handling of animal manure."
- $51,000 for drinks and meals at a Los Angeles athletic club as part of the federal financing of the Los Angeles subway.
- Millions for free rides ($240 each) for federal employees on the Washington Metro.
- $4 million for a Japanese-American museum in Oregon.
- $50,000 for travel by the Architect of the Capitol, whose sole responsibility is the Washington area.
- $25 million for research to trap the energy of the aurora borealis.
- $1.5 million for renovation of private theaters in Manhattan.
- $1.5 million for the expansion of the Worcester, Massachusetts, exhibition hall.
- $8 million for the World University Games.
- $100,000 in federal funds to connect a mobile home park to a Minnesota city water supply.
- $15 million for the preservation of antiquities—in Egypt.
- $2 million for Walk on the Mountain skyway in Tacoma, Washington, in order to see Mt. Ranier, which is only visible one out of six days.
- $744,000 for the Glass Ceiling Commission.
- $744,000 for the National Center on the Workplace.
- $3 million for an Oregon Territory historical center.
- $2 million for the restoration of two theaters in Savannah, Georgia.
- $250,000 for a water tower in a privately owned Joplin, Missouri, industrial park.
- $248,000 for an outdoor education center in California.
- $3.6 million for gardens in cities.
- $700,000 to monitor ultraviolet light.
- $1 million to study brown tree snakes.

• $1 million "small business" grant for a Kentucky high school.
• $12 million for "Toward Other Planetary Systems."
• $3.2 million for the Center for Poultry Excellence.
• $4 million for the Cosmosphere in Kansas.
• $200,000 to celebrate Smokey the Bear's fiftieth anniversary.

Is there an answer to this political trichinosis, the disease that afflicts congressional dispensers of pork?

Yes, it's really quite simple. All Congress has to do is pass a House rule that no member of a committee—especially an appropriations committee—can use a bill to authorize any additional monies for his district, or for the district of any member of the same committee.

What about horse trading between committees? "You put in a little pork for me, and I'll shoe your horse, or whatever."

If Congress has the guts to pass such a law, horse trading can easily be stopped by the two ethics committees in Congress. And they should reprimand violators with more than a slap on the wrist; perhaps large fines, the easiest way to shape up Representatives and Senators. Constituents can help as well. They should understand that robbing the national treasure to beef up their district is not the answer to anything.

How much can be saved by halting the pork epidemic? Probably $8 billion a year, or much more than a sow's ear.

The government waste trough has no bottom. I think it would be instructive to follow up some of the items I discussed in my first book. And I'd also like to take a new look at useless agencies of the federal government that should be closed.

PERKS. Like love and marriage, perks and pork go hand in hand. There has always been a little something extra for politicians, but old-timers didn't seem to abuse the privilege as much. As I've mentioned, when Harry Truman was Vice President, he was frugal (actually cheap). He had a staff of four and lived in a two-bedroom apartment on Connecticut Avenue, for which he paid the $140 a month rent out of his own pocket.

Today, of course, the VP lives royally in a mansion on Navy grounds and enjoys a motorcade of cars, a jet plane, a $90,000 entertainment allowance, sixty employees, and four government offices, including one in Tennessee, which has nothing to do with his being Vice President.

And now he's costing us even more money.

The VP's Victorian mansion has been undergoing a transformation since the days of Dan Quayle. Now Al Gore is involved and the total price tag is approaching $3.5 million dollars to fix up this old house built one hundred years ago. It is proving to be an expensive ritual, which is peculiar because Mr. Gore is supposedly a waste cutter, especially of ash trays and floor wax. The super-expensive repair includes $278,000 for the veranda (southern for porch) and a storage area underneath.

Some of the money comes out of private donations, but most of the millions is taxpayer cash. The Gore decorator has ripped up the Quayle flowered wall-to-wall rug and replaced it with beige carpeting, along with a $100 a yard stair carpeting. They have repainted and reupholstered, a common habit of Washington biggies.

They are also doing $200,000 of custom work, ostensibly paid for by donations, including $15,000 for a cherry cabinet, "faux green" wall finishes, and a steam shower.

I could save the government a fortune by tearing down the old mess and building the Gores a brand-new six bedroom, 6,000 square foot mansion for only $850,000 on the same grounds. But, of course, I couldn't include a $278,000 veranda.

There's an interesting sidelight on vice presidential waste. Both Mrs. Quayle and Mrs. Gore have had sizable staffs, including several on the federal payroll. (Is that legal?) Mrs. Quayle had ten people under her, more than twice as many as Vice President Truman's whole staff. Attempts to learn the size of Mrs. Gore's retinue have so far failed.

Too much for a VP in a democracy? I think so, particularly when this one is so concerned with waste and "performance," as he should be.

AIRPLANES. When I reported that federal agencies had 1,300 private planes, many used to ferry bureaucrats around the country, sometimes with spouses and guests, some people looked at me curiously.

Now, Secretary of Transportation Federico Pena has announced that he was surprised to discover that his own department owned 304 of those planes.

Equally surprising was that two of the planes were personally assigned to him. They sit on the tarmac at National Airport in Washington. One of them costs taxpayers $24 million, and God knows how much to keep up.

"I don't use them," Pena told the press. "I fly commercial coach."

Great! When's the auction sale on the two planes? And how about the other 302, Mr. Secretary?

An even more upsetting follow-up comes from a recent report from the Inspector General (IG) of the General Services Administration (GSA), the organization that handles the planes. When the report, done for Senator James Sasser of Tennessee, chairman of the Subcommittee on General Services, came in, it startled everyone, if not me.

It seems that the GSA has lost track of how many planes they own, if they ever knew. By checking Federal Aviation Administration (FAA) records, the IG unearthed a total of 1,384 planes, including 237 missing "ghosts" the GSA didn't know they had. The auditors found 31 planes registered to four agencies who weren't supposed to have any. Another 152 had disappeared, but turned up illegally in the hands of state and local governments.

This $2 billion cache of planes, which cost another $1 billion a year to maintain, is part of an operation that the IG estimates wastes a half billion dollars a year. That's an understatement. The majority of the planes—those not used by the FBI, or for fire fighting or drug interdiction—could be sold with a saving of several billions.

Believe it or not column: The U.S. Forest Service *gave away* twenty-eight of the planes to private contractors, one of whom then had the chutzpah to lease a plane back to the government for Operation Desert Storm, collecting $920,000 along the way!

Was all this confusion part of an overworked fleet? Hardly. One hundred and eighty planes flew less than a hundred hours per year—two hours a week. Bureaucratic sloth is apparently contagious.

The solution is to sell all the planes that are not involved in technical missions and have the big shots with sense, like Secretary Pena, fly commercial coach.

DECORATING. My revelation that the government spent between $1.3 and $2 billion a year on furniture and decorating surprised everyone, and brought an angry denial from the General Services Administration. As it turns out, not only were they wrong, but in typical government fashion they were obfuscating—a polite euphemism for what they really did. And my federal informant, a patriotic citizen, lost his job helping me learn the truth about government extravagance.

When I first called the Office of Management and Budget (OMB) and asked about the cost of furniture and decorating, they shook their head. "There's no such item in the federal budget."

They also assured me I'd never find out the cost because each agency had its own allotment, and they'd never tell anyone.

My resolve was sharpened. I called around to some contacts and finally found a Mr. Mike Bielski, an official in the National Furniture Center (NFC) in suburban Virginia. The NFC, he told me, was part of the GSA. It didn't buy any furniture, *but* it had contracts with manufacturers for discounts. Agencies could do their business through the NFC and maybe save money.

"So how much furniture and decorating business do you do?" I asked.

He didn't know, but he was happy to find out. A few days later, after a computer run, he told me. The NFC alone, in a recent fiscal year, tallied $676 million in purchases of furniture, rugs, desks, lamps, pictures, and so on.

"What part of the government total is that?" I asked Mr. Bielski.

He didn't know, but he guessed one-third to one-half. The Defense Department tended to buy their own, he explained.

So I multiplied his $676 million by two and three, and came up with my published estimate of $1.3 to $2 billion a year.

Not long after, the television magazine show "20/20" started to film a segment on me. They questioned the GSA about the decorating, and the agency spokesman intimated that I was a "liar." They told a worried "20/20" that they "could only account for $515 million" in decorating that year. "Account for" was the operational gimmick.

Quickly, I called Mr. Bielski at his office. He confirmed his $676 million part of the cost, and said he would stand behind it. But, he said, he didn't remember saying it was one-third to one-half the total.

"Then what part of the total is your $676 million?" I anxiously asked Bielski.

"It could be more than half, but it could also be as little as one-eighth."

One-eighth? That would make the decorating bill *$5 billion* a year.

The cost to Mr. Bielski came the next day. The "20/20" people could not reach him at his office; they were told to contact GSA public relations. They did and were asked to come to a meeting where GSA would explain all.

"We had our meeting," relates the "20/20" producer. "I told them what you had learned. Suddenly, it was no longer $515 million. They found another $250-plus million, and their amount was no longer all of the government decorating bill. They figured maybe it was 80 percent. So now they were suddenly admitting that the annual decorating bill was about a *billion*. It had almost doubled in a half-hour meeting."

The head of Federal Program Management, a company that helps furniture manufacturers obtain contracts with the U.S. government, estimates the real decorating cost at $3 billion.

A quick aside: When the "20/20" producer was up at the Department of Interior, he admired the nice furniture. "Oh," said the D of I spokesman. "We didn't want it. We had perfectly good furniture, but the government *insisted* that we buy new stuff."

Federal Program Management, incidentally, is suing the government because their low-bid work was turned down by GSA, which, he says, have their own, favored, higher-priced suppliers.

Whatever happened to Mr. Bielski? The very day after I checked back with him, he was kicked out of his job and transferred to some cockamamie duty involving credit cards—his reward for honesty and patriotism.

(Note to Vice President Gore: This kind of ruthless bureaucratic punishment for good work belongs in your next Performance Report.)

(Note to President Clinton: Forget about Bielski's old job in the National Furniture Center. Bring him over to the White

House where he can kick ass on the waste-ridden General Services Administration, and maybe save billions in the process.)

So much for truth-in-government. How do we fix it? One answer is for the Inspector General in GSA, and other agencies, to have *police power*. They should be able to recommend the firing of employees who lie to the press or go after whistleblowers. They need to publicly expose anything they think is remiss. To trust the integrity of government to regular bureaucrats is naive, and worse.

OTHER SERVICES. One of my best contributions to reducing waste in government was the exposure of this enormous miscellaneous item in the federal budget.

The amount for "Other Services" appears in virtually every agency subbudget in the 1,500-page 1994 document, and is often the largest item shown. (The Clinton version of the federal budget, circa Fiscal Year 1994, is shorter than the 1993 2,000-pager. The historical tables, which enable you to compare, are gone.)

There's no total for "Other Services" in the federal budget document, but that's not unique. There are no totals for anything—personnel, pensions, equipment, overhead, travel, decorating, consultants, whatever.

The reason is simple. This way, Americans won't have easy access to the horrible truth. But I finally obtained the totals.

How much was it for 1993? A mind-crushing *$246 billion*. It's almost equal to the entire deficit and exactly 20 percent of the 1994 federal budget without Social Security! In fact, it's $17 billion higher than last year, all done without benefit of an appropriation. America is being miscellaneoused to death.

"Other Services" is the government's open-ended slush fund. While Congress may argue about a billion here and there, agency bureaucrats can dip into this pot for whatever reason, whenever they want. The amounts will be secret. It's a major national scandal, which must be addressed and corrected. (Understandably, it was not mentioned in the Vice President's recent report.)

For the last two years, I have been asking OMB for a breakdown of the "Other Services." They've sent me a breakdown by agency but not by function. They claim that *nobody* in the central government has it, that these are agency budgets over which they have only general oversight. At first glance, this appears to be a lie. But considering the ignorance of the operation, even that is in the realm of possibility.

(We must assume that the CIA budget of about $30 billion is hidden in there, which may be one reason for the government secrecy. But the CIA is only one-eighth of the total.)

The OMB sent me a Circular A-11, which generalizes about the items in "Other Services," but it's of no real help. It only indicates that a good part of the $246 billion is spent on maintenance and outside contracting, items that are a swamp of waste, inefficiency, and deceit.

What can Congress do to change it? Force the OMB to reveal all.

How much can we save? See Chapter 12 on the budget.

CONSULTANTS. This category of experts for hire, particularly Washington lawyers at up to $600 an hour, is part of a "shadow government" that no one knew about. It's especially galling legalwise because the government employs more than 14,000 full-time attorneys.

Traditionally, the cost of consultants has been hidden in sneaky "Other Services." But I explored "consultants" and revealed that it cost taxpayers almost *$5 billion* a year.

Surprisingly, my revelation produced some White House action. In the 1994 budget, for the first time, it has been pulled out and given a separate line, where it can be seen and whittled away. The new budget loosely figures it at $3 billion, which is still much higher than it should be. In a frugal bud-

get, consultants would cost less than $1 billion, a savings of
$2–4 billion a year.

LAND SALES AND PURCHASES. The government
style of "buying high" and "selling low" when it comes to our
natural resources troubles me greatly. Equally troubling is
that the government owns 30 percent of the land mass of
America but still spends $300 million a year buying new land.

Since I wrote about it, new items have come to my attention. In preparation for a television program, I called the
National Park Service and learned that a new 7,500-acre park
was being created in Albuquerque, New Mexico.

Called the Petroglyph National Monument, it will preserve Indian carvings on rocks. But there are two problems.
The first is that most of the land being bought does not have
any Indian markings. The other is that the land is not in the
middle of the far-away desert and cheap. It's mainly *within
the city borders of Albuquerque and very expensive.* In fact,
part of it is made up of zoned building sites.

"What are you paying for the land?" I asked the Park Service.

"Some of the one-third-acre lots go for $30,000 in the
real estate market and that's what we're paying for them," a
spokesman responded. One large homesite parcel was bought
for $90,000. I was shocked, though I should be unshockable.

When the money was appropriated in 1989, Congress
was told that the land would cost $58 million. The estimated
cost is now up to $90 million. A local real estate man believes
the park is much too large considering that it's mainly within
the city. One thousand acres would do nicely, he believes.

"I don't think the government should spend all that
money," he says. Amen. And remember, it's all borrowed
deficit funds.

The land situation of the federal government is a nationwide scam. One of the most extraordinary wastes in American history is the purchase of *extra* land to enlarge the

Manassas Historic Battlefield in Virginia, the site of a Civil War conflict. Things were fine until someone in the National Park Service decided that a new shopping center going up *outside* the battlefield was an eyesore.

"Why not buy it?" the Park Service asked Congress, who agreed.

Now the 600-acre parcel has been bought and the park people are happy. How much did it cost, a million or two? Dream on. The cost so far, as they continue to clean up the area, is *$130 million,* or $200,000 an acre.

I asked what will happen when a shrewd entrepreneur who knows the government's mind puts up another eyesore shopping center outside the *new* boundaries. Will the government buy that one too for another $130 million? They just tittered.

The battlefield mania is far from over. Right now, the Park Service is considering enlarging another 250-plus sites of Civil War strife. When it's all done, the battlefields may end up costing us as much as the original war.

The land obsession of the federal government, which owns 60 percent of California and over 80 percent of Nevada, is a strange one. As I've said, the Department of Interior likes to buy high, but also likes to sell low, even for a pittance. This includes parcels near Nevada gambling resorts worth a fortune.

The problem is that Washington is giving away vast natural resources. When mining land is "patented," or deeded, the price is $2.50 to $5.00 an acre, a figure set way back in 1872. I've since learned that when the minerals are taken out of the ground, the unshrewd government doesn't get a copper cent of the profits. Neither do they get a nickel in royalties, even if the new owners are foreigners. Of the twenty-five top gold mines in the United States, by the way, sixteen are wholly or partly owned by foreign corporations or individuals.

In a 1993 report, the House Committee on Government

Operations estimated that Uncle Sam has given away $91.3 *billion* in mining land just since 1987.

An outrageous "patent" now going through the Bureau of Land Management demonstrates, in living dollars, how stupid—or uncaring—Washington is. The Stillwater Mining Company, owned by Manville Corporation and Chevron oil, has found platinum and palladium on National Forest land.

They are paying Uncle Sam a total of *$10,810 for 2,000 acres.* How much is it really worth? According to estimates, there is *$32 billion* worth of the minerals in the ground!

How much will the taxpayers get in royalties?

Zippo. Zilch. *Rien. Nada.* Nothing.

The House Committee estimates that $4 billion in minerals are taken out of federal public lands each year. Just a 12.5 percent royalty would bring a half billion dollars to the public treasury. In addition, placing fair market prices on the patented land could bring in another $1.3 billion a year.

(Failing that, maybe Americans should form a profit-making mutual mining fund and see how much they can extract from the government.)

There has been a lot of rumblings in the White House to change the mining law, but so far nothing, absolutely nothing, has happened.

BUILDINGS. I've already reported that despite 15 million square feet of vacant space, Washington has authorized fifty new buildings around the country at a cost of $5 billion.

To update that waste is painful. The vacant space is now up to 19 million square feet, and according to the General Services Administration, there are now *eighty-four* new federal buildings agrowing.

One of the most outrageous pieces of waste is in downtown Washington at 13th and Pennsylvania, only three blocks from the White House. It is currently the largest hole-in-the-ground in the Western world, costing taxpayers a needless *three-quarters of a billion dollars.* Just to stand there and stare is an excruciating lesson in government indifference.

(I suggest that President Clinton jog by one morning to see what GSA and Congress have wrought—if his prebreakfast stomach can take it.)

The hole is eleven acres in girth and six stories deep. Eventually it will be eight or nine stories tall above that, and take up a space equal to two regular city blocks. It will hold about 2 million square feet of finished space—not an inch of which is needed.

How did this fiasco get born? In typical Washington style: through a series of compounded errors.

Congress started out to create an International Trade Center, most of which was to be rented to foreign companies and governments. But along the way the numbers didn't work. Congress appropriated approximately $780 million, which included construction loan interest. Using paper and pencil after they started construction (didn't they have any before?), it became clear that the building was going to be uncompetitive.

With $13 a square foot for services, plus the mortgage payments, they would have to rent it for about $46 a foot, which was way out of line for that area.

So, what to do? Simple. Uncle Sam has taken over the whole building, even though we need this hole-in-the-ground like a hole-in-the-head. The Goliath of the GSA will soon house thousands of federal employees who will have to be transferred out of other buildings. Score one for federal mismanagement.

An even larger building scandal, this one costing almost a billion dollars, erupted in the summer of 1993. Despite the efforts of an honest Senator, the forces of darkness won out—again.

It all began when the appropriations committee in the Senate handling the GSA appropriated money for the construction of still another twenty-three federal buildings. Senator John McCain of Arizona, a dedicated waste watcher, was surprised. The buildings had not been "authorized" by the subcommittee in charge of GSA, which is usual Senate practice.

Despite the fact that one of the pork items included a large goodie for Phoenix, the Senator quickly introduced an amendment to stop the sneaky practice of appropriating money for nonauthorized projects.

He lost, naturally, because a seat on any of the twenty-six appropriations committees (thirteen in each house) is the way to snare the bacon and impress voters down home. Actually, voters should be angry that the national treasury is being looted, supposedly on their behalf, a little at a time.

Meanwhile, the Croix de Courage for Washington war hero Senator John McCain.

What to do? Simple. (1) Sell the hole-in-the ground and cut our losses; (2) put a five-year freeze on *any* new government buildings; (3) cancel the plans for the 100-plus buildings already authorized; (4) follow that by selling off the present buildings as we downsize the manpower.

GOVERNMENT TRAVEL. I've already exposed the government travel racket, which sets us back $7 billion a year—a ridiculous sum.

The tab for travel-loving bureaucrats has reached $3,000 for *every* employee, so one can imagine what government executives (GS13–18 and the Senior Executive Service) spend. They must be on the move continually.

Comes "September Madness," the frenetic travel pace speeds up even more as federal employees try to beat out the October 1 deadline, the beginning of the new fiscal year. To get at least the same budget the following year, they must spend every cent. A study of government travel in September, for example, shows a 48 percent rise in trips to anywhere, particularly to nice resorts.

Since my first report, I've come across a travel story that shows that near the top there are no restraints at all—nor any respect for the taxpayer buck. Take Secretary of Defense Les Aspin. In May 1993, he boarded an Air Force 707 and, with a staff of nine, took off for Brussels for a meeting with his European counterparts. So far so good, and quite legitimate.

But wait. From there, the group went to the Aviano Air Force Base in Italy, where Aspin inspected the operation. Now it was time for vacation—in nearby Venice. The Defense Secretary and a female companion checked into the Hotel Danieli, a famed $300-a-night luxury lodgery on the Grand Canal, where they personally paid for their five-night stay. So what's wrong, Mr. Skinflint?

Plenty. The government staff of nine was not shipped home on the 707. Instead, they too were given a government vacation (without cutting into their official leave time) for five nights at the same swankery, all courtesy of Uncle Sam. While Aspin and friend paid for two, Uncle Sam was paying for nine. They too played while they waited for Aspin to complete his vacation. And back at the base, the twenty-two crew members of the 707 also had to suffer five days of vacation, at lesser accommodations, on the government's big nickel.

So, how much did Mr. Aspin's romantic vacation cost the taxpayers?

Nobody knows, and the Pentagon is not talking. But counting the time of thirty-one federal workers on impromptu R&R, and the upkeep of the waiting jet, $150,000 is a good guess. It makes President Clinton's haircut look cheap.

Al Gore avoids the whole travel issue in his report, but he recommends that if bureaucrats have money left over in any budget, they need not spend it. They should be able to roll it over to the next year. But that solves nothing. If they spend less than the $7 billion, someone will catch on that they don't need it, which they don't. So they'll spend it anyway. Besides, spending madly is how they got the budget so high in the first place.

Cutting budgets up front, deeply, and across the board is the only way to beat the wily bureaucrats. Virtually everywhere in his report, Mr. Gore avoids discussing how much we can cut agency budgets—the core of the monster problem. GROSS'S LAW—CUT IT IN HALF THEN LOOK AT IT AGAIN LATER, AND MAYBE CUT IT AGAIN—WOULD APPLY MAGNIFICENTLY IN THE CASE OF GOVERNMENT TRAVEL.

OUTDATED AND USELESS FEDERAL AGENCIES. There are scores of agencies and subagencies that should be closed and eliminated from the budget—some because they've finished their job and others because they were no good to begin with. In my previous work, I suggested closing the Small Business Administration, the Rural Electrification Administration, and the in-house Government Printing Office, among others. Here are a few more:

APPALACHIAN REGIONAL COMMISSION. This one began because John Kennedy won the 1960 West Virginia Primary and promised to help out. When it finally got started with LBJ's Great Society, the commission was designed to handle thirteen states along the Appalachian Mountains, from southern New York to Mississippi. But, of course, West Virginia, home of Senator Robert Byrd, still gets the mountain share.

The agency was created as a temporary response to poverty. After twenty-seven years it has spent over $7 billion with no sign that it has helped the area. Appalachia had a per-capita income some 20 percent less than the nation at the time. And now? It's the same. Shutting it down will save $780 million over five years.

ECONOMIC DEVELOPMENT ADMINISTRATION. The EDA was formed in 1966 as one of the stellar Great Society projects. It was designed to help the poorest areas of the country with the highest unemployment. Today, the

money doesn't just go to poor towns but to anyplace with
"pork power." According to the Congressional Budget Office,
areas containing 80 percent of our entire population are now
eligible for EDA grants. Because the program has changed
into just another pork pie, cities like Raleigh-Durham, which
are more prosperous than most, have received some of its
flowing cash.

The program has been plagued with defaulted loans to
private businesses and countless failed development schemes.
One small horror story involves Dartmouth, the Ivy League
college in New Hampshire. The school received $15 million
from the EDA with which they created thirty-nine jobs—at a
cost of *$384,615 each.* So much for poverty.

EDA has labored hard for twenty-seven years, spending
our billions, and has little to show for it. Let's close it down
forthwith and save its annual budget of some $230
million—or almost $1.2 billion in five years.

INTERSTATE COMMERCE COMMISSION. This is a
symbol of pure government obsolescence. The agency once
made sense, because it closely regulated railroads, trucks,
barges, buses, etc. Created in 1887, it was the only way a car-
rier could be licensed to operate.

But now? The surface transportation business has been
almost completely deregulated, with the trucks the last to go.
Trucking prices, once set in Washington, are now controlled
by the market. The commission's staff has been cut by two-
thirds since 1981, and now it's time to say sayonara to the
rest.

Its 1994 budget is $53,184,000. Once it's closed, that's all
found money.

CONGRESSIONAL "LSO"S. One extraordinary activity of Congress involves what are known as "LSOs," or Legislative Service Organizations. These are really clubs, or
caucuses, in which the members band together to work and
enjoy themselves. There are twenty-eight of them, everything

from the Space Caucus to the Hispanic Caucus to the House Wednesday group.

The LSOs spend taxpayer's money to the tune of $5 million a year on meetings, luncheons, and parties. The money comes from Members' dues—some as high as $10,000 each—which in turn come from the taxpayers through the Congressmen's two expense accounts—"Clerk hire" and "Official Expenses."

They are really a Congress within a Congress. They even have their own staff, totaling eighty-eight employees, some of whom work in separate caucus offices on the Hill. (Just what Congress needs is more people and more offices.)

And they're not frugal with our money. The Pennsylvania State caucus-delegation, one of the twenty-eight official LSOs, spent $7,688 of taxpayer money for a single cocktail reception. The New York delegation honored a retiring member with a $1,466 Steuben glass eagle. (You didn't know you were so generous, did you?)

Not only are they generous, but they also tend to be careless, bookkeeping-wise. "Our office has conducted a ten-year study of the LSOs," says a spokesman for Congressman Pat Roberts of Kansas, "and we found that up to $7.7 million dollars is just plain missing or could not be accounted for."

What to do? This one is real easy. Close it all down and use the $5 million dollars to reduce the deficit. If Congressmen and women like to be clubby, be my guest. But let them pay their own dues, and give away their own statues.

ESSENTIAL AIR. I brought this boondoggle to the attention of the American people, first in my book, then on television. There are over a hundred communities that get government subsidized air travel, because they're more than forty-five miles from the nearest scheduled airliner.

The EA, which costs $38 million a year, should be closed down as "unessential Air."

Mr. Gore agrees, but only a little. He's recommending

cutting out only one-third of the pork, including nine routes that have only five passengers a day or fewer. He's also for reducing the maximum subsidy from $433 a passenger to $200. How about "0"?

COMMUNITY DEVELOPMENT BLOCK GRANT. This was supposed to be one of those "new federalism" programs in which Washington gave money to the states and cities with almost no strings attached, except that 70 percent of the funds had to be used to help the poor and relatively poor. The program is administered by HUD, the Department of Housing and Urban Development, and now costs $4,223,675,000 (that's billions). And it's grown 25 percent in just two years—four times faster than inflation.

The funds go to 875 entitlement cities with over 50,000 population, and a third of the money goes to the states to give to smaller towns.

The idea sounds reasonable if you're a very rich government. But considering our plight, and what can happen to the money when it gets there, it's not such a good idea.

A congressional investigation into CDBG gives it less than good marks. The City of Miami spent $200,000 to finance a theater production in Coconut Grove. The same city used $5.4 million of federal funds to give a loan at 1 percent interest to a rich Saudi renovating an office building.

In Delaware County, Pennsylvania, millions were misused on liquor, banquets, Broadway theater tickets, and gifts. The City of Troy, New York, proved as versatile. It loaned $1.65 million to a professional hockey team, while an Indian reservation used $404,000 of Washington's cash to build an off-track betting parlor, perhaps a forerunner of the new Indian gambling empire.

Even super-affluent Greenwich, Connecticut, gets a piece of the government pie. A wealthy town in Westchester County, New York, used $5,000 of Uncle Sam's money for trees around the railroad station. They could have just as easily passed the hat.

In many cases the towns hand much of the money over to nonprofit charities, which is not what people had in mind when they paid their taxes. After all, we already give $128 billion *voluntarily* to charities, and they're tax free besides.

Close the whole CDBG program down *now*, and use *all* $4.2 billion to reduce the deficit. A very good head start.

HELIUM RESERVE. This strange project, which costs about $100 million a year net, is so silly that it received an extraordinary amount of publicity when I first reported it. Simply put, we have a billion dollars' worth of helium underground in Texas, enough to last *one hundred years*.

The Vice President seeks to "improve" the operation and save about $2.5 million a year, about 10 percent of the operating cost. Nonsense. Close it down completely.

A piece of advice for Washington: Stay out of business— you can barely deal with government.

FEDERAL ADVISORY COMMISSIONS. What are these? They are *700* different, rather strange, organizations created by the White House and Congress to advise the government on everything from "cultural property," to animals, to "Rural America," to a presidential commission on "Public Diplomacy," and all at the taxpayers' expense. Some are exotic, all are unnecessary, and they cost us $150 million a year.

There is the Advisory Panel for Animal Learning and Behavior, another for the Dictionary of Occupational Titles, and even the U.S. Board of Tea Experts. The latter costs $133,000 a year and has a $68,000-a-year tea taster.

By eliminating them, we gain twice. We're saving $150 million and cutting off one more source of bad advice.

U.S. INFORMATION SERVICE. This organization, which includes the Voice of America, did a magnificent job during the Cold War, infiltrating democratic ideas behind the Iron Curtain. Now that the wall and Communism have fallen in Europe, it's time to retire almost all its activities. That includes the 200 information offices in 140 countries, and the broadcasting operation, except for perhaps the radio programs beamed at Cuba.

We need not advertise the glories of America anymore. All we get in return is more unneeded immigration.

This is not a peanut budget. The USIS costs us $790 million a year, and almost all of that should be saved.

The list of agencies to be closed and drastically cut back could make up a catalog, and we'll look at more of them in the sections on cabinet reorganization (Chapter 11), and the chapter (No. 12) on a balanced budget.

Meanwhile, it's most important to remember one maxim: Waste is not the exception, nor even just the rule in Washington. It's the *only* way the federal government knows how to operate.

To excise it will require knowledge and work, two things the American public can be expected to handle once they're given the tools.

Chapter Three

The Tax Monster

HOW TO DESTROY
THE MIDDLE CLASS

It is 1950, the era of Happy Days, car tail fins, and a successful, buoyant country. Our hero, who we shall call Mr. Mort Stevens, is a veteran of World War II who had gone on to technical school for two years on the GI Bill of Rights. Now an electronics specialist in a little company on Long Island, he is married, has two small kids, and a wife who stays home—what *Good Housekeeping* euphemistically calls a "homemaker."

Life is good because his paycheck is reasonable and the government—at all levels—is small and untaxing. There is enough money to pay the bills, even enough to take vacations and put some in the bank. The most pressing problem seems to be the recurring, damn crabgrass.

In 1950, the suburbs were mushrooming, converting dusty potato fields into miles of almost identical homes. The baby boomers were being born into pink and blue nurseries in two- and three-bedroom ranch-style homes rising out of the ground like so many spring tulips.

It was a happy day as prams, gossip, an occasional extramarital affair, and heated school board meetings enlivened the bucolic scenario.

What stood out the most, however, is how inexpensive it all was and how absent was the tax collector. Mort's house cost $8,000, which he paid for with a "good faith" down payment of $10. Secured by a 100 percent VA loan (his neighbor's was a 90 percent one from the Federal Housing Authority [FHA]), his house was a notch above those in nearby Levittown.

His mortgage interest was 4 percent and his payments to the bank were $31 a month. Mort's income was $5,000 a year. Par for Long Island, it was considerably higher than the national average, which was $3,300. By and large, wage-earner Mort had it made in the shade—a touch of which he had under the newly planted maple tree.

What about federal taxes? Didn't they cut into his little piece of heaven? Heavens no. At the time, every American, adult or child, had a personal exemption of $600 on the tax forms. That immediately took $2,400 off the taxable amount. When he added the mortgage interest on his house, the local taxes, deductions for loan interest, and other miscellaneous items, including a small veteran's exemption, Uncle Sam didn't get much of the pie.

Mort's federal tax that year was $350, or 7 percent of his income.

How about state taxes? New York began that misadventure in 1919, not long after the federal government. In 1950, the top rate was 3 percent, but at his level of about $2,000 taxable, Mort's entire state tax was $45.

The local bite—from Nassau County, the town of Oyster Bay, and school taxes combined—was $220, or 5 percent of his income, all of which was deductible from his federal taxes.

Mort, who had a working-class background, had in one fell swoop leapfrogged into the new middle class, one that came to signify the glories of postwar America.

His total tax burden, federal and local, was $615, or 12 percent of the family income. With *annual* mortgage payments of $372, that left over $4,000 in disposable funds—or 80 percent of his income. Three years later, Mort and his wife took part of the nest egg they had saved and, after leaving Alice and Todd with Grandma, went off on a two-week tour of Europe.

Middle American Blues

Who lives there today, and how is he doing after forty-three years of American politics and politicians, of both parties? How do his governments—federal, state, and local—treat him, his wife, and two small children? What's life like in the tax-happy, high-cost civilization we call modern America?

Not too good, and in many cases even disastrous, as middle America shoulders the burden of bloated governments designed for everyone but it.

That same little house in Long Island, according to the real estate experts in the town of Oyster Bay, has a present market value of $210,000. The new owner, Mr. Sam Green, bought Mort's house ten years ago (the Stevenses moved to Florida) and has a thirty-year fixed-rate mortgage of $100,000 at 8.5 percent interest, double that of his predecessor.

Sam works in the same electronics factory as did Mort, and gets paid $41,000 a year. It doesn't take a software genius to realize that's not enough to live nicely anymore in the suburban tri-state area around New York City.

So how does he manage? Obviously, Mrs. Green goes to

work every day. Nancy's a clerk-receptionist in a local real estate office, where she's paid $17,500 a year. Their combined
income of $58,500 a year puts them smack in the center of the
household range for suburban Long Island, New York.

Plenty to live on, right? Wrong. Life is no longer comfortable in that little house not far from the Long Island Express-
way. There's more shade in the backyard, but the old cliché
no longer means a thing. And Sam Green has a lot more to
worry about than the dog running out between cars on the
curved suburban street.

Let's look at his economy, one now heavily controlled by
five governments that have their fiscal hooks into him
through *seven* basic taxes: the local school district, the town
of Oyster Bay, Nassau County, New York State income taxes,
federal income taxes, FICA payroll taxes for Social Security
and Medicare, and state and local sales tax.

In addition, there are excise taxes on gasoline, telephone, liquor, plus tolls (they're taxes, too!) on the Thruway
and bridge levies—like in the days of the highwaymen. Because they're not expert swimmers, when they visit their in-
laws in New Jersey they're forced to pay $4 every time they
cross the George Washington Bridge, a structure that, despite
the propaganda, has been paid for scores of times over.

What does our 1993 resident of Laurel Lane pay in local
taxes? These levies have skyrocketed, several times more rapidly than inflation. The Nassau County, town of Oyster Bay,
and local school taxes come to a whopping $5,700 a year for
his small house, some twenty-five times what it was in 1950!
It alone takes 10 percent of their income, almost as much as
all taxes paid by the previous owners of the home.

What about the next level of taxation, the state of New
York? Here, the Greens are in the top 7.8 percent bracket
(which is crazy for such a modest income). With the permis-
sible deduction, that will cost them $2,603, another 5 percent
of their income.

Washington, meanwhile, takes its money first. The FICA tax of 7.65 percent for Social Security and Medicare is deducted from Mr. and Mrs. Greens' paychecks up front. That costs another $4,500, none of which is deductible.

(Next door, if you'll excuse the diversion, is Mr. Brown, a self-employed graphics artist. He makes $59,000 a year, and his is a modern sad story, repeated throughout America's hard-pressed self-employed network of millions. His Social Security payment is not 7.65 but 15.3 percent—just as if he were employer and employee combined. This invention of an irrational taxer is hardly an incentive for highly touted, super-American entrepreneurship. With a minor tax deduction, his FICA payment is $7,800, and all nondeductible!

What does Mr. Brown think of his government? That's not printable in a family volume.)

The Greens are now up to 24 percent of their total income, and we haven't even confronted the big monster, the Washington Establishment, which becomes larger each year as its *contributors* become poorer.

Washington's Exemption Racket

Let's look at the Greens' combined income of $58,500 as the tax man would. What deductions are allowed? First, there's the personal exemption of $2,300. How does that compare with the $600 exemption Mort Stevens had in 1950?

Poorly. So poorly that we're staring at one of the government's most insidious tricks—raising taxes not by open legislation but through inflation and other secret manipulations. The foremost of those is the sneaky change in the *personal exemption.*

Six hundred dollars back in 1950, it is now $2,300. But just by correcting it for forty-four years of inflation, it would now be *$8,700!* If the four-person Green family could receive that same personal exemption today, they'd have an automatic $34,800 deduction going in. Shades of former happiness in the USA.

When we add in Mr. Green's other deductions: $5,700 in local taxes, $2,603 in state taxes, and mortgage interest of $5,500, they wouldn't *start* to pay taxes until they had passed $49,000 in income, thumbing their noses at Uncle Sam all the way to the bank. Their whole federal income tax would be less than 2 percent of their income, a near-exact return to the good old days.

But no such luck today. That glorious dream vanished as we created the bloated giant we call Washington.

The actual federal income tax on the Greens is, instead, $5,525, plus the $4,500 in FICA taxes, or a total of $10,025 to Uncle Sam. All told, the taxes paid by the four-member family is somewhat frightening: $5,700 for local taxes; $2,603 in state taxes; approximately $1,000 in sales taxes; $520 in gas taxes (two cars); $200 in telephone and other excise taxes; $160 in tolls; and over $10,000 to Washington. The total—$20,208—is three times as much, in real dollars, as the amount paid by their 1950 counterparts, the Stevenses.

Could the Greens' burden be unusual, one larger than most? Hardly. New York City residents, who pay an extra 4.2 percent marginal tax in their bracket, or about $1,500, push the edge of the misery envelope.

In fact, the Greens are getting off easy. The typical New York State resident pays a higher tab to his governments than they do. The Tax Foundation maintains a "Tax Calendar" that shows, by date and state, how long a person must work just to meet all tax liabilities—that is, before he can put a single slice of pizza in his mouth.

The national "Tax Freedom" date is May 3. In New York State, that date is May 22, or 142 days into the year. That's 39 percent of the year—and just four days short of 40 percent. Connecticut is a close runner-up, with May 14 as the dreaded cutoff date, with New Jersey and California not far behind.

The "Spending Freedom" day, the amount of time Americans have to work before they can pay off the total government tab, including the deficit, actually comes twenty-three days later, *May 26*. In New York State that day is June 17, almost half the year. Little wonder the natives are restless.

So "typical" Mr. and Mrs. New Yorker (not including masochistic New York City residents) would be paying $21,450 on the Greens' income—an amount shaped by legislators who don't have to strain to find $20 for the baby-sitter to go to a $7.00 movie, which with popcorn and diet Coke sets the Greens back $40 or so, not counting the price of gas.

Like so many Americans today, the Greens are struggling from paycheck to paycheck to support an enormous panoply of governments, several of which are unseen. In the deadly triangle called the tri-state area (New York, New Jersey, and Connecticut), the burden is not only great but continually growing more painful, as it is in most of the country.

And the pain is not subjective. It is easily countable without an abacus. In just the past decade, the tax burden in that area has risen 35 percent. In Connecticut, a new 4.5 percent state income tax, which does not allow for most federal deductions, is making life intolerable for a community decimated by cuts in defense contracting.

That story is repeated elsewhere in America. Only seven states—Texas, Florida, South Dakota, Alaska, Washington, Wyoming, Nevada—have no state income tax, and the courageous list gets smaller every year. In 1991, Connecticut bit the dust.

As we've seen, the Greens spend over $20,000 on taxes, plus another $920 a month, or $11,000 a year on their home mortgage payments. Together, that $31,000 takes up 54 percent of their income, or three times as much tax-mortgage burden as handled by the Stevenses in 1950. Instead of 80 percent of their income being tax and mortgage free, the Greens have only 46 percent with which they must pay for food, insurance, telephone, utilities, clothing, car payments, baby-sitting, gasoline, credit card payments, etc. There's *no* money left to save for the kids' education or anything else.

What about vacations? Sure, the Greens intend to take one. They'll be going with the kids to Disneyworld—in 1996.

What's the difference to them? Only the quality of life, something the government and its tax monster have stolen from the American people.

The Shrinking Pay Raise

Now let's say the Greens have good luck (God forbid) and increase their income by $20,000 to $78,500 a year, then become courageous (or foolhardy) enough to buy a new home with an extra bedroom. What is the marginal rate of taxes they'll pay on the extra money?

First there is the 28 percent federal rate on all taxable income over $36,900, which is a ridiculous idea because it doesn't take into account the 7.65 percent FICA tax, which makes that rate 35.6 percent. (What about food money?) Then there's the yearly hidden increase in FICA taxes, in which the maximum rises each year, to some $59,000 in 1994. Next there is the new Medicare tax of 1.45 percent on *all* income above the FICA limit, still another yearly federal income tax hike. That will cost them another few hundred dollars. Then there is the top 7.8 percent New York State tax on the full extra $20,000, or another $1,560.

We also have to add in the extra $3,000 for county, town, and local school taxes on the new house, which is assessed on a percentage of "market value," a figure that cleverly escalates with each new "reevaluation."

We should not forget the new federal gasoline tax, which brings the total up to 18.4 cents a gallon, which, with state gas taxes, costs Sam Green and his wife an extra $100 a year. Also, there's more sales taxes, on and on, ad infinitum.

What happened to the extra $20,000? It was mainly eaten away by governments with greasy, itchy palms. The Greens, people of modest means, are fast approaching the catacylsmic 45–50 percent marginal rate that is the symbol of total depression—psychological and fiscal—for hard-working middle-class people.

Realizing that various governments have gone into partnership with their bank account creates a powerful disincentive for Americans who hope to rise into the upper middle class, the socioeconomic description of the American dream.

In that one tax equation, read the death of the middle class.

That bite on the Greens' extra income is nothing compared to what would happen to their neighbors, the Joneses, if they had the "good fortune" to jump $20,000 in income and move into the middle class, an endangered species not protected by the Environmental Protection Agency.

The Joneses earn $37,000 a year, and are thrilled, temporarily, by their luck. Mrs. Jones, who had been unemployed, has just found a job for $20,000 a year. That extra money is even more vulnerable than the Greens' extra earnings. It has catapulted them into the higher federal bracket—from 15 percent into 28 percent. The Joneses also have to pay 7.65 percent on the additional $20,000 for Social Security taxes. With state taxes in the higher bracket, that $20,000 increase has been cut down in its tracks.

We've been dealing here with property owners. What about a single person, say a woman, who has been successful and is renting an apartment in New York City. What happens to her $60,000 gross income?

Read 'em and weep. First, she must pay federal income tax, FICA tax, state income tax, and New York City income tax. With the standard deductions, her taxes are as follows: federal, $12,975; FICA, $4,528; state, $3,896; city, $2,187.

That's a frightening $23,586. (If she itemized the state and city taxes, she'd save $300.) When it's all done, adding in sales, excise, and gas taxes, we're talking about a tax bite of $24,500!

So this $60,000 salaried woman now has only a $35,500 net income—a figure that is askew from the lifestyle she developed under the false illusion that she was "successful."

Could anyone expect her to love her government?

And what of the family that has "made it," the legendary Americans with two $50,000-a-year salaries, for a gross income of $100,000. They're no longer such an object of envy. Their costs have risen dramatically with a new standard of living—one they can no longer really afford. Property taxes are now $8,000. Their state taxes are $5,500. Their FICA taxes, for two, are $7,500. The rest of the federal tax, after deductions for property and state taxes, in the 28 percent marginal rate (fast approaching the 31 percent rate), is $17,000, for a total federal bite of $24,500. His nondeductible sales taxes, including those paid on the occasional new car, averages over $1,000.

The total, including gas, telephone, liquor taxes, tolls, etc., comes to a frightening figure: *$40,000.*

And what if the couple has the nerve (or ignorance) to follow the well-advertised American dream and become a *self-employed* entrepreneur: contractor, interior decorator, small businessperson, consultant, architect, whatever? What is Uncle Sam's reward for the good citizen's attempt to stimulate the economy?

You guessed it. A giant penalty. They have to pay virtually double Social Security and Medicare taxes, which are now $13,000 for the couple—a nondeductible bloody sacrifice to the government tax monster. Their net tab, even with deductions for property and state taxes (but not sales taxes), comes to almost $45,000, just enough to make life miserable—courtesy of Uncle Sam.

(If he is a renter, the self-employed person would save

the $8,000 property taxes, but loses the deduction and pays $2,400 more in federal taxes. And he has no house.)

Perhaps there are no dry eyes for the couple with that majestic income, but isn't that what all Americans are striving to make? And won't they be miserably disappointed when they arrive, holding only the *illusion* of wealth, or even true comfort?

What happened? How did the upwardly mobile working American of 1950 become the oppressed modern American?

Death and taxes. We love to talk about their inevitability, but we don't think about them as one and the same—at least not yet. Perhaps we should, especially as we watch the not-so-slow, insidious murder of the American middle class through excessive taxation.

Jefferson's Warning

It was Thomas Jefferson who reminded us that a "wise" and "good" government "shall not take from the mouth of labor the bread it has earned."

Jefferson was advising his colleagues, our Founding Fathers, to be watchful of taxes as they drafted the Constitution. Government, he warned, could not afford to impoverish its own citizens. When they met in Philadelphia, that sage handful of men (much brighter than the present crop) wisely drew on Jefferson's philosophy.

What happened to his counsel? Fortunately, it ended up in a historic codicil of the Constitution—Article I, Section 9, Subsection 4—which protected the fledgling nation from the fiscal sins of Europe. It simply stated that there shall be "no capitation" or "direct" or head or income tax instituted in these United States.

With that phrase, and the absence of income taxes, America became the shining beacon for the world. While Europe was saddled with despotic levies, America alone was spared. The result is history.

By and large, the typical citizen's presence was unknown in Washington, and he was subject, almost exclusively, only to local taxes that he and his neighbors could control. With that single stroke of political genius, nothing could hold back the fledgling nation. And nothing did.

Then what happened?

During these innocent years, only the Constitution restrained politicians eager to get their fiscal hooks into the burgeoning middle class by passing an income tax law. Lincoln did put in an emergency income tax, legal or not, during the Civil War, but it expired just a few years later. In the 1890s, Congress tried again, but the Supreme Court ruled the levy unconstitutional.

Finally, in 1913, President Woodrow Wilson turned his back on the Founding Fathers and sought to repeal the Constitution. He succeeded, and with the Sixteenth Amendment, the federal income levy became legal. By a strange twist of irony, it was instituted by progressive politicians, such as Wilson, in an attempt to get the "robber barons" of the era to pay more taxes. But though it was designed to take *only* from the rich (and taxpayers were absolutely assured of that), the amendment has boomeranged against the working and middle classes, the very people it was designed to help.

The new federal income tax rate was set at 1 percent, with a 7 percent ceiling, and was enforced against only those rich enough to qualify. Up through the 1920s and 1930s, nothing much came of it. In fact, by the outbreak of World War II in 1941, only one in seven wage-earners even filed with the government.

But that ill-advised change in the Constitution has now come back to haunt us. The individual income tax has evolved into a machine expert at milking the cash cow—the American middle class, who now pay over 80 percent of the $515 billion the Treasury receives in individual taxes. Meanwhile the rates have regularly escalated from that meager 1 percent to its present 45 percent plus when FICA taxes are figured in, even though they are often ignored by the press when talking about income tax rates.

This, of course, is in addition to the sizable income taxes levied by forty-three states and even many cities. There are several thousand government units in the United States— states, counties, cities, towns—that now levy income taxes.

Given the go-ahead by U.S. Supreme Court decisions that ruled that the Sixteenth Amendment applied to them as well, local politicians saw that the cash cow could serve up equally rich milk, even cream, for the locals. So what started out in 1913 as an often-overlooked constitutional amendment has now become the tax monster, the progenitor of big, nation-destroying government.

During the last thirty years, the metamorphosis of the income tax bite has been one of the cleverest manipulations in history, one shaped in Washington by the masters of legal pickpocketing.

As we've seen, the first step in destroying the middle class was *not* to raise the personal exemption by simple "indexing," which would have kept it on a par with inflation.

Bracket Racket
The second step was even more insidious. Called "bracket creep," it moved ordinary Americans from low brackets into the sacred ground once occupied only by the wealthy—the 30, 40 percent bracket, and more—not because their real income moved ahead, but because their salaries increased with inflation. While their purchasing power remained the same or decreased, their taxes kept escalating as they *unprospered*.

"Bracket creep," which could more properly be labeled "the bracket racket," began in earnest in the 1960s and reached a crescendo in the 1970s, especially during the administration of Jimmy Carter. With inflation at 13 percent, people *falsely* zoomed ahead in earnings, placing themselves back where they started from in *real* dollars. But they were still propelled into a higher bracket for income tax purposes, both federal and state.

What started out as a nibbling away of disposable income became a carnivorous attack on the family pocketbook. It was not until 1983 that President Reagan and Congress "indexed" tax rates for inflation.

But by then it was too late. The middle class had already been snookered into high-tax purgatory.

Still, Washington was not satisfied. It developed other arcane devices to destroy the middle class. One of the worst was taking away benefits—now you see it, now you don't—that had been previously granted.

In the 1960s, working Americans were finally given two excellent tax breaks: the IRA retirement system and Income Tax Averaging. Under the IRAs, anyone could save up to $2,000 a year in a special account and deduct it from their income. With the continual changes in the rules of Social Security, which was being refashioned from a pension plan into a welfare scheme, the IRA gave the taxpayer a way out from dependency on an untrustworthy government. It became extremely popular and zoomed upward to several billion a year by 1986.

Income tax averaging, created in 1965, was fashioned for those taxpayers with fluctuating income, whether they had been laid off the year before and were finally regaining their stride, or a self-employed person with a inconsistent cash flow. Suddenly hitting it big in one year didn't become a tax tragedy (instead of a victory), because the income could be averaged out over three years.

But in 1986, with one stroke of the pen, both the tax benefits of the IRA and income averaging were eliminated in the so-called Tax Reform Act, another swipe at the middle class. The law actually *increased* the taxes of millions of wage-earners. "Most of my clients found their taxes went up, not down, as a result of the law," says a busy Connecticut CPA.

That same law contained several bitter pills for middle-class Americans. They lost *all* interest costs except home mortgages. That meant that interest money spent on credit cards, buying a car, and getting a loan to send children to college were no longer deductible. In a nation built on debt, that became another nail in you know what, and a disincentive to spend. As a going away swipe, they even took away the deduction for sales taxes, which made buying a car or a refrigerator that much more expensive.

The government seems to look for, and find, as many ways possible to penalize citizens trying to make—and keep—an honest buck. It's as if there's a devilish little man with a green eye shade in the basement of the Treasury Building on 14th and Pennsylvania who works overtime dreaming up an obstacle course for life in the United States.

One hidden penalty is geography. The government fails to take into account regional cost of living differences when setting tax rates. A family with a combined income of $60,000 can just make out in a New York suburb, while a similar family is quite comfortable in Arkansas on $40,000. (If you recall, the former Governor of that state made only $33,000.)

But Washington couldn't care less. We are all Americans, they say, and must pay our share of income taxes. Meanwhile, a $60,000 New Yorker quickly moves from the 15 percent rate at $36,900 taxable into the 28 percent bracket, while the $40,000 Arkansas family, who may be much richer in purchasing power, stays at the comfortable 15 percent level.

So much for tax intelligence in the Great Beltway Universe!

The tax laws are written by men with considerable net worth, and with little understanding of what wage-earners must do to make ends meet. As if that were not enough, these august legislators continually pass new tax laws, as they did in 1982, 1986, 1990, and 1993.

An antitax group in Michigan has concocted a slogan, "Not One More Dime," which could become a rallying call for bumper-sticker aficionados. It should also be a warning for legislators that they're in danger of losing their seats to the wrath of an awakened electorate.

If not, there may be another remedy. Should we fix the pay of the entire political class, from President to Mayor, to the household income of the average American? We can then sit back and smile as we watch them fall over each other to reign in the tax monster.

In the meantime, what can we do? What is a sensible tax plan to heal the pain of working middle-class Americans?

It's really not difficult. As we reduce the size of government (see Chapter 12) we will not only eliminate the deficit but be able to cut the taxes on the middle class as well. Here's an interim plan to make our income taxes less painful:

1. Raise the personal exemption immediately to $3,500 for each adult and child. Then increase the exemption each year twice as fast as inflation until it reaches the *real* dollar amount of $600 in 1948, which in 1994 would be $8,700.

2. Reinstitute the income averaging law.

3. Eliminate double Social Security payments for the self-employed, freeing up entrepreneurship.

4. Change the income tax law from two initial levels to three, making the tax bite smaller and more gradual. The present tax rate is 15 percent on the first $36,900, which then jumps to 28 percent up to $89,150, then to 31 percent above that, then to 36 percent at $140,000 for a married couple filing jointly. At $250,000 it jumps again.

The new rates for people earning less than $89,150 should be changed as follows: the 15 percent rate until

$50,000, then 20 percent to $65,000, then 28 percent up to $89,150.

5. Reinstate the IRA retirement plan for all.

6. Reinstate deductions for the interest on *all* loans, credit cards included.

7. Eliminate the 1.45 percent Medicare taxes above the FICA limit, which is approximately $59,000 in 1994.

8. Make the bracket ranges reflect different regional living costs by using average property taxes as a guide.

9. Let's begin to talk about repealing the Sixteenth Amendment, and eliminating the income tax altogether— substituting it with a fair consumption or sales tax. (Think of the blessings of not even filing!)

What would this scheme do for a family of four with a household income of $50,000?

It would, almost immediately, cut their federal taxes by almost 20 percent. That savings would grow each year as the "double indexing" of the personal exemption clicks in, eventually reducing their taxes by one-fourth. Having accomplished that on a federal level, we can turn our attention to the states, cities, counties, and towns, and reign in the junior tax monsters.

Can we really afford to do this?

That's not the question. The question is: Can we afford not to do it?—to continue the erosion of the middle class perpetrated by an uncaring Washington. We had better be prepared to do it if by the year 2000 we want an America we still recognize.

To learn how we can manage this miracle, please read on.

Chapter Four

Government Without a Theory

STATES AS COLONIES, CITIZENS AS SUBJECTS

It happened at the near edge of the United States, so you might think that the irrational tentacles of Washington wouldn't reach that far.

Think again. It was in Anchorage, Alaska, directly on Cook Inlet and the Gulf of Alaska. This city of 240,000 has a waste problem, and like a lot of other coastal towns, it empties its water waste into the ocean.

"We have a waiver from the Environmental Protection Agency [EPA], so we don't have to build a secondary treatment plant," says Paula Easley, city governmental affairs officer. "That would cost us as much as $150 million, which is three-fourths our entire annual budget. But to keep the federal waiver, we have to follow EPA regulations.

"We have to treat a certain percentage of the organic material in our waste water to meet Washington's standards. The trouble is that our waste water often doesn't have enough organic material in it. It's too clean, because from time to time it gets diluted by the snow run-off. So we had a problem: How do we treat what we don't have?"

I was surprised. "Why don't you just explain to the EPA that your waste water was too clean?" I asked, naively.

I could sense Miss Easley's smile over the long-distance phone wires. "You're kidding, right? We're dealing with Washington!"

Instead of fighting the City Hall down east, Anchorage found a way out.

"We got the fish companies to dump fish guts into the waste water to pollute it," explains Ms. Easley, "then we cleaned that up—and kept our waiver."

Obviously, the federal government is unstable. But we already know that. What we may not know is how it operates its latest and perhaps most expensive racket.

It's called *unfunded mandates*, and it's bankrupting the states and cities and making a mockery of the Constitution. One of them is Washington's mandate to Anchorage, and cities throughout the nation, to clean up their waste water, or else. Apparently, it doesn't make any difference if they're clean to begin with.

Well, doesn't the government put strings on all their programs? Like Medicare and Welfare? Yes, but there's a big difference. Those programs are supported by matching grants from Washington—anywhere from 50 percent to 100 percent of the money. But not these.

When a series of high-sounding programs were signed by two recent Presidents—the Clean Air Act, the Clean Water Act, the Americans with Disabilities Act, and more—the me-

dia responded with huzzahs. Who doesn't want clean air and
water, and to help the disabled? Washington was doing a job
for the American people, right?

Wrong. The federal government was talking with its
mouth, not its pocketbook. Washington was taking the bows,
but the states and localities were paying the *entire* bill. In actuality, this is the blossoming of a new era in Washington irresponsibility, one that threatens to bankrupt the states and the
cities, and bring them down into the same fiscal morass as
the federal government.

This new phenomenon in government is virtually unknown to most Americans. *Unfunded mandates* is a concept
in which the cities and states are treated as vassals of a
power-mad Washington. Less polite, it means that a dictatorial
central government makes the laws, which the states and cities not only have to obey but have to pay for, heavily and
forever, by themselves.

Meanwhile, Washington contributes nothing except aggravation.

"As the federal budgets get tighter and there's less and
less money to spend," explains a General Accounting Office
[GAO] official, "the government passes the buck for programs
it originates. It pulls back its money but leaves the strings attached."

New York City, one victim of this federal scam, agrees.
"The government's goals are admirable, and the Washington
politicians love these programs," says Judy Chesser, director
of New York's Washington office. "They take the credit but
don't have to raise the taxes. We have to pay for it all."

Are these mandates just petty cash, few, and short-lived?

Quite the opposite. The National Conference of State
Legislatures (NCSL) conducts a Mandate Watch to keep tabs
on such Washington excesses. They have found *172* federal
mandates covering virtually every area of local government:
education, environment, criminal justice, health, handicap

problems, communications, transportation, energy, taxation, and so on.

And they keep coming, fast and furious. Just in the last Congress, says the NCSL, 115 new bills were introduced that "would make the states pay for a program designed by the federal government." As we've mentioned, just seven proposed new mandates would cost localities almost $2 billion.

Not only are states forced to put up the money, but each mandate weakens, or "preempts," state authority, increasing Washington's control over ordinary Americans.

Washington As Big Brother

What kind of micromanaging is Washington doing?

Everything. The list is endless, but here are a few minor examples recently passed or being considered in Congress.

States are being prohibited from starting new lotteries based on sporting events. States are being required to provide bilingual assistance to voters if more than 5 percent of the voting age population speaks a foreign language—even if they don't vote.

Fishermen, anyone? A new law will prohibit the states from letting anyone catch striped bass if the state action is inconsistent with the federal Interstate Commission on Striped Bass. Consumers? A new law prohibits states from enacting *stricter* consumer and privacy protection than permitted by federal law. Toys, anyone? A new federal law preempts state authority to label toys and games.

States have to pay for energy conservation plans for apartment houses and office buildings; they must do the same with school antidrug policies; eliminate asbestos hazards; inventory and check underground storage tanks, like gas stations. States can no longer regulate marine mammals, and they must service and pay for aid to handicapped infants and toddlers. Once the federal Superfund cleans up a toxic site, the state must maintain it and treat the groundwater.

Just one new bill, the widely hailed Motor Vehicle legislation, will cost the states $20 million a year, which is Wash-
ington's low-ball figure. The NCSL places the cost at $58
million, plus a onetime state cost of $25 million for putting it
on computer.

Some mandates are nuisances, picking away at what little sovereignty the states have left. But most are big package,
budget-breaking items in the fields of environment, crime, education, and transportation.

The new federal burden is really unconscionable. Estimates put the costs anywhere from $100 billion to $500 billion
a year, and growing. The result? States and localities have to
raise property, sales, income taxes and user fees in order to
please an insatiable Washington.

It also pushes up the cost of government nationwide, a
figure that takes forty-two cents on every dollar in 1994. With
the costs of mandates (which you won't find in the federal
budget), it could reach fifty cents on the dollar by the year
2000. That could signal the end of the United States as we
know it—and possibly cause a systemic depression that
would not yield to a new New Deal.

New York City, for one, doesn't know how it is going to
pay for the mandates. A recent worksheet shows how much
it will cost New York to appease the Big Bad Brother in the
Beltway, figures that will surely go up.

Eight dewatering facilities will cost New York City $860
million, plus $22 million a year to operate. Land disposal re-
quired by Washington will cost $125 million each year. Con-
struction of a long-term sludge disposal facility will cost $1.2
billion.

What will Washington contribute? The professionals call
it NFD—No Federal Dollars. A cabdriver in Brooklyn might
better label it IYF—"In Your Face."

What about clean water? New York City has three plants
that don't meet the Clean Water Act's Secondary Treatment

requirements. To upgrade just *one* of them will cost $800 million, and more later. That's big money, but the future is even more threatening. New York has a federal waiver on a water filtration plan. It's eventual cost? *Four to eight billion dollars.*

Federal contribution? NFD, Nada, Zippo, In Your Face.

Like clean air? Doesn't everyone? Ask New York City, which is desperately trying to conform to federal regulations. Just for downtown Brooklyn, $50 million of the city's money has already been budgeted. Wait a few years. It'll take more than an abacus to add up the costs.

New York City is still working on estimates for other mandates, including education and criminal justice. (The city's cost of two *shared mandates,* Aid to Families with Dependent Children [AFDC] and Medicaid, has just passed $3 billion a year!) One scary estimate is that it will take a billion dollars a year just to conform to Washington's criminal justice requirements.

Federal contribution? NFD.

The problems of Anchorage, Alaska, are small by comparison. But not for it. That city figures that it will cost $25 million this year to conform to federal environmental requirements alone. That cost will rise rapidly, taking $4,649 from *each Anchorage household* in this decade. The total tab to this medium-sized city will be $428,628,000, almost a half billion dollars. And that doesn't include the cost of conforming to recent amendments to the Clean Air and Clean Water acts.

Multiply that by cities around the country, and by other federal mandate areas, and the future looms frightening.

Reckoning is also going on in the heartland of Columbus, Ohio. They're not optimistic. Just conforming to federal environmental mandates is costing the city $82 million a year. A lot of money? Sure, but Columbus estimates that for the decade it will be $1.6 billion! Just pleasing Washington on fourteen environmental acts will take 23 percent of the city's entire budget.

Where's the money going to come from? Nobody knows, and a dictatorial Washington couldn't care less. As one federal employee says, "Washington's trying to balance the budget on the backs of the people."

Is all of this constitutional? Not likely.

The Forgotten Tenth

The powers not delegated to the United States by the Constitution, nor prohibited by it to the States, are reserved to the States respectively, or to the people.

That's the entire Tenth Amendment to the Constitution, the last item in the Bill of Rights, ratified on December 15, 1791.

It was no minor accident of history. Carefully drawn by Madison and Jefferson, its purpose was to quiet their fears that Washington, D.C. would someday become a monster to rival the centralized autocracy of Europe. Without that safeguard, they worried, the government in the new "federal city" could use its powers to oppress the American people.

The amendment was part of an exquisitely developed theory that distinguished us from the rest of the world. The American system blended state sovereignty and local independence with the uniting umbrella of a federal government that had limited powers.

It was checks, balances, freedom, and common sense all wrapped up into one magnificent phrase.

Did it succeed? Yes, for most of our history. In fact, the theory worked so well that Americans not only surpassed Europe in freedom but in the material well-being of its people as well.

So things are still good, right? We are still bound by the genius of that document, aren't we?

Hell, no.

The Tenth Amendment might as well be a piece of discarded newspaper. It is laughed at in the White House and in the halls of Congress as an "outmoded" principle. Washington is the center of the empire, they crow, and we must step to its call as our Founding Fathers were once forced to yield to London. The day Jefferson and Madison feared has arrived.

Every day, the federal government exercises more control by issuing regulations and mandates that must be obeyed. It also seduces the states with matching grants, which some falsely see as "free" money. Instead, the states and localities are lured into the federal web.

In its drive for power, the federal government strives to homogenize the nation, to force it into McDonald-like imitations of the central government. In the process, it not only robs the states and people of power, but makes them pay for their own oppression.

There is no doubt that the long-range plan of Washington is to convert the states, the cities, the counties, and the towns of America into colonies of the federal government.

As the violations of the Constitution continue daily, the theory that made America great is rapidly being lost. Without the original American concept, what do we have in its place?

A Made Up Government

That's best described as a *poor imitation of Europe*, coupled with some remnants of the old American system. It's not Jefferson and it's not really Europe. It's a newly cobbled, made-up method of government that exists nowhere else in the democratic world. It operates without a theory and combines the failures of the American and European systems into the worst of both worlds. Without a sound concept behind it, the new Washington-directed American government is doomed to practical failure, which, of course, has already begun.

The basic difference between the European system and our present ad hoc one is that theirs is designed, at great expense, to deliver enormous services to the middle class on a centralized basis. Washington seeks to ape them with a centralized system, but while it makes the mass of middle-class Americans pay for that scheme, it delivers the services elsewhere.

Let's compare, for instance, how the European and American governments treat their children. In his swan song to Congress, the January 1993 "Economic Report of the President," former President George Bush spoke proudly of how we take care of our own. That year, he said, the government would spend almost $90 billion on children, boasting that it was an increase of 67 percent in three years, a figure since raised by the Clinton administration.

Admirable, surely. But whose children?

Few Americans have ever seen that largesse. If we ask average parents if they've received any of that enormous bounty, they'd look at you curiously, then answer, "no." The money, as usual, is always going somewhere else.

But how about Europe? If we travel to Germany or France, supposed models of the new centralized Washington government, we'd get a resounding "yes" from the working middle class. In Germany, every month, every German family (without any means test, as in our GI Bill, the last piece of near-universal social legislation in America) receives a check from the government for all its children.

Called *Kindergeld*, or Children's Money, it's substantial. In the envelope are 70 deutsche marks for one child, 120 for two, and 150 for three. Only now, with the crush of costs from East Germany, is the government contemplating cutting out the wealthy. But the middle class, up to a yearly income of at least $67,000, will still receive the stipend.

The great distance between the European and American systems today is that our Constitution did not set up near-total rule by Washington. The result is that the present central functions of Washington, except for those mentioned in the

Constitution (interstate commerce, immigration, defense, inland waterways, etc.) are mainly hollow, making the American imitation of Europe a joke, even if an expensive one.

An Impotent D of E

In France, for example, the Ministry of Education educates all the children of the nation, and not only has control but accountability. In the United States, the Department of Education doesn't educate *one single child*, and has no accountability. It does not contribute directly to the budget of the school districts, because education in the United States is constitutionally a state function, and is handled primarily by the towns and cities.

Washington has no power over school curricula. If Paris wants trigonometry taught in the tenth grade, it merely sends out a directive and it is done. If the Department of Education in Washington did that, it would bring on smiles and a good set shot of crumpled paper flying into the circular file.

Then what does the U.S. Department of Education do?

It only pretends to be an educational body. Instead, it tries to control the situation through mandates to the states and localities, accompanied by cash. In all, it picks up only 6 percent of the total tab nationally for elementary and secondary education, and almost all of that is wasted. Since the scheme is based on no known theory of government, it is a miserable failure.

The cabinet agency started out as the Office of Education, a group within the Department of Health, Education and Welfare (HEW). In 1979, President Carter created the Department of Education with the goal of improving education in America. Since then, educational results have deteriorated considerably. The department can hardly be blamed for that, but it surely has had no beneficial effect, and has yet to demonstrate any reason for its existence.

Without teaching a single child, the D of E spends $31 billion a year on 230 different projects. It spends $130 million a year on research and statistics, which have yet to improve schooling one iota. It has almost 5,000 employees and, at last count, spends an additional $60 million a year on outside consultants.

One of its major programs, Chapter I, is aimed at disadvantaged children, but they're not designed in the localities— the 15,000 school boards around the country. Instead, Washington brings strings along with its mandate.

The money, about $6 billion, doesn't go to the schools to use as they please. Washington pays the salaries of Chapter I teachers, for example, and tells them how to help poor and academically deficient children.

How do they do it? There are various methods, including "in class" instruction, where the Chapter I teacher circulates in the regular class and helps out the Chapter I kids involved. But in most cases, they use the "Pull Out" system in which the Chapter I kids are taken from their regular class and segregated in another room for special instruction. They lose one hour and gain another. Big deal.

How much special instruction do they get? An hour or less a day.

Is the program any good? Not really. The Department of Education itself has evaluated Chapter I and found it wanting. It says that Chapter I had some small value in its early years, but the benefit disappears as the children get older.

(The Head Start Program, which some educators believe helps, is not even part of the Department of Education. In strange Washington logic, it's run by Health and Human Services.)

Hollow Agencies
The same problem—important titles, Cabinet-level pageantry, and vast budgets, but little to do except spend vast amounts of money—is also true in the Department of Transportation. This is another poor imitation of European governments, which ac-

tually run much of their public transportation facilities, while in the United States transportation is a private function.

So why do we have a DOT? No one really knows, except that's it a grab bag of regulatory agencies put together for Washington's convenience. The only thing DOT runs is Amtrak, a failure that costs taxpayers almost a billion dollars a year. Otherwise, it tries to control transportation in localities in scores of ways, most of which are wasteful.

The interstate highway system, which is actually made up of connected state roads, is controlled by Washington, yet it forces the states to pay for part of the system through matching funds. (There are no federal roads, except in national parks and forests.)

While supposedly helping, the federal government regularly increases its control: it regulates the speed limits and raises the cost of road construction through federally determined labor costs (Davis-Bacon Act); it steals the enormous gas tax surplus and uses it for nontransportation purposes; and it adds billions of dollars in congressional pork to the highway budget each year.

The Department of Energy is another fake-European-style fiasco, a grab bag, made-up agency that handles everything from making atomic bombs to welfare for people who can't pay their electric bills. And in its attempt to centralize energy, it also dictates to the states, even though it provides only 6 percent of the nation's energy, and at an enormous cost.

Taxpayer-created electricity from federal dams, for example, is sold to utilities for less than two cents a kilowatt, while regular consumers pay eight to fifteen cents a kilowatt for their nonfederal power.

The Reason Why
Why do Americans permit Washington to micromanage American life when most Americans (76 percent) do not believe the federal government knows what it's doing?

The answer is complex, and goes deep into the American soul. Part of it comes from the propagation of the *big lie*, a technique perfected by the likes of fascist Germany and the totalitarian Soviet Union.

In the United States, the big lie is that Washington knows best, and that the states and localities are incompetent and cannot handle the governing of the country, as they did for most of our history—except for national emergencies.

How did the lie start? Mostly from the national unconscious, the memory of what used to be good and relatively inexpensive.

The first mass experience of modern times was the New Deal, which fed the nation in crisis, followed by the collective victory in World War II, then the postwar recovery and the success of the GI Bill of Rights, all of which strengthened the federal position. Following that, it was Washington, not the states, that provided the victory in the civil rights revolution.

Using all this accumulated prestige as a wedge, Washington has—front, center, and aggressively—been telling the American people that it is needed everywhere. For a time, the people bought the argument, which is only now being demolished by the results. Rule by Washington, in virtually every area of life, has now become standard operating procedure and it is destroying America in every way, from debt, deficit, and taxes to the seemingly inability of the nation to solve *any* problem.

It appears that the end result of federal intervention is only to exacerbate the problem with dire results. Instead of waste and inefficiency being an occasional byproduct of bureaucracy, Washington is rapidly becoming a symbol for institutionalized stupidity.

What Americans have forgotten is that during the period of grandiose federal activity, the states and localties kept the nation and its basic functions going rather effectively and at a somewhat lower cost.

In fact, today, the states are far ahead of Washington in innovation and method. Hawaii has pioneered health insurance, as has Oregon, while New Jersey, Wisconsin, and Massachusetts are far ahead of the federal government in welfare reform. Many states are consolidating departments and reducing overhead at a rapid rate. Governor Carroll Campbell of South Carolina has cut his state agency roster from seventy-nine to seventeen. The National Governors Association—and not Washington—is in the forefront of reform.

The argument of Washington versus the states was once an ideological one between liberals and conservatives. This is no longer true as *all* government threatens to overwhelm us. It is now an argument of intelligence versus ignorance, and in that battle—and only that battle—Washington is losing.

Bloated Local Government
In its attempt to micromanage American life, the federal government is a *direct* cause of high state and local taxes. But the smaller governments should not be left off the hook. As we've seen, the cost of state and local government has gone up *350 percent* in real dollars since 1960, with little to show for it. Just since 1980, nonfederal government employees have increased by 3.5 million people, a major cause of rising state taxes.

When it comes to income taxes, states love to imitate Washington. Today, 43 states have income tax laws, along with 867 cities, counties, and towns, plus multiple governments in Pennsylvania. State income taxes vary enormously nationwide from a low 1 percent to an outrageous 12 percent.

With their coffers overflowing during the 1980s, state spending went out of control. In 1960, state budgets took only 4 percent of the GDP. By 1970, that figure had jumped to 7 percent. Today, it's 9 percent of the GDP—a total of over a half trillion dollars.

The cost of state governments, not counting localities, averages about $4,600 per family of four. But some states, like Connecticut, are more flamboyant. The Nutmeg State spends $8,000 per family—quite a hefty burden on taxpayers, who, for the first time, have an income tax.

On top (or under) this, is the enormous cost of running our excessive number of cities, towns, counties, villages, and so on. Their cost has also risen from 4 percent of the GDP in 1960 to 9 percent today.

Part of that outlay is due to America's obsession with government. Whenever possible, and whatever the level, we love to institute a government, no matter how small, or large. This leads to so much duplication that we now have a giant network of local governments numbering 86,743—with 3,043 counties, 19,296 municipalities, 16,666 townships, 33,131 special districts (from pool to day-care centers), and 16,044 school and related districts, a few thousand of which are duplicated.

Historically, the massive enterprise was designed to assure local independence and to make up for what was once a relatively small operation in Washington. But now, with a mammoth federal government, we're saddled, even cursed, with both giants.

Let's take New York State and look at a typical governmental pyramid. At the bottom, the city of White Plains, for example, has the usual high cost of cities burdened with environmental, health, and school problems. But on top of it is another government, the county of Westchester, which includes White Plains. On top of that is the state of New York, then, naturally, the federal government in Washington.

Take any function, and multiply it by four, and you have a picture of American governmental waste. White Plains has a Department of Public Works, but so does the county of

Westchester. So does the state of New York, and Washington has the Federal Highway Administration. There are even country roads within the city of White Plains, including part of its main street.

Is it all necessary? Hardly. In fact, the whole concept of one of the layers—county government—is a carry-over from the squiredom of old England and is outmoded. We might even speak with authority about the "county racket." The 3,043 county governments in the United States have a payroll of 2.3 million people and total budgets of $150 billion, much of which is unnecessary.

Surprisingly, we can do very nicely without counties. In fact, two states, Connecticut and Rhode Island, have *no* counties at all, and no county budget. And they don't miss them. The famed name of Fairfield County, Connecticut, the symbol of affluent suburbia, is only a line on the map. In 1960, then Governor Abe Ribicoff presided over the *elimination* of all counties in his state. Instead, Connecticut has 169 municipalities under its state government. One whole layer was removed with the stroke of a pen.

The Great Crazy Quilt

Not only is there excessive duplication among local, state, and federal governments all over America, but within local government there is a crazy quilt of separate jurisdictions. In affluent Westchester County, New York, which sits just on top of New York City, there are six cities (Rye, Yonkers, White Plains, Mount Vernon, New Rochelle, and Peekskill), fourteen townships, and twenty-three villages, each with its own overlapping government.

Suburban Nassau County, Long Island, is flooded with government. The score is two cities, three towns, and *sixty-four* incorporated villages, plus numerous unincorporated areas under the town governments, plus school and special districts. Some households can be taxed by as many as five local governments, plus New York State and Washington, D.C.

Nearby Suffolk County is another giant crazy quilt. Under the county government there are ten towns and thirty incorporated villages, plus other unincorporated areas. And each of these three counties has a County Executive structure as well as full-sized legislatures.

Little wonder that America has become a government-politics-tax-crazy nation.

If New York State didn't have such giant subdivisions as Nassau, Suffolk, and Westchester County governments, which have a combined budget of $5 billion, it could return the power to simple municipalities as in Connecticut, and reduce both the complexity of government and the tax rates.

The story of America's counties is inexplicable except as historical accident. There's no rhyme or reason in their size or jurisdiction. Los Angeles County has 8.86 million residents, while little Loving County, Texas, has 107 people.

Counties made sense back in the nineteenth century when America was largely a rural country. It was an attempt to create quasi-municipalities out of disconnected villages. It worked then, but today urban areas have intruded on the counties, and they're all wrapped up in a skein of confusion.

In some urban areas, as in New York City, the counties (boroughs) are smaller than the city, while in others, like Los Angeles, the county is three times as populous. Los Angeles County includes eighty-eight cities (like Los Angeles, Beverly Hills, Long Beach, Pasadena, etc.) plus about a million people in "unincorporated" areas, who rely on the county as their municipality.

We've grown used to it, but woe to the taxpayer. It's an inefficient, illogical, overlapping, and expensive system.

But despite this crazy quilt, hasn't federal aid to the states and localities eased the burden of local governments?

No. In fact, exactly the opposite. States and localities

keep crying for more federal aid, but they're making a mistake. They forget that with the seduction comes control, followed by even larger local costs.

The infusion of federal money has only *increased* the cost of local government. The two have risen in tandem, somewhat like the effect of third-party insurance on the cost of health care. The Cato Institute, a Washington think tank, has examined the relation between federal aid and state taxes and concluded that there is an almost exact one-to-one relationship between rising state taxes and federal aid in the last forty years.

One of the reasons is Washington's *606* categorical grants—$225 billion in programs that states and localities can apply for. But in most cases, there are two strings attached. The locals have to follow federal guidelines, and usually have to put up matching funds. In only 2 cases out of the 606 is the money sent without strings.

There's no end to the "grants." They range from Medicaid to Job Training to Airport Improvement to Geosciences to Abandoned Mine Reclamation to Wildlife Restoration. Vice President Gore's "National Performance Report" hopes to better organize the 606 so that states can get the money easier, and with less bureaucracy.

Well and good. But that's far from a solution. The grants don't come cheaply, and the people usually can't afford them.

Medicaid is a case in point. The federal government pays 50 percent of the cost in Connecticut, for example, but the state has little to say about how the money in spent. When a welfare mother gives birth, for example, the usual reimbursement for doctors is not high enough to attract specialists to handle the delivery. What did Washington do? As part of the Omnibus Reconciliation Act of 1989, they mandated that the Medicaid reimbursement for doctors delivering babies of unwed mothers on AFDC be upped from the typical 50 percent to 90 percent.

The result? The state must now pay its fifty-fifty share of a much larger doctor fee, costing taxpayers millions. "This means we have to pay out about $2,500 per delivery," says a Connecticut Medicaid spokesman, "and we can't afford it."

The equation has been proven again and again. The more federal aid that comes in, the more state and local money that goes out, and the higher local taxes become.

Well, can't Connecticut tell Washington where to go?

Surely, but then Washington will really tell Connecticut where to go. The state will lose *all* of its Medicaid money for not conforming to that one mandate.

For the time being, Washington has the upper hand in its crusade to run, oppress, and possibly destroy the United States. But occasionally a state will stand up to the federal government. California recently was mandated to take more lead out of its drinking water. The state said "fine," but they couldn't pay for it. If they wanted the lead out, the Governor's office told the EPA, you pay for it. So far, it's been a Mexican standoff.

New York Sues
New York State has gone even further on one environmental case. It sued Washington in federal court. The case, *New York* vs. *the United States, et al.* involved an EPA mandate that would force the state to seize and take title to a piece of toxic waste property. After that, the state would have to assume liability for the clean up and any environmental damage.

New York sued on the basis of the Tenth Amendment, that the federal government was violating state sovereignty according to the Constitution. The lower courts decided against New York, but on June 19, 1992, the U.S. Supreme Court ruled in the state's favor on one aspect of the case—with the ghosts of Jefferson and Madison all over the document. In the majority opinion delivered by Sandra Day O'Connor, the court decided that *the federal government did not have the power to force the state of New York to take title to anything.* Thus they were not required to assume any liability.

This is a beginning. The future must hold out the following promise: That states and citizens will sue the federal government on specific violations of the Tenth Amendment whenever Washington overplays its hand, as it regularly does. And that federal and state legislators will understand that "grants" and "mandates" end up first in coercion, then in bankruptcy of both Washington and the states.

We cannot expect the Supreme Court to quickly make a sweeping decision upholding the Tenth Amendment and chastising, and reigning in, the federal government. That would wipe out at least half of Washington's programs. But little by little, if the O'Connor decision is any guide, the court can side with the people and first halt, then whittle away at, the embryonic dictatorship we call Washington.

Meanwhile, are our Congressmen, supposed representatives of the people, doing anything to help out?

Most are working overtime against the people. They are seeking to make Washington into a centralized city of total power, a kind of London, Paris, or Bonn all in one. But those foreign capitals provide many services for the mass of their people, while our version is not only ineffectual, wasteful, and antitheoretical but geared to everyone *except the working middle class.*

But other Congressmen are fighting the good fight. Right now, there are over twenty bills in the congressional hopper that want to stem at least one aspect of Washington hubris—the use of unfunded mandates.

The mildest one is by Congressman James Moran of Virginia, a former Mayor. It would require the federal government to estimate the cost of each mandate beforehand, in the hope this would slow down Washington. Congressman Christopher Shays of Connecticut also has a bill that requires cost estimates for mandates, including any changes made in committee or floor debate. Congresswoman Olympia Snowe of Maine wants the states to be free of any unfunded mandates unless Uncle Sam pays the cost in full.

HR. 140, proposed by Congressman Gary Condit of California makes it complete. It says that a federal mandate, including the requirement to meet "national standards," shall be legal "only if all funds necessary to pay the direct costs incurred by the government in conducting the activity are provided by the federal government."

Amen.

So, what can we do to slow down the aggressive Washington monster? And what can we do to reduce the cost of state and local government, which is silently eroding the nation's pocketbook?

Here is a six-point program:

1. Pass the Condit bill and make all federal unfunded mandates illegal.

2. In the case of shared mandates, like Medicaid, states must be given the right to refuse *any* part of the federal aid and still keep those parts they want.

3. State powers must be strengthened and federal powers reduced as part of a concerted campaign. We need to make clear, if necessary with a new constitutional amendment, what the federal government can and cannot do to preempt the powers of the states and the people.

4. All the states should follow the Connecticut plan and move toward the elimination of all counties. That antique form of government should be replaced with a single layer of municipalities under the states.

5. The cost of state and local government, now eighteen cents on every dollar in the GDP, must be cut by at least one-third. The first step is to eliminate 5 million of the 16 million state and local government employees through attrition. By

rehiring only 20 percent of those who leave, die, or retire, the reduction can become a reality in a six-year span.

All these proposals should be enacted, but I have one last proposal. It is quite revolutionary, yet it is the only true solution to the oppression from Washington.

It is, simply:

6. Washington shall be required to abide by the Tenth Amendment to the Constitution, which will limit it to functions outlined in the Constitution. If it wants to do more, it can send all the checks it wants to the states and localities—for Medicaid, environment, education, or anything else.

But the money must come *without any conditions or regulations whatsoever*. Then, and only then, will the states and the people be free to spend their money as they see fit.

The choice is ours. The present centralized, made-up theory of American government is failing. To reinvigorate our nation, we must make Washington weaker, less oppressive, and less expensive. Only then will our politicians get the people's message: In Your Face.

Of course, we don't have to do it, either because of fear or inertia, or a recalcitrant President and Congress. But neither do we have to survive as a free and sound nation.

Chapter Five

Welfare Slavery

HOW TO KEEP THEM— AND EVERYONE ELSE—POOR

"POVERTY SUCKS!"

That bumper-sticker slogan might as well be the national anthem. Americans hate to be poor. The nation was built on upward striving, a compulsion that has had models from Horatio Alger to Bill Gates, the thirty-eight-year-old Microsoft billionaire.

Success is the great bitch God. Every man a millionaire. Every man a king. But Americans are a generous people who want to help those who cannot seize the dream. Last year, we gave $128 billion to charities, quite voluntarily.

We can't demand charity from the Salvation Army, although it seldom refuses. But state charity—what we call "welfare"—is a different proposition. In modern society, we consider that a right of the poor. So really big charity becomes an *involuntary* activity, one whose goals are decided by our politicians, our duly elected representatives.

Most citizens go along, to a limit. They gladly pay taxes for some social programs, including sustenance for blind and disabled, unemployment insurance for the out-of-work, and various other fringe programs, such as student loans.

But (and that's important) state welfare is still not fully trusted in the United States. The country didn't become great because the government gave anybody welfare. And surely no one ever became rich on the dole. If the millions who struggled their way through Ellis Island—Irish, Greek, Jew, Italian, Pole, Hungarian—had been given welfare, they'd probably now be victims of capitalism instead of its masters.

This is a practical country, one reason welfare is driving the nation batty. More and more, there's a groundswell of discontent about government charity that's too generously dispensed. Taxpayers are convinced that all is not right with Washington's attempts to stem poverty by handing out checks. They grumble: What in the hell is going on?

The discontent has filtered back to the politicians. The campaigning President made a hollow pronouncement that, in two years, welfare as we now know it will no longer exist. Other pols are loudly mouthing welfare reform. The citizens listen, dubious about promises for change. As far as many are concerned, they work and others unfairly get the benefits of their sweat.

Is it true? Is the government mishandling the money meant for the poor? And if so, how?

To answer that we should first explain that since there's no bottom line, government lives more off perceptions than reality. And behind that is the federal government's attitude about virtually everything. It is based on two premises: (1) good intentions; (2) bad theory. Washington would rather not have bad theory, but they're used to it. Still, they do know that if they don't *project* good intentions, they're finished. At least that has been the rule.

Why? Because in America today, government is the secular religion of millions. To them, the desire to do good is more important than the outcome. Doesn't state charity count as much spiritually in the life of the giver as in the material gain of the taker? they ask.

Good or bad, there has to be a theory. The one for the present welfare system started with a simple question first posed seriously in the early 1960s at the height of American affluence. What about a plan to *totally eliminate* poverty in America? asked our politicians. Yes, most enlightened Americans answered. That's a good idea.

How would it be done?

A Search for the Poorest

Simple. We'd first try to isolate the poor, which make up 14 percent of the nation, about 35 million Americans. Some are in rural areas, others are in the suburbs, and large numbers are in what's called "the inner city." Poverty, as defined by the U.S. Bureau of Census, involves those families of four with an income of $14,700 or less.

Who are the poorest and most disadvantaged of all? Generally those young people who are fatherless and whose mothers are unemployed.

How can we lift them out of despair? Education, surely. But the schools are failing. Another route would be to create two-parent working families. That's hard, because many families have only one parent, and good jobs are hard to find, especially among the poorly educated.

Then try this idea, theorists said, as if shouting "Eureka." Let's find the young women of these disadvantaged families and encourage them first to avoid marriage, then to engage in premarital sex, as early as age thirteen. We know the inevitable result: teenage pregnancy, high school dropout, and birth of a child out of wedlock.

Now, we've isolated our clients for the dole: unwed mothers, teenage and older, with small children.

But, we ask the theorists, how can you be sure these youngsters will oblige? Not to worry. Pay them. First with cash, then food and housing, then with a marginal lifestyle in which work is not only undesirable but antiproductive.

How long can they be persuaded to live that way?

Apparently for a long time—*if* you can convince them to continue. How do you do that? Just add money and rewards for each additional child born out of wedlock, making sure the system helps the young women avoid marriage, work, permanent ties with men (at least openly), and traditional families.

Then, of course, try to make the system jump from generation to generation. The result? More fatherless, uneducated children born out of wedlock. And most important, more poor new families, and more clients for the welfare system and its social workers and bureaucrats.

Of course, now there's *more* poverty instead of less. But we don't talk about that. And besides, as I pointed out, results are less important than intentions in Washington.

Crazy? Yes, quite. But of course the theory didn't develop that way, or that openly. In many ways, it just evolved as a concession to inner-city poverty. But in its fulfillment, it has become perhaps the most destructive concept in the history of American post-slavery society. If truth be known, it has been the greatest *creator* of poverty ever conceived, and the destroyer of families, civility, and dignity.

Besides, it violates the American credo: Poverty Sucks.

But what happened to the original intent of *curing* poverty?

Apparently, it got lost in the social work theory that the poor are "clients" that need to be rehabilitated. Many politicians swallowed that quackery, and are only now beginning to lament it, if belatedly. They're racing backward, away from the social work bureaucrats, and hoping voters will forgive them, which they shouldn't.

Give the theorists an *F.* Give the politicians a kick you know where. But what about the victims, the abused poor people swept out of the mainstream of American life? At least give them apologies and try to make up for ruining their lives.

What we've just described, in its simplest form, is one of the basic welfare programs of the federal government, Aid to Families with Dependent Children (AFDC), which boasts a roster of 14 million people and 5 million families.

Why would the federal government want to do such a thing? That's not an easy question, but in any case, the victims of this failure are twofold: those who pay, and those who receive.

One of the worst side effects of welfare is that it has become a buzzword for "minorities." Those who dislike them point to welfare as proof positive of their foibles. To those who defend nonworking minorities, welfare is retribution for sins committed by society against them.

What are the facts? Is AFDC a minority program?

The first, surprising, fact is that there are slightly more whites on welfare than Afro-Americans. About 39 percent are white; about 38 percent are Afro-American; and the remaining 23 percent are everyone else, with Hispanics predominating. But the minorities are heavily overrepresented. Even though they are close in actual numbers, proportionately there are six times as many Afro-Americans as whites in the basic AFDC program.

What has actually happened? Is the government paying out a fortune to support the victims of out-of-wedlock births? Or is government welfare actually a stimulus, even the cause, of the condition?

Washington As Villain

The evidence seems quite clear. Welfare, as we now know it, is the villain. In a poor society, no force can defeat the steady revenue stream of checks in the mail for not working. The result is that many of the people in the inner city, both Afro-Americans and Hispanics, and whites in rural areas, have changed their normal behavior to satify the government's demands.

From a behavior that used to be typically American—if poorer—and based on family, work, and church ties, many have become somewhat dysfunctional in order to please the Great White-and-Black Father in Washington and his marvelous check-writing machine.

The numbers leave no room for argument. Out-of-wedlock births among Afro-Americans and Hispanics have directly followed the growth of the welfare program. At the outset of World War II, the black out-of-wedlock birth rate was only 19 percent. It was higher than the white rate but far from crippling. The extended family was easily able to handle that number of children.

The figure rose to 28 percent by 1965, then to 49 percent by 1982. Courtesy of Uncle Sam's "generosity," it grew constantly until it is now, according to the Census Bureau, up to 67 percent. That's too overwhelming for any group to handle. (Even the white out-of-wedlock rate has jumped to 17 percent.) What could be a better recipe for poverty?

There's no doubt that the misguided welfare programs of Washington have badly misfired. Despite the expenditure of a trillion dollars over the years, the number of people in "poverty," as defined by the U.S. Bureau of Census, is *larger* today than when the antipoverty programs went into full gear.

Eleven percent of Americans were labeled "poor" in 1973. After twenty years of welfare, the number has risen to 14 percent. In the case of Afro-Americans, welfare has clearly been a giant obstacle to success, holding back their entry into the mainstream more than any policy since slavery.

If Alexis de Tocqueville, that great French observer of America, were to revisit these shores, as he first did in 1835, he might even conclude that the welfare policy was an attempt to keep minorities out of the working middle class. With his flair for phrases, he might well have dubbed it "Welfare Slavery."

In fact, charges that the government program is racist (if not consciously) should not be easily dismissed.

Minority Stereotypes

The first victim of this strange scheme is racial tolerance. Welfare has heightened friction between blacks and whites, who too often associate blacks with the AFDC stereotype. The same holds true for tensions between whites and Hispanics in inner cities such as that of Los Angeles. It is a strong image, but it is a false one.

AFDC, in fact, does not involve most Afro-Americans. The 5.3 million blacks on AFDC make up only one in five of that minority. We often overlook the fact that the great majority of Afro-Americans are gainfully employed, and that many with education are moving into the upper middle class. Quite surprisingly, Afro-American female college graduates now earn almost as much as their white counterparts.

The second victims are the AFDC clients themselves. White or black, they have been seduced away from family and work life. Instead of young women looking to marry young men, they've chosen an older suitor with more money—Uncle Sam. It seems that only those who escape his seductions can follow the American dream.

Who are the welfare clients? Is the single mother stereotype really true?

Yes. Of the 5 million families, over 90 percent are headed by unmarried mothers. The majority have never been married and one-third are divorced, separated, or have been abandoned. The entry age of clients gets younger every day as teenagers increasingly give birth to out-of-wedlock children.

The typical AFDC mother has two children, but 30 percent have more, which increases their cash rewards in all states except New Jersey. The government likes to claim that AFDC is only a "temporary" condition, but their figures, which cover only "one spell" on welfare, are misleading.

The true numbers were compiled by researchers at the Kennedy School of Government. The average stay on AFDC is actually *twelve* years, and this includes young mothers just joining the welfare world. Twenty percent have been on the dole for at least fifteen years.

The third victims are the children on AFDC, who see their mother's abnormal lifestyle as normal, perhaps even desirable. Studies show that AFDC children are three times as likely to bear children out of wedlock, and then to go on welfare themselves, continuing the cycle of poverty. They are also more likely to give birth as teenagers. If they do marry, they are 92 percent more likely to get divorced.

Antisocial behavior is another uninvited guest in the AFDC home. Welfare children are two to three times more likely to commit suicide, use drugs, and become criminals than those in two-parent homes of the same education and income.

The fourth victim of welfare is the American taxpayer, of all races, who has to pay for it. And as we shall see, the tab is enormous.

The Fake Welfare State

Perhaps most disheartening is that America is falsely called "a welfare state" in the belief that most citizens are provided for by the government. Nothing could be further from the truth. The average working American falls between the welfare cracks. In Europe, the working middle class has national

health insurance, day-care centers, long-term unemployment
benefits, free universities, substantial pensions, and other programs that don't exist here for the majority.

Our two working-middle-class programs, Social Security
and Medicare, are not welfare. They're self-supporting from
the FICA taxes. In fact, their large annual surpluses are
tapped by Washington (read: "stolen") to pay for the welfare
of others.

What happens in this so-called welfare state when a
working person falls on hard times and turns to the government? More often than not, he's humiliated.

Let's take Medicaid—health care for the poor—which
automatically goes to unwed mothers on AFDC. In Connecticut, if working people lose their jobs and health insurance,
they can get Medicaid on two conditions: *if* they give the
state a lien on their house, and *if* they don't mind walking.

The value of their car is checked in the wholesale Blue
Book, then the remaining payments are subtracted. If the "equity" remaining is more than $1,500, they are refused Medic-
aid. They can always sell the car, but the cash would put
them over the amount of allowed liquid assets. And without a
car, how could they look for a job in spread-out suburbia?

Fortunately, the government is as stupid as it is bureaucratic.

Let's take the case presented to a Medicaid specialist in
Connecticut. A man of forty-five with a wife and two children
has been laid off from a job that paid him $60,000. He's still
unemployed and has gone through his savings; he applies for
Medicaid. He has two cars—with a combined equity of
$18,000, which puts him *way over* the $3,200 liquid assets he's
allowed to have. What can he do, I asked the specialist? He
desperately needs medical care for his wife and children.

"There are several ways of handling this," he explained,
almost in a confidential tone. "First, he can sell the cars and
get the $18,000, which makes him ineligible."

"So what good is that?" I asked, waiting for the punch lines. They were soon in coming.

"All he has to do is get rid of the $18,000. He can spend it or he can just give it to a relative. Transfer of funds are completely legal in the Medicaid system as long as you're not going into a long-term nursing home. But there's also a legal second way."

I listened closer.

"He can go to the bank and borrow out the equity on the cars. Then he can keep the $18,000 and won't have to transfer it away, and he'll still be eligible for Medicaid. We do not consider borrowed money as assets."

What? This absurdity goes beyond Ionesco. It began because the applicant is only allowed to have $1,500 equity in *one* car, and $3,200 in assets (aside from his house). Now he has $18,000 in cash from the sale of *two* cars, can rent a car for $4,000 a year, and he is suddenly eligible for Medicaid. Of course, if he didn't know these ropes, and was not a pregnant teenager, he'd be out of luck. Only in America.

I'm happy for the man without a job because he deserves medical care for his family. But what about the taxpayer paying for all these legal shenanigans?

Cornucopia of Programs

Is AFDC the only welfare program? And does the average citizen really know about the others?

The answer to the second question is a distinct "no."

The answer to the first question is that there are *seventy-eight* certified federal welfare programs. They're all cataloged in a semisecret government volume, *Cash and Non Cash Benefits for Persons With Limited Income*, which is not available to the general public. Put out by the Congressional Research Service, a citizen can only get it through an accommodating Congressman.

The table of contents is a compendium of taxpayer cash

going everywhere, from Rural Rental Assistance Payments to Migrant Education Program to Child Development Associate Scholarship Program to Weatherization Assistance and many others.

Are these seventy-eight welfare programs coordinated? As any student of Washington knows, the answer is "naturally not." They are a crazy quilt, run by numerous agencies, with a confusing maze of thousands of rules. Each program has its own eligibility requirements, with no common denominator.

AFDC is central. Its clients can tap into dozens of benefits run by a half dozen agencies—Health and Human Services, Department of Agriculture, Department of Energy, Housing and Urban Development, Department of Education, and Department of Energy—the closest America comes to cradle to grave care.

As we've seen, AFDC clients automatically receive Medicaid, a program run by HHS (Health and Human Services) that now costs $130 billion a year in federal and state money, and is increasing at almost 17 percent annually.

One reason is that welfare benefits keep expanding, often beyond those available to most working people. All AFDC clients receive monthly cash, ranging from about $200 a month in Mississippi to well over $1,000 a month in Alaska, with the average running about $500. AFDC clients are also eligible for housing provided by HUD (Housing and Urban Development), either for apartments in the "projects" or in private housing, paid with vouchers that can run over $1,200 a month for a welfare family.

(Of course, that's topped by putting welfare clients up in downtown city hotels, which can run $1,000 a *week*.)

That's far from all. The unwed mother will receive food stamps for herself and her children, a program run by the Department of Agriculture. When the kids trot off to school, she needn't bother with making breakfast or preparing a lunch box. The children will receive both free breakfast and free lunch at school.

Pregnant welfare clients and those who have children up to age five are also eligible for WIC (Women, Infants, Children) supplemental food. It is either dispensed with vouchers or comes in actual packages, à la Tammany Hall, which are sometimes delivered right to the home.

AFDC clients are eligible for several Department of Education low-income programs, including sizable cash Pell grants (in addition to loans) for the college bound, along with TRIO, a group of six programs for low-income students. One program, Upward Bound, gives students a cash stipend of $40 a month year-round and $60 a month in the summer.

There is also Head Start for preschoolers and a kiddy "graduate" program called "Follow Through" for the early elementary grades, plus Chapter I special education for poor children, whether formally on welfare or not.

There are Perkins college loans at very low interest for those in "exceptional need," Fellowships for Graduate and Professional Study, and State Student Incentive Grants, plus Health Professions Student Scholarships for poor youngsters who want to become everything from doctors to pharmacists.

AFDC clients can count on free government legal assistance, subsidies for utilities (the LIHEAP program from the Department of Energy), job training (Department of Labor), and several others.

Strange Government Rules

What must AFDC clients do to receive all this bounty? It's quite simple. All they have to do is have a baby, or two, or more, *out of wedlock.*

Equally important is what they must *not* do if they want to stay in the program: (1) they must not get married; and (2) if they do get married, it must not be to someone who's gainfully employed.

So what's wrong, Mr. Skinflint, in helping the poor?

Nothing. But this is *not* what America does. Poor people are those who are working at indecently low salaries, and those who are unemployed, or those who are disabled. *Our present system helps those who we've encouraged to enter poverty by creating new poor nonworking families.*

Naturally, such a program is highly counterproductive, for themselves and society—socially, philosophically, and economically. The rules provide powerful incentives for the mother not to work, not to get married, and for the father to abandon his family so that Uncle Sam can support them.

This distorted approach quickly spreads like a sociological infection, offering an *alternative* to the American system even though rational people know there is no alternative to work and family.

People counter that single mothers who work sometimes elect to have children out of wedlock. That's fine, but there's no suspicion that the child was created as "a way of making a living," as one welfare mother explained to a New York reporter.

Welfare, it might accurately be said, has changed the position of the young male in the inner city and rural poverty areas from a breadwinner into a pariah. Marriage, not illegitimacy, becomes a dirty word. "Maleness" comes to represent a threat and not the essential half of a partnership of two people fighting together for a place in the world.

To put it candidly, the AFDC program, as it's now administered, is an *evil* operation with strong overtones of racism. It is an operation that helps destroy the cultural backstop of the Afro-American community—church and family—and substitutes detached social workers and bureaucrats. The clients become the victims, not the beneficiaries, of Washington.

At one time, as part of The Theory, a man couldn't even live in the AFDC home with a welfare mother. The rules have been liberalized, but if a woman, or her husband, does work, they're still heavily punished by reduced benefits. If the young father moves in and works, say at a fast-food restaurant for $5 an hour, his income—$10,400 a year—would exceed the limit and the young family would get the bureaucratic boot. The checks from AFDC would stop, cold.

Defenders say the government is not really killing the work ethic among the poor. But all evidence points in the opposite direction. The destructive impact has been confirmed by several studies including one by Washington's own Office of Economic Opportunity. Using Seattle and Denver as their sample, they found that for each $1 increase in welfare benefits, the recipients worked less. The income from labor decreased by eighty cents.

Studies also show that extra welfare benefits are like a harsh mother-in-law—they squelch the desire for marriage. University of Washington researchers showed that when welfare benefits rose $200 a month, teenage out-of-wedlock births went up 150 percent. Cornell University studies showed that for every 10 percent increase in benefits there was an 8 percent drop in marriage among single mothers, the likely candidates for AFDC.

How is all this possible in the civilized USA? How could the government of all the people do this to the poor and taxpayers alike?

Easily. Uncle Sam's welfare system, circa 1993-94, is the confluence of every bad sociopolitical idea proposed over the last fifty years. Naturally, the AFDC program is under attack. Not just by taxpayers but by politicians who rant about "reforming" a program they themselves enthusiastically put into place.

"We must make the able-bodied work," insisted former President Bush. During his campaign, President Clinton vowed to "end welfare as we know it," implying that after two years, unwed mothers would be kicked off the rolls if they didn't have a job. Both men, of course, were lying. Welfare, in its worst form, has become an indigenous part of our irrational political environment.

Welfare is a national disgrace and perhaps America's greatest failure. But before we look under the hood and try to fix it, we might take a peek backwards at how the multibillion-dollar fiasco began.

How It All Began

Welfare was almost nonexistent before the Great Depression. Local governments had some funds for the extremely poor, private charities chipped in, and the cities ran free hospitals and clinics for those who couldn't pay.

But faced with the Depression in 1933, FDR improvised a plan aimed mainly at people who were, or had been, working: Social Security, Workman's Compensation, Unemployment Insurance, plus support for the blind and disabled. For widows with children he established a little-known program called AFDC, Aid for Families with Dependent Children.

But the pressing problem was unemployment, which reached the 25 percent level. FDR decided on a cash concept called "Home Relief," in which heads of households received about $15 a week, just enough to keep them from starving. But within a few months men sitting at home became nervous, as did a watching nation.

Always the pragmatist, FDR scrapped the relief program as debilitating and substituted work as part of the now-famous Works Progress Administration (WPA). (There was also a PWA, Public Works Administration.) Men just showed up for work and were given a pick and shovel, a rake, or a paint brush. They were paid about $21 a week, enough to get by on.

The program was hooted as "make work" by the press, but in retrospect it's starting to look real good. At its height, 5 million men (including this author's father) were building post offices, bridges, dams, laying asphalt and concrete high-

ways, even painting murals in public buildings. In my own
community center, an out-of-work musical director helped us
put on a revue.

The WPA died an honorable death as World War II created a labor, not a job, shortage.

Most New Deal remedies like the WPA disappeared in
the postwar boom, but AFDC hung on by transforming itself
from a widow's program into its present single-mother incar-
nation.

The early postwar period was short on welfare, but by
the time of JFK, the picture had changed. Influenced by Michael Harrington's book *The Other America*, a study of hidden poverty in a time of great affluence, Kennedy drew the
outlines of several programs. They didn't become reality until
after his death, when Lyndon Johnson became the Father of
the War On Poverty.

Now, almost thirty years later, an even larger, more expensive, equally ineffective welfare program is in full swing.
Besides the AFDC and its single mothers, several of the
seventy-eight welfare programs offer benefits for what is
called "the working poor," people at, or somewhat above, the
poverty level of $14,700 for a family of four. Help for the
working poor can make good sense, but, as we shall see, it often comes into conflict with The Theory.

Each of the seventy-eight programs has its own rules, eligibility, and income limits. The Weatherization Assistance
Program of the Department of Energy, for example, gives families about $2,000 to insulate their homes. The money goes to
those who earn up to $18,500 a year. Above that you're on
your own when the cold snap hits.

The energy program to help families pay for fuel
(LIHEAP or Low Income Home Energy Assistance Program)
is more generous, with a cap of $22,000 a year. Above that,
you can sit in the dark.

In many ways, the seventy-eight programs are a redistribution of wealth, away from the middle class to first the poor, then to working people with lower wages—sometimes to the point of blurring the difference between givers and getters. Unlike Robin Hood, the federal government takes from one worker to give to another.

The cut-off points for low-income welfare come perilously close to the income of regular wage-earners. The WIC vouchers for extra food for pregnant women and children, for example, can go to families who earn up to $27,000 a year. Others can ostensibly buy their own food baskets.

Arkansas Is Not Connecticut

One relatively new welfare scheme is based on income redistribution and is called Income Tax Credit, or EITC. It gives tax reduction, and even checks in the mail, to families far above the poverty level. In broadest strokes, it sends checks to working suburbanite families—via Uncle Sam—that have been paid for by their only slightly more successful neighbor.

The maximum a recipient can make is now up to $27,000, and EITC's $6 billion budget has been raised to $17 billion. The plan is unusual because it is *national* in scope and doesn't take into account enormous regional differences in income and living costs. To Washington, we're all Americans, whether we live in Connecticut or Arkansas—even though a house in the President's poor state costs only $70,000 and the same one in Connecticut carries a price tag of $200,000.

In Arkansas, $27,000 is a good living, as shown by the then-Governor Clinton's salary of only $33,000. Even today, the Lieutenant Governor makes only $29,000, and the Speaker of the Arkansas House only $14,000. A future Speaker would automatically be eligible for EITC and other welfare programs. If his wife should get pregnant, she'd be in line for WIC, where eligibility runs up to $27,000. In fact, the food basket could be delivered right to her Little Rock hospital bed!

The $4 billion National School Lunch program, another of the seventy-eight, has an even higher income ceiling of $28,000. That might make sense in Connecticut, where $28,000 won't take you very far. But in Arkansas, with a little shove, the Lieutenant Governor, whose salary has just been *raised* to $29,000, could get his children some of that good ol' Washington welfare.

In effect, the Eastern or Midwestern suburbanite who makes $35,000 and is struggling desperately with high taxes and living costs, is subsidizing the Arkansas family who makes $27,000 and is living reasonably well but still receiving EITC and other welfare. We're robbing Peter New York to pay Paul Arkansas, when Peter may be much poorer than his welfare beneficiary.

Washington's topsy-turvy math is best shown by the AFDC and Medicaid matching grant system. Washington *mandates* that federal funds be matched according to a formula, a system that is destroying the fiscal health of many states and forcing local taxes up.

So-called rich states (where are they?) are burdened even further because Washington can't do simple arithmetic. New York, New Jersey, and Connecticut, for example, pay substantial amounts to AFDC clients. Connecticut's cash payment to an AFDC unwed mother (in addition to housing, food stamps, etc.) comes to approximately $600 a month. Meanwhile, Arkansas pays her $200—$194 to be exact.

Does Washington care? Do they compensate Connecticut because they have to lay out so much money?

No way. In fact, it's exactly the opposite.

Washington gives Connecticut 50 percent of its outlay, so that it costs the state a net of $300 a month. But under some logic not yet taught in school, it gives Arkansas 79 percent, supposedly because it's poorer.

But the math doesn't jibe. Net, it costs Arkansa only 21 percent of the $200, or $42 a month. But Connecticut is spending $300 net, or *seven* times as much. Arkansas may be poorer, but it's not Bangladesh. In a rational government, the compensation would be the same 50 percent—or maybe a little *more* for the richer states, to reflect the cost of living. But that would be asking too much of the best and the brightest.

The Real Tab

What does it all cost the taxpayer? The government tries not to add up the tab, or even to talk about it. When it comes to welfare, politicians are ignorant, or evasive. Governor Mario Cuomo of New York recently played down the cost, saying it was insignificant.

Is that true? Think again. The real numbers are found in the Congressional Research report, and they are staggering. The reality is that welfare for low-income people, on the city, on the farm, in the rural areas, *is the single largest item in the nation's budget,* larger than defense or the interest on the federal debt!

The latest numbers available, Fiscal Year 1990, show a total of federal and state spending for welfare of $210,630,000,000, translated as $210-plus billions. Roughly three-fourths of the spending was federal and one-quarter state and local—almost all of it dictated by Washington.

Now that it is four years later, the total cost is obviously much higher. Can we estimate it?

Yes, and easily. From 1989 to 1990, in one fiscal year, welfare costs rose 13 percent. Medical benefits, mainly Medicaid, rose 17 percent. Cash benefits increased 11 percent and food aid went up 15 percent. Being conservative, we'll use only an 11 percent annual increase to bring us up to Fiscal Year 1994, which began October 1, 1993.

That magically moves the $210 billion to $318 billion, the present yearly cost of welfare. (That's one of the marvels of compound interest, an equation taught in the eighth grade—or used to be—but apparently unknown in Washington.)

Vice President Gore just assured the public that the 1993 Omnibus Bill will increase the welfare total by $40 billion over the next five years. But to keep it current, we won't include that.

So what's the bottom line? How many people are on welfare and what does it cost for each of them?

The number of welfare clients is known only to individual programs. Some people might be on a dozen programs, but there's no coordination—no central computer that might show that someone is getting AFDC, food stamps, WIC, energy help, college grants, or special relief for Cuban immigrants.

We do know that there are approximately 30 million people on Medicaid, 14 million on AFDC, 25 million on food stamps, and several million on other programs. But as the government admits: "An unduplicated count of welfare beneficiaries is not available."

Let's take an educated guess. The Census Bureau has classified 35 million persons as "poor." They exist in 70 percent of the households that receive some help. An educated guess is that there are 23 million people—about 9 percent of the nation—somewhat dependent on welfare.

By dividing those 23 million into the $318 billion, we get $14,500 as the cost of the average welfare client. That comes to *$58,000* a year for a family of four! It's 80 percent *higher* than the average working family's income of $36,000, which generally comes from two wage-earners.

The welfare family surely doesn't see that kind of money. In Connecticut they could receive—in cash, food, housing, special grants for energy, school breakfasts and lunches, WIC, Head Start, and college grants—as much as

$32,000 tax free—and without work. But that's high for the
nation as a whole.

So where's the money?

It flows into the great pit of Washington waste and ignorance, into the maw of duplication and bad administration,
into the pockets of bureaucrats and overhead on the federal,
state, and city level. It is part of the scores of unnecessary
and inefficient programs that work at cross purposes and
waste hundreds of billions of dollars, creating great social
damage in the process.

*As we project into the twenty-first century under the
present welfare system, there will never be enough money in
the world to cure American poverty, let alone slow its rise.*

But The Theory continues unabated despite failure.
Why? Greatly because of misapplied ideology. To many Americans, welfare is a symbol of "goodness." No amount of
money thrown down the drain is enough for them, or too
much to assuage their guilt. To the callous, on the other hand,
any interference in the free market economy is ideological
blasphemy.

Meanwhile, the American middle class, caught between
the two, continues to pay the growing bill—in money, crime,
and social damage—for programs that must fail because of
faulty theory.

What About Reform?

Is there a real answer to this $318 billion annual fiasco?

The federal government is toying with reform. Toying is
the operative word. The Family Support Act of 1988 (better
known as the JOBS program) offered the states $1.2 billion
for education and job training to help welfare people get off
the rolls. It was both a carrot and a stick for the small
number required to participate, or lose some of their benefits.

How is it doing? So far, the states have not been overly
enthusiastic about Washington's remedy. They have to put up

half the money, which they don't have. For those who are involved, the preliminary results are in, and they are *insignificant*. In one supposedly successful training program, it increased AFDC client's real income about $200 a year. The most optimistic prospects envision a 5 percent reduction in welfare, but at an increased cost. Surely this is no answer to the dilemma.

On their own, states are doing better, as they generally do when left alone. New Jersey is the first state not to extend the benefits beyond one child, and others are considering similar legislation. Still other states are thinking about putting a time limit on a client's benefits—that is, instituting a cut-off date. Still others are lowering benefits, hoping to make the program less attractive to unmarried women looking to start a family on the dole.

But faulty government theory cannot be wiped away by reform. As long as the AFDC (which is at the core) pays for children out of wedlock, the damage, fiscal and social, will continue.

Is there, then, a real solution? Yes, and it's a money saver besides.

First, let's look at the idea of eliminating *all welfare and all poverty with one quick stroke*—with checks. A check for $14,700 (the poverty level) sent to all 7.7 million poor families, which includes all AFDC families, would cost us only $113 billion. If we include the single folks, young and old, that adds about 5 million more people, at a reduced $9,000, or $45 billion.

All told, that brings the poverty-ending cost to $158 billion, just half our present outlay. That solves all poverty more than once over, because the poor have some income of their own. The real cost of this approach, therefore, would probably be only $100 billion dollars.

But we spend three times as much under our present

system and solve nothing. We only massage, nourish, and keep poverty going.

Under the "check-for-everybody-poor plan," we've cured it all, and we're over $200 billion to the good—money in the bank. It also takes the guilt off the head of the working middle class, who can then turn all their attention to working forty, fifty, sixty hours a week, with two paychecks, just to keep up with the mortgage and the oppressive local, state, and federal taxes.

So what's the disadvantage of such a scheme? Only moral. We'd be creating a giant, nonworking leisure class. We'd no longer have any guilt, but there'd be a lot of psychic aggravation.

The True Remedy

So, what's the real answer? It's what everybody who thinks about it knows is the *only* solution: We must replace welfare with work, and discourage others from starting along its downhill path.

The solution is quite simple. I call it: THE GROSS EIGHT-POINT ANTIPOVERTY, ANTIWELFARE PROGRAM TO RESTORE SANITY AND DIGNITY TO AMERICA THROUGH AN OLD IDEA—WORK.

The plan comes in eight broad strokes to be implemented one at a time, and cumulatively designed to wipe out all poverty in America and save multibillions in the process.

1. Take all welfare programs out of the hands of the different federal and state agencies and place them under one roof—a Department of Welfare. Citizens can then see what is being done, and at what cost, for whom.

2. Bring back the WPA of New Deal days and offer decent paying jobs above the poverty level for all nonworking Americans—especially those on welfare. They can help rebuild the infrastructure, work as assistants in schoolrooms

and hospitals, rebuild houses and facilities in the inner cities and rural areas, and work with the aged.

3. The WPA should build a string of day-care centers, where formerly idle welfare mothers can work, taking care of their children and those of other working mothers. The French model would be worth studying.

4. Once these three programs are in operation, *totally* eliminate AFDC and move the 5 million families into the work world. For pregnant mothers, offer maternity leave from WPA work.

5. Provide health insurance for all WPA workers, paid for by the government at $1,800 for a single person and $3,500 for a family, using HMOs. This will take more than half the people off the Medicaid roles.

6. Take student loans out of the welfare system by eliminating the means test, as we did with the GI Bill, then require an IRS payback. This will bring the cost down to virtually nothing.

7. Provide proper aid to the blind and disabled.

8. Finally, close all seventy-eight welfare programs, except for unemployment insurance and aid to the disabled. Period.

This plan will provide work, supply health insurance, and eliminate all poverty at the same time.

Should we force people to work? Of course not. Those who want to join the voluntary poor, can be our guest, which is their right in a free society. But without squawks or TV documentaries, please.

But what about the cost of this extravagent work system? Can we afford it?

Oh, yes. Actually it will save money.

The first positive result will be that there will be fewer poor people to support. An unwed young woman faced with the prospect of working all her life to care for a child without

a husband will not look so kindly on out-of-wedlock pregnancy. Second, the WPA program, which fits much better into
our Judeo-Christian ethic, will stimulate the work ethic, increase the possibilities of advancement and self-improvement,
and provide less leisure time for aberrant behavior, including
crime.

But what about the cost?

Let's do the arithmetic together. Let's say it costs $15,000
a job, plus $2,500 for health coverage on average. That's
$17,500 times the 5 million families on AFDC—if everyone
elects to join the WPA. That's less than $88 billion, less than
the present AFDC cost when you add in housing, food
stamps, WIC, and Medicaid.

Now, let's extend the WPA to another 5 million families
who are poor, or unemployed, or who just want the jobs.
That's another $88 billion. The total? $176 billion. When we
add in help for the disabled, and other miscellaneous projects, we've still *saved $100 billion*.

The problem? We need to convince America to be rational and to forget social work theory and false ideologies of
the Left and Right, the puerile arguments that have gotten us
into our present trap.

There is, I can state categorically, no way to "reform" the
welfare system. That's like learning to live with untreated can-
cer.

Social work types like to believe that with a little twist
of technique—generally referred to as "education and job
training"—these dependent families will enter the mainstream
working culture. No way. The federal government would love
to repeal human nature, but it can't. No program can compete
with the allure of free checks in the mail, sent to otherwise
normal, healthy people.

A False Philosophy

Why, then, do we continue as we do, spending vast sums and getting nowhere fast?

I think the answer is philosophical. It also explains a great deal about the general failure of government in America.

We live in a world in which politics has replaced philosophy. Many powerful citizens, including our government leaders in Congress and the White House, seek a kind of religious expiation through their government, which they view as a giant foundation or charity.

The need to feel good about themselves replaces inner convictions and pushes them to invent schemes to spend billions of other people's money to satisfy their charitable instincts, without ever considering the value of what they're doing or its harmful results.

For too many politicians it is part of a scheme for false glory, a kind of distorted Messianic drive. Everyone wants to be FDR without a Depression (but they might make one to accommodate themselves), or JFK without his charm or the prosperity of his era.

What should our politicians do? They should seek religion in church and synogogue, if they want it, and try to bring the poor up into the working class—as the immigrants did on their own—with practical ideas and without subjecting those in need to false, punishing social work theories. The next step is to encourage them to move into the middle class—if that class still exists by the time they get there.

The poor need work experience before they can leave poverty, if the government ever lets them have it. Again, nobody ever got rich on the dole. Work, and not the failed welfare schemes that are destroying both the poor and those who support them with their tax money, is the ultimate answer.

But, of course, we have to consider one other thought.

Is it possible that those in power, from administration to administration, like "Welfare Slavery" just the way it is?

Chapter Six

Money, Money, Money

IT MAKES CORRUPTION
GO ROUND

Guess how much money American politicians—of all ideological stripes and federal jurisdictions—spent in 1992 in their hunt for public office?

Ten million? One hundred million? Give up?

Well, here's a hint. The four-minute mile of campaign financing has finally been breached by money-hungry politicians.

The answer is *over $1 billion*!

That dismal day has been coming for sometime. The price of office has been escalating so rapidly that an outside observer from Mars—or France or Germany—could only conclude that elections in the United States are not won. They are bought.

Money is so much the lifeblood of American politics that it doesn't take a Diogenes to understand that Elections, USA, are the least democratic (small *d*) in the civilized Western world. The nation that gave birth to democracy has evolved into what can now only be described as the pits of electoral indecency, the epicenter of philosophical corruption.

The record-breaking billion-dollar vote-buy of 1992 is split three ways, all governed by a compendium of complex, barely comprehensible election finance rules that make the IRS code look like a kindergarten game.

The U.S. Congress, that arena of bounced checks and postal scams, is of course the champion. In 1992, according to the Federal Elections Commission (FEC), the 535 representatives of the people spent *$678 million* trying to get elected or reelected to their $133,000-a-year job, a spending increase of 52 percent over the last cycle.

The average member of Congress is quite royal in wooing the bombarded voter. The typical House winner spent $550,000; the typical Senate victor almost *$4 million*. The losers, of course, were outspent about eight to one by the incumbents, some 93 percent of whom won their races for the House.

Who were the champion raisers-and-spenders? In the Senate, Alfonse D'Amato of New York spent $11,331,301, while the newly elected Barbara Boxer of California went through $10,368,600 to gain her seat. The campaign black-belter in the House was Michael Huffington, also of Los Angeles, who spent $5,435,177, or over $40 for each vote cast. (In Tammany Hall days, votes were bought more directly, and much cheaper.)

But what about the antichampions, those who relied on themselves instead of the big buck?

The undisputed winner there is Representative Bill Natcher, Democrat of Kentucky, the new chairman of the House Appropriations Committee. Mr. Natcher is a dichotomy. As a dispenser of the people's tax money he is a mad spender who has earned a lowly "0," the lowest possible grade, from the watchdog Citizens Against Government Waste.

But as a candidate, Natcher is a skinflint personified. He refuses to take any campaign donations, from anybody. He spends only a few spare dollars getting reelected, and all of that comes out of his own pocket.

In the Senate, the champion campaign nonspender was William Proxmire of Wisconsin, founder of the "Golden Fleece Award," who has since retired. In 1976, when he ran for reelection, Proxmire took in *no* dollars in contributions and spent $175. On what? On stamps and stationery to *return* the unsolicited donations. He won with 70 percent of the vote, a performance he repeated in 1982, again without any campaign funds.

What does Senator Proxmire think of the present election finance system?

"It's disgraceful," he says. "Members of Congress put themselves up for sale."

The second part of the billion-dollar blowout was money spent on the presidential race. According to FEC law, the government matches, up to $27 million per candidate, all individual contributions of $250 or less during the primary campaign. This cost Uncle Sam $42,742,815 in the 1992 presidential sweepstakes.

But there were also nonmatching primary contributions from individuals of over $250 and up to $1,000, and $5,000 from the Political Action Committees (PACs).

The national conventions convened soon after the primaries, and once again we were there, check in hand. The Federal Election Commission handed each of the parties $11 million in taxpayer money for the *entire* cost of these staged affairs—which proved to be superfluous. The primaries had already settled the nominations. When those carnivals were

over, George Bush and Bill Clinton were each given a government check for $55 million to spend as they saw fit. Unfortu-
nately, the largest piece of our money went for inane television advertising—as Americans paid for their own political
stupefaction.

Ross Perot, the third candidate, garnered more than 5
percent of the vote, and would have also been eligible for the
$55 million, if he hadn't exceeded the federal spending limit.
But he never claimed a nickel.

When the Presidential race was over, what had it all
cost?

If we estimate Ross Perot's campaign at $65 million, it
was $330 million dollars. That brought the total, including
Congress, just past the billion dollar mark!

Where does all that presidential campaign money come
from? Mostly from taxpayers in the form of the $1 checkoff
on their IRS forms. At one time, 28 percent of Americans voluntarily gave, but the voters are increasingly turned off. In the
last election, the $1 contributions dropped to 17 percent,
which the FEC estimates will create up to a $100 million
shortfall for 1996.

But wait. There's a third category of big cash spent in
1992 federal elections, which takes the mark well over $1 bil-
lion. That's the totally legitimate, but absolutely sneaky, donations called "soft money."

The government permits individuals to give only $1,000
to a presidential candidate for his primary battle, and he can
give $20,000 to the party of his choice. Is that all? How about
the fat cats?

Oh, there's an easy way around that. In a typically irrational, and devious, Washington scheme, that same individual
can give *all he wants* to the political party of his choice at any
time.

All That Soft Money

What's the secret? Easy. The big money becomes uncontrolled as long as it goes into the party's "Non Federal Fund" and is not used *directly* for candidates. It's then called "soft money," and it's suddenly transformed into cash out of the government's jurisdiction. It can be directed for such activities as "party building" or "getting out the vote." But heavens to Betsy, they can't print the *name* of the man or woman up for office.

Who are they fooling? The parties can take all the soft money they want and use it for staff, rent, ads, anything, and still not violate FEC rules. They can get out the troops, as in 1992, by asking people to "vote democratic" when they meant Bill Clinton, and "vote republican" when they meant George Bush.

The FEC apparently doesn't give a damn and the voters do have some idea of who's running for President.

It's a giant loophole through which rich contributors can, and do, drive a gold-laden Wells Fargo wagon.

Is it called "soft money" because it's small and insignificant?

Hardly. The FEC reports that in 1992, the two major parties took in $290 million. In addition, there was $63 million in "soft money" at the federal level, and more given to the state parties. Despite the scrim of non-candidate backing, or maybe because of it, soft money has become the great joke of modern campaign financing.

Laughing at the limit for plebians, the wealthy gave from $50,000 up to almost a half million to their favorite party in 1992 without breaking any election laws. Edgar Bronfman, the chief of Seagram's, is the champion soft money Republican with a donation of $450,000. (The family covered both sides of the street. His son gave a $100,000 gift to the Democrats, as did senior Mr. Bronfman himself.)

Who's the champion Democrat? That honor belongs to a

Rockefeller heiress, Alida Rockefeller Messinger of Minneapolis, who gave the DNC $300,000.

Like the Bronfmans, some companies like to play both parties. Atlantic Richfield gave $171,000 to the Democrats, but $305,000 to the Republicans. (How do they explain that to Bill Clinton?)

Hollywood loves the Democrats. Sony film chief Peter Guber gave $75,000. Disney's Katzenberg donated $70,000. David Geffen gave over $100,000, as did Lew Wasserman of the Music Corporation of America (MCA). Sony's business side gave the Republican National Committee $100,000 and, to balance the books, $130,000 to the Democrats.

Each member of Team 100 gave $100,000 to the Republican National Committee, and Clinton's group of big givers approached the same level for the DNC.

The power of these large donations is that they can command privileged access to the White House top command, Cabinet-level officers, and even the President himself. When the donations are overwhelming, it can even result in an ambassadorship.

Little wonder that the usually diffident *New York Times* has relabeled "soft money" as "sewer money."

No Limit Here

There's still another loophole in the irrational campaign finance laws. This one is called "24E," or "individual expenditures," and it's so potentially massive that it can make all other federal restrictions meaningless. Under 24E, anyone can form a committee to *directly* help the candidate, as long as it's without the candidate's cooperation.

Hah!

With a wink between sponsor and candidate, a whole new campaign can be financed—legally—to run alongside the official one, with no financial holds barred. Unlike the President's own campaign, there are *absolutely no spending limits here*.

Mr. Floyd Brown did just that for George Bush in 1988 by raising and spending a lot of money, under 24E, to run a series of television ads during the election. You may remember them. They featured a fellow from Massachusetts named Willie Horton, the parolee who helped sink Mr. Dukakis.

Neither does this billion-dollar-plus tab include hundreds of millions spent on state and city elections, which have now entered the big time alongside Uncle Sam. State legislator seats, which can pay very little—$18,000 in Oregon, for example—can cost a lot of money to gain. One state candidate in Florida spent $880,000 and several local California elections have gone over the million-dollar mark.

Money has turned American elections into a system of legalized neo-corruption. Says political scientist Tom Cronin of Colorado: "Money doesn't talk. It shouts." Fred Wertheimer, president of the citizen-oriented Common Cause, laments, "When you add up all the influence money flowing in Washington in all the various ways, you end up with a corrupting way of life—and citizens know it."

One Senator, Rudy Boschwitz of Minnesota, who was defeated in the last election, at least was frank about the power of campaign money. He actually converted its influence into a formal system. Every person who gave him a $1,000 gift received a book of "access" stamps. By placing the stamp on a letter to the Senator, they were assured of swifter, more expeditious attention than that given to mere folks in his state.

When Charles Keating, the S&L scammer who gave $1.3 million in campaign contributions to Congressmen, was asked whether his money had influenced politicians, he was taken aback.

"I want to say it in the most forceful way I can," he commented. "I certainly hope so."

Raising the money for their campaign chests not only

keeps politicians busy, but it can drive them somewhat mad. Congressmen become "full-time fund-raisers and part-time legislators," sadly declares Senator Robert Byrd of West Virginia. Collecting the typical $4 million senatorial bankroll means ignoring much of the work in Congress in order to take in $13,000 a week for the entire six-year term! One Representative, who finds the experience demeaning, calls it "panhandling."

As Al Hunt of the *Wall Street Journal* observes, "Most members of Congress think a lot more about their own campaign budgets than about the federal budget."

A good part of congressional campaign money comes from PACS, the Political Action Committees created as a supposed "reform" in the aftermath of 1974's Watergate scandal. Instead, the PACs have become among the most corrupting influence in the system. In fact, most campaign finance "reforms" by Congress have resulted in still more influence-buying, a debate not unlike the intra-Mafia discussions about which vice to exploit that year.

PAC money is cash raised specifically by special interest groups. The richest of these can garner the most influence or, as one also might view it, wreak the most havoc. Without PACs, Congressmen, especially House members, would feel unloved and unbacked.

As of 1993, there were 4,700 PACs in various categories, including disguised "leadership" and "back pocket" varieties, as we shall see. There are PACs run by corporations; labor unions; health, membership, and trade associations; cooperatives; privately owned companies. Even politicians start their own so as to funnel money to other politicians who can be helpful.

PACs are perfect tools for lobbyists, who can monitor the outflow of money from their clients to their most cooperative Congressmen. The PAC cash involved is enormous: $269 million in 1992. *Each* PAC can give *each* Congressman or challenger $10,000—$5,000 for the primary race and $5,000 for the general election.

It adds up: The average House member took in $260,000 in 1992 from PACs. So fluid is the money flow that Congressmen can't even spend all they get. At the end of the last election, they had a $76 million *surplus* in the bank. (Not the House Bank!) Naturally, those politicians who don't cooperate can find their campaign funds cut off the next time around.

Who are the champion PAC-takers? In Congress, there is no contest. It is Dick Gephardt of Missouri, Democratic Majority Leader and former presidential candidate. In the 1991–92 election cycle, he took in $1,240,597 in PAC money. In the Senate, it's probably Republican Arlen Specter of Pennsylvania, who raised $2,038,057 from PACs for his reelection bid.

The big contributors in the PAC business are big names: The National Rifle Association (NRA), $6 million; the American Medical Association (AMA), $5.4 million; civil service workers union, $4.7 million; the Trial Lawyers Association, $4.5 million; the realtors, $4.4 million; the United Auto Workers (UAW), $4.4 million; AT&T, $2.8 million. Naturally, the groups tend to favor specific parties: corporations for Republicans; labor for Democrats. In 1992, the National Education Association (NEA), a labor giant, not only gave $300,000 to the Democrats, but answered their phones for a full day during the campaign like this: "NEA—Clinton and Gore!"

"I can't say that PACs are buying these elections," says former Senator Proxmire, "but you'd have to be a fool to believe that they aren't buying something."

There's also the danger that the need for PAC money will submerge the Congressman's interest in his own constituents. Senator David Boren of Oklahoma fears just that. "Our constituents know what happens when there's someone who's able to control the flow of PAC money waiting to see us," he says. "And you have five minutes to see one person or an-

other, and six or eight constituents are also competing for our
time, and we're desperate to raise all that campaign money."

The Secret PACs

The open, if brazen, PACs do regular damage. But perhaps
even worse are the usually secret "leadership" PACs. Cleverly,
these are *not* usually registered in the name of the true
owner. Instead, the fund is registered in the name of the trea-
surer who may be a friend, relative, or associate trusted to
keep his mouth shut. These PACs usually have glorious
patriotic-sounding names such as Campaign Democracy, or
Participation 2000, or the ultimate, I Love America Committee.

The real owners are politicians, most of whom are quite
prominent. Their motives are far from exalted. These secret
PACs collect huge sums, then give their $5,000 gifts to other
politicians in the hope of influencing their votes or controlling
them within the party.

Is the real sponsor's name actually kept secret?

Not really. In a bureaucratic twist that's strange even for
Washington, one part of a government agency—in this case
the Federal Election Commission—snitches on another part.
The FEC issues a list of the *real* PAC sponsors, along with
this disclaimer: "This is an UNOFFICIAL list. . . . The information is compiled by the FEC Press Office from media reports
and not official agency records."

Who's on the list of secret sponsors? Virtually every important person in Congress—about a hundred members of the
House and Senate, from Speaker Thomas Foley to House Minority Leader Robert Michel. The list also includes virtually
all living former Presidents, from Jimmy Carter to George
Bush, although secret presidential PACs are generally discontinued after they leave office.

This approach to politics is symptomatic of the whole
diseased election finance system. It makes sense to politi-

cians who use the secret PAC money to endear themselves to fellow Congressmen, and even to buy clout with the party back home.

Money often goes from a Congressman's leadership PAC to his state's Governor and state legislators, even Mayors. It reminds the locals that he is *the* Washington big shot, and in some cases it can even help ward off a primary race within his own party. (Such a catastrophe can dump a politician in mid-career as swiftly as term limits.)

It made a lot of sense to Congressman Dan Rosten-kowski, whose America's Leaders' Fund collected and handed out $203,761 to 113 candidates for office, mostly House Democrats. The "state account" of one of his PACs gave $8,500 to the campaign funds of ward committeemen, county assessor, and state legislators back in Chicago, his hometown.

But it makes a lot less sense to voters. For them, this *extra* money for political power is just another touch of the philosophical corruption that dominates so many American lawmakers.

Is that the end of this madcap money race? Far from it. There's still another series of sneaky, but absolutely legal, PACs. Officially, they're called "nonconnected" PACs. But in the marketplace of ideas they're more aptly labeled "back-pocket" PACs, a reflection of their common misuse.

The Perfect Loophole

What *are* these things? First, as kids would say, they are "major-major" loopholes in the election law. Officially, they have nothing to do with the political race, but that's just a Washington fantasy. Many are designed as "issue-solving" PACs related to environment, or law enforcement, or civil rights, with names as high-sounding as the secret PACs. But in actuality, they're perfect ways to get around FEC rules.

Who could object to the Committee for a Clean and Safe America? According to Common Cause, that was formed in

1987 by people friendly to Jim Florio, then chairman of a House commerce and consumer protection subcommittee. In 1989, he ran for Governor of New Jersey. The PAC raised money for a cleaner America, but some of it ostensibly found its way into the Florio campaign. The "back-pocket" PAC reportedly gave $5,000 to two south Jersey Democratic organizations, and after Florio became Governor, turned $50,000 over to the state Democratic committee to help pay off a Florio campaign debt.

A spokesman for American Cyanimid, one of the contributors to the "clean air" PAC, was quoted as saying, "If we had thought this was a campaign financing organization, you wouldn't have seen a penny from American Cyanimid."

Still another way to make an end run around the FEC is to use the "state accounts" of PACs. When the "federal account" is "maxxed out," as campaign experts say, contributions can flow into the state account, which is not regulated by Washington. In many cases, neither is it controlled by the states.

A relatively new form of PAC has injected foreign affairs into the debate. The Congressional Research Service tells us that $2.8 million of foreign money, mainly from Japan, is now given to American politicians through PACs. Though run by Americans, these PACs represent American subsidiaries of Japanese firms. One such PAC, organized by car dealers handling Nissan, Toyota, Honda, etc., gave $2 million to seven Senate campaigns. The donations were challenged but the Justice Department ruled them legal because American citizens were involved.

For every FEC regulation, there's an equal and opposite loophole. One is called "bundling," a warm word that evokes the love lavished on it by politicians. The loophole starts from the frustrating fact that politicians can take only $1,000 from an individual, no matter how filthy rich he is. *But*, asked some inventive people, why not collect a lot of $1,000 individual gifts, *bundle* them into a nice package, then hand them to the candidate?

Instead of a $1,000 limit, there's no ceiling for bundlers. As much as $100,000, or much more, becomes a convenient, easy, packaged *legal* bundle for politicians.

The popularizer of bundling was Emily's List, an organization formed to elect Democratic party women to office. In the last election they raised $6.2 million through direct-mail solicitations and gave an average of $110,000 to each of fifty-five women running for Congress. Twenty-five won.

The Emily people call their successful scheme to get around the law a "donor network," but others are skeptical. Margaret Tabankin of the Hollywood Women's Political Committee disagrees. "Bundling loopholes will undermine real campaign reform," she contends.

Because Emily's List is fearful of reform, it has already hired a top Washington gun, the lawyer-lobbyist firm of Patton, Boggs, and Blow, once home to former DNC chairman Ron Brown, to save "bundling" from its critics.

No wonder they want to save "bundling." That business is even potentially bigger than people know because any individual can give $1,000 to each of twenty-five bundling PACs every year, reaching an individual's $25,000 legal giving limit.

Whatever the gimmick, defenders of the system say that at least the money is going into campaigning and not into the pockets of our politicians.

Oh, yeah?

It's All Mine

Hundreds of politicians regularly dip into their campaign funds for their personal use, something the voters, and the contributors, find hard to take. Campaign donations are regularly used to pay for everything from cars to mortgages. What is, and what is not, allowed is decided by the six commissioners of the FEC (three Democrats and three Republicans). So far, they've waved few red flags at campaigners. Naturally, politicians have taken advantage of the implicit "go ahead and take it" signal.

Senator Daniel Inouye of Hawaii ate $892 worth of campaign meals in Jakarta and Taipei, not really inside his Pacific constituency. In the 1992 race, four congressional challengers had their mortgage payments picked up by their campaign committees. One congressional campaigner started a media company composed of himself and his wife, then hired and paid himself and his wife with campaign donations. Congressman Bud Shuster of Pennsylvania spent $3,000 of campaign funds for gifts to constituents and donors.

It's apparently great to be an Ivy Leaguer and use donations from ordinary people to pay your way in that cloistered world. Senator Terry Sanford of North Carolina paid $674 to the University Club in New York City from his campaign coffers, while Congressman Les Aspin, now Secretary of Defense, did the same for his membership in the Yale Club just a few blocks away. Both clubs, of course, are miles away physically and socially from those politicians' regular hunting grounds.

Creative politicians have used donations to pay for everything possible for personal use: a tuxedo and ball gown, golf fees, money to play the commodities market, even to pay off gambling debts. Senator Frank Murkowski of Alaska charged his campaign for moving his family to Washington. He now belongs to the exclusive 116 Club in Washington, which is also paid for by contributors. A *Los Angeles Times* study showed that ninety-four congressional incumbents had cars bought for them by their campaign committees.

Sometimes the FEC commissioners disagree as to what is proper when it comes to personal use of other people's money. One candidate signed a contract with his own campaign making himself manager at a $3,000-a-month fee. The commissioners split, so he couldn't pull it off. One unemployed Californian who wanted to make an independent race for the Senate asked to live on his campaign funds while he collected petition signatures. He came close, but the commissioners split again.

Going Home with a Smile

Diverting campaign funds to personal use is not nice, but is it the worst violation of the social contract between citizens and their elected officials?

Unhappily, no. In a welfare program unrivaled in the Western world, many Congressmen have left office with a veritable black bag stuffed with leftover campaign cash. Up through the end of 1992, *all* unspent campaign money became the personal fortune of Representatives once they left Congress!

This scheme made old-fashioned political pork look like dog food. In the last ten years, Congressmen, in addition to their sizable pensions, took home $6.4 million in old campaign donations when they retired or were defeated. Those elected after 1980 were out of luck, but Congress "grandfathered" those who were in the House beforehand.

The results are shocking. Gene Taylor of Missouri went home with $345,000, and Sam Stratton of New York left with a gift of $198,000. Even former Speaker Tip O'Neill, since enriched by a book, television commercials, his sizable pension, and taxpayer-supplied Office of Former Speakers digs and staff in Boston, took away the $65,000 that was still in his campaign kitty.

Fortunately, there are a handful of Congressmen who wince at stuffing people's contributions into their own pockets. Congressman Manuel Lujan gave his $117,000 to a scholarship program. Two honorable Congressmen, Harley

Staggers of West Virginia and William Brodhead of Michigan, actually sent the money back to donors.

The world of campaign finance is not only disturbing, it is fascinating. There are myriad ways the taxpayers can be duped because of the lack of wisdom displayed by the federal government. One strange gambit is racking up enormous bills while running for office, especially for President, then not paying them if you're not elected.

As of now, there are many unpaid campaign debts of presidential candidates including Alan Cranston, $220,000; Alexander Haig, $290,000; Bruce Babbitt, now Secretary of Interior, $130,000; John Glenn, $2.3 million; Tom Harkin, $140,000; Jesse Jackson, $120,000; Paul Tsongas, $130,000. The principals needn't worry about being dunned. If they have taken public money, another peculiar federal law limits to $50,000 the amount they can pay back out of their own money.

There's no longer a real debate among intelligent, right-minded people. True campaign reform, not the dabbling, ineffectual variety we've seen to date, is sorely needed.

Elections are obviously rigged in America. Not in the old manner of Mayors Daley and Hague, who specialized in creative arithmetic and the registering of tombstones. Today, corruption is aboveboard. Money, in most cases, simply determines the outcome of who wins and who loses.

Schemes for Reform
How can we change it?

Reform is in the air, but we shouldn't take it too seriously. Even if everything proposed is enacted, it still won't change an election system that spends over a billion dollars in one election year. That's not decent, no matter how much it's tinkered with by frightened politicians.

They are fearful that without reform, voters will "throw out the bums," especially them. But they're equally frightened that if the reform is real, the money—which they fervently believe is the true source of their power—will dry up.

Protected by six-year terms, the U.S. Senate is in the forefront of whatever limited reform will take place. S.3, the election reform bill proposed by Senator Boren, was passed overwhelmingly in the Senate in June 1993. But now, as it wends its way through the House, it is being heavily diluted.

Originally, reformers wanted the PAC maximum gift cut back to $1,000, but House pressure forced it to stay at $5,000. The Senate voluntarily cut their PAC limit back to $2,500, but PACs contribute only 20 percent to the Senate funding. The presidential PAC limit was cut back to $1,000, which is also meaningless. The FEC picks up the entire $55 million presidential general election tab and the $11 million convention costs.

The real fighting ground is in campaign spending limits. The Senate decided that any limit would have to be voluntary. That's based on one controversial Supreme Court decision. In 1974, in the case of *Buckley* vs. *Valeo*, former Senator James Buckley of New York sued Secretary of the Senate Valeo over the spending limit, which was then restricted to $140,000. The Court ruled in Buckley's favor, saying that money equaled free speech. Therefore the limit was in violation of the First Amendment.

The ruling seems somewhat farfetched, but because of it, the new Senate version of the reform bill makes the limits "voluntary." The limit in the Senate is $1.2 million to $5.5 million for the general election, depending on a state's voting age population. For a primary, it is two-thirds as much.

The reform is rather meaningless. The sums are not much different from the present spending average, and may even turn out to be more in some states. Overall, it makes little, if any, difference in the money pollution of the election environment.

In the Senate version of the reform bill, PACs would be

outlawed in federal elections, which would be a good step forward. But no one believes the PAC-happy House will go along. One small, positive gain is that lobbyists who have lobbied a member of Congress within the previous year would be prohibited from making donations to them that year.

Of course, this is easily evaded (as are other FEC rules) merely by skipping years, or through a clever wink from lobbyist to client, who can then produce the same donation themselves.

Another provision would try to cut down on "soft money" to national parties in federal elections. This will reduce it somewhat, but the amount taken in by the national committees is overwhelming. They will survive nicely, thank you. Two other new reforms in the Senate version are quite positive: the elimination of bundling, and the end of leadership PACs—if it ever becomes law.

The Green King

What happens if a candidate refuses to abide by the proposed voluntary spending limits? Nothing too much. All the new law does is charge the campaign committee a gross receipts tax on its contributions.

But in such cases the plan is designed to help the opponent, if he will abide by the rules. Those who conform will receive a few public-financed benefits including lower cost mailings, broadcast time at half the regular rate, and a bonus of one-third the general election limit when the opponent breaks the spending limit.

Should S.3 pass the House, how will it change the amount of money now spent corrupting the system?

Very little. Money will still be green king in Washington. In the case of the presidential campaign, it will actually *raise* its cost somewhat. Under the proposed new law, a candidate who wants primary matching funds would have to raise

$15,000 in each of twenty-six states ($390,000) instead of the present $5,000 in twenty states (only $100,000).

As far as the Senate is concerned, it'll make little difference anyway. *If* candidates hew to the voluntary curb, it will probably cut the cost of the average senatorial campaign from $4 million to $3 million, no dramatic reduction. It will help challengers a bit through low-cost advertising and mailings, but that won't supply the millions needed to fight an incumbent.

If the PACs were totally eliminated, which is very doubtful, it would make a difference in the House, at least at first. PACs now provide 40 percent of campaign funds raised by the House. But since the new spending limit will be $600,000, the restraint is rather meaningless. In fact, the limit is actually *higher* than the average amount incumbents now spend on getting reelected. All they have to do is find the same amount of money elsewhere. You can bet the farm they will.

What, then, is the answer? Is there a way to take the money corruption out of the election business?

Yes, it's really quite simple. All we have to do is remove *all private money* from American politics.

Absurd? Hardly.

To accomplish this, there is only one plausible possibility: THE GROSS CLEANUP PLAN TO MAKE POLITICS CLOSER TO A LEGITIMATE ACTIVITY, AND SAVE THE SOULS OF POLITICIANS—AND THE NATION—BY REMOVING CASH (AND CHECKS) FROM THE PRESENT CORRUPT, ROTTEN CAMPAIGN SYSTEM.

The scheme, which costs nothing extra, goes as follows, in twelve simple steps:

1. All political contributions of any kind for any candidate for any federal office in the United States of America shall be deemed illegal. Criminal penalities will be attached to the giving of contributions or loans connected with an election campaign.

2. All the money now raised in the voluntary IRS $1 check off for presidential campaigns shall continue to be taken in and dispensed by the Federal Election Committee.

3. That money, and no other, shall be used to pay not only for the presidential campaigns, but for *all* federal races in the United States—President, Senators, and House members. If less money is raised in the IRS check-off, less will be dispensed. Congress shall not appropriate any additional money for federal elections.

4. Each political race will receive a portion of the pie, according to voting age population. That money, and no other, shall be divided equally among all candidates for the race. For example, if a congressional seat is to receive a total of $250,000 according to this formula, all candidates, including the incumbent, will share equally.

The typical House candidate will spend approximately $100,000 (one-sixth the present amount) on the general election—all supplied by the FEC. The typical senatorial candidate will receive about $400,000 (one-tenth the present amount).

5. One-third the allotted money will be spent in the primary; two-thirds in the general election.

6. In the general election, no one will be allowed to spend any of his own money, eliminating the power of wealthy people to influence the political process.

7. In the primary, candidates may not take any contributions but may spend up to only $2,500 of their own money in a race for the House, $7,500 in a race for the Senate, and $35,000 in a race for the presidency. Not a nickel more.

8. None of the allotted campaign funds may be spent for personal use.

9. All political television and radio advertising shall be declared illegal, as liquor and cigarettes are at present, which is a perfectly constitutional restriction.

10. The Federal Communication Commission (FCC) shall direct all television and radio stations to give a generous amount of free time equally to all candidates for all federal offices, including candidates in the primary races.

11. Political parties and individuals will not be allowed to spend any money to influence any election races, nor spend any money in which candidates of either party, or independents, are named or alluded to.

12. The plan will *not* pay for political conventions.

Such a plan, if my arithmetic is any good, will provide about $25 million in public funds, in toto, for the presidential race instead of the present $175 million, about $1 million for all candidates in each of the thirty-three Senate races that come up in the typical two-year cycle, and about $250,000 for each of the biennial 435 House races.

Critics may complain that the 1974 Supreme Court decision will make this plan unconstitutional, but we should keep in mind that the Dred Scott Supreme Court decision at one point in our history reaffirmed slavery.

An intelligent Court should realize that the American people, and our democracy, are now being held hostage to money: more than a billion dollars of it every presidential year, and almost as much in off-years.

A breakthrough such as the GROSS plan, and not the latest piddling, diddling, failure-prone piece of reform enacted by Congress, is the only way to free us from the present corruption of our election system, and restore our democratic spirit as well.

If the Fourteenth Amendment guarantees "one person, one vote," then the flood of cash from private interests violates that rule. Rich individuals and special interests have, in effect, more than one vote. To reinstate democracy, that imbalance must be corrected.

If by chance the GROSS plan is declared unconstitutional (which would be a shame), all that would be required is a corrective constitutional amendment for true election reform—one of the many moves needed to save our nation from corrupt elections and unwise government.

Chapter Seven

Whatever Happened to Democracy?

THE TWO-PARTY DICTATORSHIP

It was Wednesday, so it must be WHIP day on Capitol Hill.

In Room H107 on the House side, the Majority Whip waited as his lieutenants, the Chief Deputy Whip and the lesser Deputy Whips, filed into the room and took their seats alongside the other Democratic Congressmen.

It was 10:00 A.M. and they were ready to get down to serious party business. A staff aide, salary $66,000, ordered a junior aide to set up a breakfast of muffins, croissants, and coffee—all paid for by the taxpayers. (In 1993, with an occasional feast of pizza at $14 per pie, that cost me and you $30,000.)

With the party's top leaders, the Speaker and the Major-

ity Leader, the room held sixty-seven people. Led by the
Whip, a cross between a college cheerleader and jail warden,
the group got their instructions on how to vote on an upcoming piece of legislation.

He laid it on the line. To pass the bill, all good men and
women had to come to the aid of the party. Solidarity. Discipline.

Down the hall, the words were being echoed by the Republican side. Party togetherness is what makes Congress go
around—and sideways and, eventually, downhill.

What happens if you don't obey? Well, a chairmanship of
one of the 251 committees will elude you, as will your favored
committee slot. That threat of near-excommunication is used
regularly, as it was in August 1993 when the Democratic
Whips *forced* the President's tax bill through Congress.

Because of negative voter opinion, fear was then rampant among Congressmen. Even so-called reform Democrats
bore down to stop defections. One Congresswoman, Leslie
Bryne of Virginia, a freshman-class Whip, went so far as to
author a stern letter demanding party retribution against
those who had defected on President Clinton's first tax go-
round.

What did she want? She wanted eleven subcommittee
chairmen who had voted "nay" kicked out of their jobs! Was
hers a wispy, lonely voice in the dark? Hardly. It was signed
by eighty fellow House Democrats.

Constituents, not parties, elect representatives. But
these goings-on, in which Congressmen almost always vote
the party-way instead of their own consciences, are a sad part
of a growing American political tradition. In fact, it has so
overtaken Congress and the state legislatures that a citizen
could validly come to the conclusion that instead of a national government, we have a *party government*.

The Parties *As* Government

The two political parties in the United States have become so mixed in with government that they've convinced voters that they *are* government. It's increasingly hard to distinguish where one begins and the other leaves off. In the confusion, democracy suffers.

In addition to his regular staff of nineteen, the Democratic Whip (now David Bonior of Michigan) has *seventeen party workers*. But, most amazingly, they are not paid by the party. *They are all on the federal payroll.* That's only the beginning. The Majority Leader, who incidentally is elected by nobody except his party pals, has twenty-six party workers on the taxpayer tab, including three foreign affairs advisers. Their job is to develop and push the party line on legislation. The bill for his party work, picked up by all of us, runs an extra $1 million a year.

The Speaker of the House is elected by all the members, is mentioned in the Constitution, and is third in line for the presidency. But the Majority Leader and Minority Leader are just inventions of the House, a convenience for the parties. They may be party men, but they've taken on enormous constitutional powers.

The so-called leadership includes six major positions: the Majority and Minority Leaders, the Majority and Minority Whips, and the Majority and Minority Chief Deputy Whips. All told, they have ninety employees, who faithfully do their party work, but collect their check from Uncle Sam—which means me and you.

These are not underprivileged staffers donating their talents to the party of their choice. One aide of the Democratic Majority Leader takes home $122,000 a year!

In addition, the parties run several other groups in Congress on the federal tab, few of which are known to the public. They include: the Democratic Steering and Policy Committee (eleven federal employees), the Democratic Caucus (twelve), the Republican Conference (forty-two), the Republican Research Committee (six), the House Republican Committee on Committees (one).

All told, how many party people in the House are living off the federal Treasury? The number is a staggering 160.

The Senate is even freer in supporting the political parties. They have 201 party workers on the federal payroll, making a total of 361 in Congress.

Party leaders in Congress get extra federal pay. Regular Congressmen receive $133,600 a year, but four party leaders get a bonus, which sounds mighty unconstitutional. Both the Majority and Minority Leaders get an extra $14,800 in the House. In the Senate, three cash in the same way: the two party leaders and one elected official, the President Pro Tem, who's fourth in line of succession to the presidency.

In addition to the cash, party chiefs are treated royally. They rate extra offices and staffs, and are even entitled to free limos supplied by the government, with Capitol policemen (sneakily off the budget) as chauffeurs.

What's the total taxpayer-paid party tab in Congress? About $20 million.

But the cost runs higher in the weakening of democracy. So cleverly have the parties intruded themselves into government that the line between them has become blurred, unspoken, and accepted. Though the whole system is probably unconstitutional, it's considered quite normal in the jaded Beltway. At its best, it's the nemesis of impartial legislation.

This confusing interchangeability—one minute an elected official, the next minute a party boss—is a magical trick that has evolved as the parties took over functions from the voters and became quasi-governments.

Fear of Party Power

Like the congressional leadership, political parties are mentioned nowhere in the Constitution. In fact, the Founding Fathers had little patience with them. In his farewell address in New York, Washington warned "of the baneful effects of party." His fear that partisanship would divide and injure the American people seems more telling each day.

In a letter to John Adams in 1814, John Taylor shared the same misgivings. "All parties," he said, "degenerate into aristocracies of interest." The public, he warned, had to be watchful about where the party "integrity ends and fraud begins."

Prime examples of this possible conflict are the chiefs of the party system, the chairmen of the Republican and Democratic National Committees. Though they run private companies, they wield enormous public power. Elected by no one, they still move in high political circles, right up to the Congress and the White House.

In his former role as head of the Democratic National Committee, Ron Brown, now Secretary of Commerce, often attended the exclusive closed-door Wednesday morning strategy meetings of the Democratic House leadership. At the time, according to The Center for Public Integrity, Brown was receiving income from his former lobbyist–law firm of Patton, Boggs, & Blow, which has approximately 1,500 active corporate clients.

Strange, undemocratic scenarios emerge from the shadow government of political bosses. Party chairmen can pick up the phone and easily reach the President. They can arrange meetings between large contributors and both elected and appointed government officials. They can use their party influence for private gain. They wield enormous power, but they are absolutely unaccountable to the people.

Since 1977, for example, half the DNC chairmen have, either before or after their tenure, been registered as "foreign agents" with the Department of Justice.

Party influence in government ranges from "recommending" major appointments, including the Cabinet, to favors for contributors. In the early 1970s, the DNC, which is

now quite wealthy, was broke. They were bailed out by Lew
Wasserman, the multimillionaire owner of the Music Corporation of America (MCA). When Lew couldn't get a room at his
favorite Washington hotel, the Madison, the DNC chairman in-
tervened with the hotel manager, but failed. Desperate, he
used his influence to get Mr. Wasserman even better
lodgings—the Lincoln Bedroom at the White House.

Party power has so permeated the government at all
levels that we often excuse it as normal. Unfortunately, this
intertwining infects the integrity of public life—from Washington to the statehouse to the town hall. In fact, much of our
system has been shaped for the convenience of politicians
and the parties, and not the voters. Too often, American democracy is subverted by the hammerlock of the parties.

Of course, not all the problems that afflict our
democracy—and there are many—stem from the parties. The
list of damage done from various sources is long and covers
many internal systems that grew up haphazardly over the
years but are still threatening the integrity of our system.

The faults and foibles are many. Here are a few that
must be changed if we are to make America a true democracy, one in which power is taken away from the political
class and returned to the voters:

• Political parties often illegally take over powers reserved for government.

• Strong party discipline weakens the power of elected
officials, often forcing them to go against the wishes of their
constituents.

• State and local rules, drawn up by the two major parties, purposely discriminate against millions of Independents,
who are virtually unrepresented in American political life.

• The ability to run for office as an Independent on the
same basis as the two parties, or to start a solid third party
movement, is cut down by the entrenched system.

• The "Initiative," which grants direct democracy to the voters, is denied to most Americans.

• The ability of citizens to reject or approve legislation through the "referendum" doesn't exist in most states or on the federal level as it does in many other democratic nations.

• Majority rule does not exist in most American elections. Candidates who receive less than 50 percent of the vote enter the statehouse, Congress, and the White House.

• The primary system for the nomination of presidential candidates is often foolish, and the result undemocratic.

• The laws that elect the President, from the Electoral College to a possible choice in the House, are irrational.

We think of our two main parties as public because of governmental support, but surprisingly, they are actually private corporations. The Democratic National Committee, for example, is incorporated in the District of Columbia under its operating arm, the DNC Services Corporation. The Republican National Committee is also incorporated in D.C. as a private entity.

Their incomes are enormous, which strengthens their hold on elections ranging from the White House down to the school board in many communities. In the two-year 1991–92 election cycle, the DNC took in $104 million, and the RNC $192 million. The two parties also had nonfederal accounts of $37 million and $52 million, respectively.

Of course, this doesn't include the funds of the state and local parties. Together, the two parties have an income of one-half *billion* dollars during each two-year election cycle.

Shadow Governments
The parties constitute a virtual shadow government, which is remarkable considering that the largest group of Americans are neither Democrats nor Republicans. According to the National Elections Center at the University of Michigan, 37 percent of Americans label themselves as Independents, while

only 36 percent are Democrats and 29 percent are Republicans.

It's ironic that as the major parties gather more power, their support is shrinking dramatically. In 1952, only 23 percent of Americans called themselves Independents. This number has increased by 50 percent, and is rising yearly as voters become increasingly disillusioned with politics as is.

The parties have cleverly insinuated themselves into the public body politic. Connecticut, the so-called Constitution State, is a typical case of the parties acting as "quasi governments." In the state's General Assembly in Hartford, the parties have 160 Republican and Democratic staffers on the state payroll. This is surprising, if only because the state has more registered *Unaffiliated*, or Independents, than Republicans, and almost as many as the Democrats. And none of the Unaffiliated are represented.

In Connecticut, a citizen registered in a major party cannot even run for statewide or federal office in his own party primary without the approval of a percentage of delegates at the party convention!

Pauline Kezer, the Secretary of State of Connecticut, has been trying to reform the system, which is perhaps the least democratic in the nation. She has tried to bring in a *direct primary*, one in which petitions alone would place a candidate on the party ballot. But politicians in the State Senate recently voted it down.

Party power sometimes reaches such extravagant heights that it's an obvious violation of the Constitution. In affluent Greenwich, Connecticut, the two political parties have *officially* split up the power of running the suburban town of 60,000.

By *town law*, the Board of Estimate and Taxation (BET), which sets the budget and tax rates for the community, has been evenly split between Democrats and Republicans. It is part of a deal that openly defies democratic rule. Section 39

of the town charter permits each political party to put up six
nominees for the BET. Citizens are permitted to vote for only
six nominees of the twelve-man board.

The result of this arrangement is not hard to figure. All
the nominees, six Republicans and six Democrats, are automatically elected even if they get only one vote. This is best
described as a new twist of the old Soviet style of democracy.

Not only is this an affront to voters, but it tampers with
common sense. In a town that is overwhelmingly Republican,
that party splits its power with the Democrats, a minority of
only 20 percent. In fact, there are almost twice as many registered Unaffiliated in Greenwich as there are Democrats.

The loaded system has been working for the politicians
for years. In fact, the Board of Education elections in Greenwich are held in the same distorted manner.

But now that Greenwich is facing a large property tax
rise, a new party—the Taxpayer's Coalition Party—is chal-
lenging the two-party gimmick by putting up five of their own
nominees for the taxation board in the coming election. Whatever the outcome, that town has to realize that they need to
honor democracy, and that the voters, and not the political
parties, *are* the government.

Keeping "Outsiders" Out

The two-party grip on the system, nationwide, is cleverly used
to keep independents and third parties from even making a
serious challenge. In many states, laws are carefully tailored
to keep "outsiders" out.

(Cynicism from independents is one reason so few
Americans vote. The usual turnout is below 50 percent for
federal elections and one-third for statewide contests, the
worst record in the Western world.)

In Florida, independents or those hoping to start a third
party, have to sign up an overwhelming number of people—
over 180,000 signatures even to get on a statewide ballot.

They must pay a ten-cent "validation" fee for each name, and collect each signature on a separate card—an obstacle course that protects the parties in power. California requires more than three-quarters of a million signatures before an independent can reach a statewide election. The number of required signatures are also excessive in Maryland, Oklahoma, and Massachusetts, among others.

One Congressman has tried to inject more democracy into the system, but his efforts have gone nowhere. John Conyers (Democrat, Michigan) offered House Resolution 1582, which would have paved the way for independents across the country. Under his bill, anyone seeking federal office would need only 1,000 signatures or one-tenth of 1 percent (0.1 percent) of the voters in the last election, whichever is greater.

What happened? Naturally, his bill is dying an unnatural death in committee.

To make an independent race for the U.S. Senate in our sample state, Connecticut, for example, the candidate needs about 15,000 signatures—not an easy task for a nonparty person. Conyers's bill would have reduced that to 1,000—a good step forward. The ideal state in which to run for Congress is Ohio, where citizens need *only fifty signatures* to get on the primary ballot. That's true democracy at work.

But professional politicians are not anxious to have ordinary citizens compete with them. Democrats and Republicans may fight, but when they're faced with an outside threat, they quickly close ranks. Term limits, a new rallying cry of the voters, tells the story of how both parties are stonewalling the people.

Voters are now convinced that politicians, like fish, spoil the longer they stay around. They begin to suffer from hubris and power-madness. Any early eagerness to represent the voters erodes with time as the pressure from party bosses, special interests, and big campaign contributors begins to wear away their soul. (A Times-Mirror poll showed that 78 percent of citizens believe elected federal officials quickly lose touch with their constitutents.)

The Fight for Term Limits

In no area are voters and politicians at such loggerheads as on term limits. It's strictly a case of *we* versus *they*. It's a classic fight between politicians and citizens, between professional politicians who see government as an interesting way to make a living, and amateurs (from *amore*, to love), citizens.

Most voters desperately want to make amateurs out of our professional pols. How do we know this? Not just by polls, which show 70 percent of Americans favor term limits, but by the ballot box itself.

In the November 1992 elections, the question of term limits was on the ballot in fourteen states. What was the result? People in all those states voted to restrict the number of years politicians could serve. Most set a limit of six years for members of the House and twelve years for the Senate.

The victory for term limits was overwhelming: a 66 percent average with two states reaching a 77 percent margin.

Some 30 percent of the members of Congress, from fifteen states, are now under the term limits passed by voters: Arkansas, Arizona, California, Colorado, Florida, Michigan, Missouri, Montana, Nebraska, North Dakota, Ohio, Oregon, South Dakota, Washington, and Wyoming.

Unfortunately, the law doesn't work retroactively for the present members of Congress. But the clock started to tick in 1993 for *all* federal officeholders elected from these states.

In fact, the top three Democrats in the House are on their way out. (By a statistical fluke, the Republican leadership was spared.) Tom Foley of Washington, Speaker of the House, will have to leave in six years. Dick Gephardt of Missouri, Majority Leader in the House, will be out in eight years.

Dave Bonior of Michigan, Democratic Whip, will be in the House only until 1998.

But they could run for the Senate or the presidency; a change of job starts the clock running again.

Politicians, of course, are not taking term limits lying down. Lawsuits have been filed against term limits in four states where they've been passed. Speaker Foley is pressing the suit in his home state of Washington, claiming the law is unconstitutional, that Congress, not the states, is in charge of such matters. But so far, all such suits have failed. The Nebraska Supreme Court has refused to hear the argument, and the others are still awaiting hearings in the Federal District Court.

Eventually, the U.S. Supreme Court will settle the argument. If it fails there, the only voter remedy will be a constitutional amendment—if they can get it started over the objections of politicians.

If voters everywhere want it, why have term limits been passed by only fifteen states so far?

The Vital Initiative

The reason is another flaw in American democracy. The states that have passed term limits have *direct democracy* written into their state constitutions. It's called the "Initiative" and exists mainly in the states west of the Mississippi. *Initiative* is a simple process that bypasses the state legislature and even the veto of the Governor.

All voters have to do is sign a petition that they want a specific law—say to hold all state and local taxes down to 1 percent of the state's GDP—and it is automatically placed on the next ballot. If the voters win, no one, neither the legislature nor the Governor, can tamper with it. It is the will of the people and the law until the people decide to change their mind with another Initiative.

Twenty-three states have the Initiative, and fifteen of

them have already voted term limits through their ballots. The remaining eight—Alaska, Idaho, Maine, Massachusetts, Mississippi, Nevada, Oklahoma, and Utah—are expected to place term limits on the ballot in 1994.

What about the others? Well, in the twenty-seven states without Initiative—and that includes most of the East, and places like the New York, New Jersey, and Connecticut area— legislators rule supreme. And they rule with an iron hand. In legislature after legislature, Democrats and Republicans have locked hands to block term limits.

Connecticut has no Initiative Law, but term-limit legislation is regularly put into the hopper—uselessly. The bills have never even gotten out of committee. Only in one non-Initiative state, tax-and-politician-weary New Jersey, are legislators considering term limits. Better short careers than none at all.

"Politicians in the non-Initiative states are fighting this down to the wire," says Norm Leahy, research director of U.S. Term Limits. "The voters are going to have to make it clear to state legislators that they either put in term limits for themselves or they'll be voted out of office."

Congressmen are no exception. They've also turned their backs on the people. In the U.S. Senate in May 1993, for example, Senator Hank Brown of Colorado tried to add a term limit amendment onto the Campaign Finance Reform Bill. But he was promptly voted down, 57–39. *Every* Senator from the tri-state New York, New Jersey, and Connecticut area—except Al D'Amato of New York—and both Senators from California, voted against term limits. (Observers were surprised Brown even did as well. The thirty-nine-in-favor votes are a sign of rising public pressure.)

As a backstop, Brown has also put in a constitutional amendment, S.J. Res.34, which would limit the terms of all Congressmen to twelve years, which some consider too long for the House. "The chances of passage are slim," an aide says. "Nobody in Congress really wants to have their terms limited. But we'll keep fighting for it."

This fight is tied to the fight for the Initiative. They go hand in hand. The battle for direct democracy is the only way American voters can hurdle the legislators who've turned a deaf ear to citizens, making a mockery of representative government.

But there's one caveat to an old cliché: *People do not get what they deserve in the American democracy.* The cards are heavily stacked against them. Instead, they get what the two-party dictatorship wants them to have. Unless the legislators yield, or are kicked out of office, the people will never get the Initiative, and term limits and other reforms with it.

"Politicians hate the idea of the Initiative. They're afraid the people will take power away from them. The only way for the people in my state to gain an Initiative law is through a state constitutional amendment. But the politicians are the only ones who can initiate that as well."

The speaker explaining this catch-22 is someone who should know. State Senator George Gunther of Connecticut has been trying to bring the Initiative to that relatively undemocratic state for twenty-seven years.

"I put in an Initiative bill almost every year, and it regularly gets killed in committee," he recounts. "This year, we made a little progress. A few people changed their mind and it got out of committee, ten to nine. But as soon as it did, the leadership killed the bill. They didn't even put it on the calendar to be voted on. I don't get my hopes up, but you can't stop fighting."

What would Initiative in all fifty states do?

A great deal. On the state level, it could demand the repeal of the state, and city, income taxes. It could set the level of state budgets based on a percentage of the state GDP. It could limit local property taxes, reduce or raise the education

budget, restrict the amount of the sales tax, reorganize the
state cabinet system, and on and on.

Amendments by the People
But what about the federal level? We've already seen what the
Initiative states have done in term limits. But one *unexplored*
use of the Initiative is to start federal constitutional amendments on their way. If the voters in these twenty-three Initiative states could work in concert with other movements, they
could revolutionize the country.

How can the people actually *start* a constitutional
amendment on its way? Doesn't Congress have the exclusive
right to do that?

Absolutely not. A constitutional amendment can be
launched in one of two ways: either in Congress, or by application of the state legislatures.

Article V of that august document explains:

> The Congress, whenever two-thirds of both
> Houses shall deem it necessary, shall propose
> amendments to this Constitution, or, on the appli-
> cation of the Legislatures of two-thirds of the sev-
> eral States, shall call a convention for proposing
> amendments. . . .

So all it requires is that two-thirds of the states, thirty-four to
be exact, can get it rolling *without the permission of the
Congress or the President*. Under this alternate, voters in the
Initiative states would direct their legislatures to make "application" for a convention for the *sole purpose* of proposing certain amendments, and not others. With the twenty-three
Initiative states in the "yea" column, it would only need
eleven more states to start it going.

What would be the first amendments on such a citizen-created agenda? That's easy. The first three would be those now blocked by Congress over the will of the people:

(1) The balanced budget amendment

(2) Term limits for Congress: House and Senate.

(3) Strict line-item veto for the President.

Through this one simple constitutional maneuver, the voters could outfox the foxy political class, and perhaps put them in their place. If not forever, at least until they learn the basic tenets of democracy.

What else don't Americans have in the way of democracy?

The answer is the "referendum." This is a chance for the people to *endorse or reject* the moves of their representatives, who may not be operating in their best interests.

We read about referendums overseas all the time. Citizens in France and Denmark voted on whether or not to stay in the European union. In Italy, voters rearranged the representative system. Even in the new Russia, a public referendum was held on Yeltsin's policies.

The only general use of the referendums in the United States is at the local level, such as the recent Florida vote that turned down legalized gambling. Many school districts require that voters approve school budgets through referendum, but they're not really binding. The Governor or the state legislature can always take over a local school district.

A true referendum would first have to be written into the law of each state. How would it work on a national level? There we would need a constitutional amendment that required citizen approval, through a national referendum, of major congressional acts, especially on pocketbook issues. A national referendum might be used to approve, or reject, raises in income or FICA taxes. Then citizens would have only themselves to blame if the tax burden was too high.

Such a referendum amendment might even require that the entire federal budget be approved by the people, much as school budgets often are now. The idea might prompt premature heart attacks in Congress, but it'd be greeted with huzzahs in households throughout the land. It might even bring fiscal stability to our bruised nation, something legislators seem incapable of doing.

Where's Majority Rule?

America has some strange antidemocratic traditions that must be corrected. One is permitting politicians who *lose* elections to be declared the *winner*. In the trade, this is called a *plurality*, but it actually means that most people voted against the so-called winner.

The practice is becoming increasingly common in three- or four-way races in which no one gets a majority, so the one with the highest vote is elected. Such strange political behavior is not possible in most democratic nations.

It happened, of course, in 1992 when Bill Clinton won the presidency with only 43 percent of the vote in a three-way split. In also happened in 1990 in our sample state, Connecticut, when former Senator Lowell Weicker won the governorship with 40 percent of the vote.

In this area, Europe is way ahead of America. In fact, almost all democracies require a majority to get elected to virtually any office. The Europeans have two ways of getting at a majority: through a coalition of parties, or a run-off between the two highest-scoring candidates. The coalition idea fits only the parliamentary system, where leading parties unite to form a majority. But the run-off of presidents and other executive officials shows what's missing in the American system.

In other nations, the top two vote-getters usually have to fight it out. In the 1960s, there was a historic battle between Charles de Gaulle and François Mitterand for the presidency of France. No one received a majority vote, so by French law, a run-off was held and de Gaulle prevailed.

In the 1988 French election, Mitterand was running

against *eight* opponents. In the first ballot, Mitterand and Jacques Chirac came out as the two top vote-getters. Mitterand had some 10 million votes; Chirac, 6 million. In the required run-off that followed, they ran solely against each other. This time the vote was closer—16 million to 14 million—with Mitterand the victor.

Had the United States used this method in the 1992 presidential election, the top two vote-getters, Clinton (43 percent) and Bush (38 percent) would have faced each other in a run-off. Basically, it would have been a contest to see who would get the lion's share of the Perot vote (19 percent)—and it might have produced a different result.

Though the Constitution now makes run-offs for President impossible, it neither requires nor prohibits run-offs at the state and local levels. Right now, there's only one state that requires a majority for election of Congressmen, Governor, and state legislators. That's Georgia. (Arizona demands it only for state offices.)

The Georgia law might seem academic, but it was recently pressed into use in the senatorial election of 1992. Because the Libertarian candidate, Jim Hudson, got more votes than expected, neither the Democrat incumbent, Wyche Fowler, Jr., nor the Republican challenger, Paul Coverdell, racked up a majority on election day. Three weeks later, Georgia held a run-off and the Republican squeaked in.

The Fake College

America has had a number of minority officeholders over the years, defying the majority will of the people. Clinton is not the first minority President. In fact, there have been eleven, the most grievous case being John Quincy Adams, who got only 31 percent of the popular vote and became President by virtue of a victory in the House of Representatives.

The American presidential election system is the most convoluted and the least democratic in the Western world. It originated in this, the world's earliest major democracy, through a series of compromises between the states and the federal apparatus. This created an antidemocratic monster, under which we have painfully lived for over two hundred years.

It is the Electoral College, which couldn't care less about how many people voted for whom in the election. It only cares about votes per state. So ridiculously askew is that ballot counting, that when Clinton skinned by with only 43 percent of the popular vote, he was Mr. State Champion incarnate, taking 68 percent of the Electoral vote!

Americans know it's not fair, but they're generally not aware of its potential for mass distortion. States are awarded an Electoral College number equal to their population, which seems reasonable. But it's a winner-take-all system. A victory of *one vote* gives the candidate *all* the electoral votes of that state. For example, the candidate who gets 6 million votes against his opponent's 5,999,999 in California wins all fifty-four Electoral votes, almost 20 percent of what's needed for national victory!

That's pretty poor democracy, but we can imagine an even worse scenario. To win California's giant Electorial prize, a majority is not required. All that's needed is one vote more than the next candidate. If minor parties were to take 4 percent of the vote in California, for example, that would leave 96 percent for the major candidates in a three-way race. The victor of that, with only 32.1 percent, or less than one-third the votes, would take the entire giant prize! Hardly a democracy.

The Electoral College stirs up nostalgic images of the Founding Fathers, but it really was one of their few grave mistakes. At the time, it seemed reasonable—a compromise favoring those who wanted "indirect" election of the President, which they finally achieved.

But its unfairness keeps cropping up. In two presidential

elections in the late 1800s, the candidates who won the Electoral College moved into the White House. But in both cases, they had lost the popular vote.

Today, more and more Americans believe the Electoral College is no longer worthwhile and is a violation of common sense. To date, two states have acted to at least make it a little more democratic. Maine and Nebraska now divide their electorial vote by the results in the congressional districts instead of winner-take-all.

If the Electoral College is undemocratic, what follows when no one gets a majority of that body is even worse. As everyone knows, the vote is then thrown into the House of Representatives—where it should never be. But what most people don't know is the devil in the peculiar details. The House can chose the President from *any one of the top three* vote-getters, regardless of how well they did in the actual election.

If a candidate received only 10 percent of the popular vote, and *none* of the Electoral College votes, the partisan House could still name him, or her, as President of the United States!

Another kicker (in the face of democracy) is that House members cannot vote individually. Only states can vote. And each state, regardless of population or the size of its delegation, gets only a single vote. So California, with fifty-one Congressmen, is only as powerful that day as Vermont with one Congressman. To win the presidency in the House, the candidate needs only twenty-six votes from the states, one greater than half the fifty cast.

Some democracy. No student of political science would even propose such an idea. He'd get a flat-out F. But it is the law of the land, and the day may not be far away when we'll have to call on it.

A second idiosyncratic idea embodied in the Constitution is the selection of the Vice President when no one has a majority of the Electoral College. According to the Constitution, the choice is to be made in the U.S. Senate at the same time the House is picking the President. But the choice is now made from the top *two* candidates for that office, which leads to an interesting, reason-defying speculation.

The Senate could choose a VP from the opposite party of the House's selection of President. Thus, as in Jefferson's day, the President and VP might be at political loggerheads. In fact, this would *always* be the case if the House chose the third-ranking candidate as President. And so on.

The only argument in favor of this strange Electoral College system is to dignify it with the adjective "constitutional."

But sooner, rather than later, we need a new constitutional amendment (number twenty-seven) for the election of the President of the United States. It should go as follows:

1. Totally eliminate the Electoral College
2. Determine the President and Vice President solely by popular vote, on a nationwide, not state-by-state, basis.
3. If no candidate receives a majority of the popular vote on Election Day, a run-off should be held three weeks later among the top two candidates. The winners would be the President and Vice President of the United States.

This three-part solution is simple. No matter how much argument or compromise is presented, there's no democratic alternative. It should be enacted into law immediately

The Crazed Primaries
There's still another hole in the logic of electing our President. Naturally, that's the present system of presidential primaries, which run from February through July and end up at the party conventions. Millions of words have been written about the strange nature of our presidential primaries, but all

that should be added is that, for irrationality, the system has few peers.

In the cold of winter, a half dozen or more presidential hopefuls arrive in small towns in the underpopulated, not overly affluent, state of New Hampshire and proceed as if they are running for Mayor of each town. Dogged by over 1,000 journalists and every major television network, cable, and hangers-on, they march from high schools to supermarkets, trying to woo a minuscule number of Americans, which the media can then "project" onto the nation as a whole.

It's an asinine activity, but it's the beginning of a march across the nation that resembles an obstacle course for the politically retarded. Following New Hampshire, a handful of Americans then meet in each other's dens and basements throughout Iowa to eat hamburgers and caucus for presidential choices.

This goes on from February through Super Tuesday in the South in March, which seems to push Southern candidates forward in the race, as per Bill Clinton, but leaves the titans of the North in the dust. By the time we reach California in June, the race has pretty much been decided. Because that giant state has been disenfranchised in the choice of President, it's considering moving its primary up to March just after Super Tuesday as part of the game of "I Want to Pick the Next President."

What to do?

Easy. Scrap the entire ridiculous state-by-state system, each with its own crazy quilt rules (some let voters cross party lines, which is difficult to predict or entangle), and substitute a national primary system in three layers.

In the first stage, in March, races should be held simultaneously in the nation in perhaps six regions to allow for local favoritism. (Mario Cuomo would not have done well in Kansas.) The top four of that race could then proceed to a national semifinals, perhaps in May. The top two primary winners of that contest would then proceed to the finals. Winner take all.

The conventions, which cost the taxpayers (not the parties) $22 million, could either be eliminated or thrown as much less expensive bashes to congratulate the winner. There's only one argument for keeping them open: a little color and charm for the political process.

So, in three well-defined primary elections, open only to registered members of a given party, each can choose its own candidate. As time progresses, and a viable third-party arrives to keep the other two honest, it can choose its candidate in this same way. Third parties will not be disruptive, because with my new "majority only" run-off election, no one who comes up with 33.4 percent of the vote would be elected to anything, including dogcatcher.

A Plan for Democracy

To change the United States from a nation that is justly proud of its democratic heritage into one whose *present* contains the best of democratic methods, we need a ten-point program to consolidate these ideas and produce a system equal to our pride.

The plan is neither convoluted nor difficult to achieve. It is not partisan, nor is it loaded in any ideological direction. But it does require courage on the part of voters, and especially from the most recalcitrant and shortsighted segment of our democracy—our politicians.

The plan, in summary, is:

1. Party and government must be separated in Congress. Eliminate all extra staff, quarters, and salaries for party leaders. Except for the Speaker, they can operate with their own congressional staffs and a notebook and pencil, which the government would be willing to pay for. *All* party workers in Congress, whether on the Democratic Majority Leader's

staff or in the Republican Conference, should be taken off the federal payroll and put into their party headquarters where they belong.

If party leaders want staff help, they can use their own personal staffs, who are legitimately federal employees.

The same should hold true for state governments. Party labels should be for identification and not for government featherbedding and undue influence.

2. Party heads of the national committees must be kept at arm's length, by law, from the U.S. government.

3. The Initiative should be given to voters in the remaining twenty-seven states. If state legislators fail to do so, they should be kicked out of office. Failing that, it should be accomplished through a constitutional amendment.

4. The referendum should become a national right of voters. Increases in federal income and FICA tax, and perhaps other measures such as the annual budget, should have to be approved by the voters in a national referendum.

5. Term limits should be put in place by all the states. If that fails, Congress should pass a law putting it into practice. If that fails, citizens should seek a constitutional amendment limiting terms of Congressmen, just as we now do with the President.

6. Majority rule should become the law of the land. All elected officials should be required to achieve more than 50 percent of the vote, or participate in a run-off of the top two candidates.

7. Federal laws should be passed to permit Independents to run and third parties to form by blocking state intransigence. The number of signatures needed to get on the ballot in any statewide election, such as Governor or U.S. Senator, should be no more than 1,000. For district office, whether state legislator or members of the U.S. House, it should be 100 signatures.

8. Direct primaries in which citizens petition to get on

a state primary or general election ballot must be the law in all states, eliminating the power of state conventions to control buddy-buddy nominations.

9. The present primary system for President should be scrapped. Instead, we should have a national primary in three stages, ending with a party run-off of the top two candidates.

10. The Electoral College should be eliminated posthaste. The President should be elected by popular vote nationwide, and participate in a run-off three weeks later if no one achieves a majority.

It's not a difficult plan to understand, even for politicians. But it will go a long way in making the United States, once again, the foremost democracy in the world.

Otherwise, we can keep going the way we are, and hold yearly postmortems on why the government and democracy don't work anymore.

Chapter Eight

Our Madcap Congress

CURBING THE SPENDERS

It was the late spring of 1992. The Bush campaign was up in the air, and the Democrat, Bill Clinton, was winning primaries.

But what was really *in* the air was a public howling for an end to excessive government spending. Ross Perot was getting on the nerves of politicians as his nasal Texas twang filled the morning TV shows like so much hot chili.

"Balanced Budget" was the name of the game. It was the main topic of commentators and the bane of badgered politicians, who were being compared to Nero. Polls showed that 70 percent of the public wanted a balanced budget and an end to the waste and deficits. Promises to hold the line were no

longer good enough. People had lost faith in the word of politicians.

What to do?

What was needed was big bandage legislation that would
stop the bleeding of dollars. An ordinary law would not do. It
could too easily be overturned later, which was the fate of the
Gramm-Rudman bill.

The obvious answer was a Balanced Budget Amendment
to the Constitution—the twenty-seventh to be exact. Congressman Charles Stenholm, a maverick Democrat from the
ornery West Texas countryside, placed the amendment, House
Joint Resolution 290, into the hopper.

"Judiciary chairman Jack Brooks generally goes with the
leadership. He had no intention of letting that bill ever get out
of committee," relates a Stenholm aide. "But we got a majority of members to sign a 'discharge petition' in record time—
less than thirty-six hours. That forced the bill out for a vote."

Stenholm had put together a formidable array of allies,
both Republicans and moderate Democrats. Even a few liberals like Joe Kennedy of Massachusetts signed on. In all, he
had 278 co-sponsors.

Since it was a constitutional amendment, a majority vote
wasn't good enough. To pass, it needed two-thirds of the
members, or 289 votes. After that, it would bypass the President and go right on to the state capitals, where three-fourths
(thirty-eight) of them could make it the law of the land.

June 11, 1992, was *der tag*. Stenholm was pretty sure he
had 292 votes, three more than they needed.

Meanwhile Speaker Foley, the Jack Armstrong of big
government, and Majority leader Gephardt, moved into action. They wheeled, dealed, and Whipped to block the amendment that would put America's house in order. Their chutzpah
was unrivaled. They even worked on the bill's sponsors, trying to twist their heads—something the congressional leadership is famous for.

Majority Leader Gephardt put in an amendment that would let Congress do deficit spending anytime it wanted with a simple majority vote. Some constitutional amendment! That ploy was defeated three to one.

Suddenly, when the final vote was taken, Stenholm's bipartisan coalition failed. They received 280 votes to the leadership's 153. They were nine votes short of the two-thirds goal.

How come? Simple. *Twelve* of the co-sponsors had voted against their own bill! The leadership had conquered again.

Dubbed the "Dirty Dozen," these twelve deserters had jumped the legislative ship at the last minute under extreme pressure (or "unction") from the congressional bosses. The losers could take consolation in one fact: five of the twelve never returned to Congress.

The fight has resumed in the 103rd Congress. Representative Stenholm has reintroduced the Balanced Budget Amendment, renumbered HJ Res.103. He's already signed up 246 co-sponsors, only 43 short of victory.

"We're optimistic that it'll pass this time, but we're letting the Senate try first," the House aide reported.

In the Senate, the bill is being orchestrated by Democratic Senator Paul Simon of Illinois, Chairman of the Senate Judiciary Subcommittee on Constitutional Law—the right man in the right place.

What are the chances in the Senate?

"We need sixty-seven votes out of one hundred to make it go," says a Simon aide. "We have about sixty so far, and there are several undecided. The leadership is strongly against it, but we're gaining anyway."

The adventure of this balanced budget amendment is a morality play about Congress. It shows that it can thumb its legislative nose at the American people and get away with it anytime it wants. It's also an insight into a world where open duplicity is commonplace, where the leadership tweaks the

ego or threatens the future of men less powerful than they, seducing or beating them into impotence.

It is a world where even the sponsors of a bill can turn
against their own creation—when the price is right.

What About Those Congressmen?

With tongue-in-cheek, political sage Will Rogers suggested
that Congress was probably the "only native American criminal class." Alexis de Tocqueville, the French genius who
hailed American democracy in 1835, was kinder, but still
viewed the House as filled with quite ordinary Americans.

Today, Americans might not go as far, except during
such brouhahas as the House bank scandal. But people are
still mightily disillusioned by the U.S. Congress.

It's rough and ready, and often less-than-informed. But
we're stuck with the institution that makes our laws and can
tax and spend us to death, a right they've overexercised. We
no longer hold them in awe, but we are apprehensive about
what they intend to do for—and to—us in order to earn their
$133,600 annual salary, plus a handbasket full of perks.

If voters are ever to outfox their rulers, they had better
understand how the U.S. Congress works, moral and intellectual warts and all.

What do Americans really think about their Representatives and Senators? When asked their opinion of the Congress
as a whole, they take on the expression of a man about to
throw up in a crowded subway. In a recent Gallup/CNN poll,
65 percent said they "disapproved" of Congress. Less than one
in four (24 percent) approved, a negative rating that no un-
popular President, not even Jimmy Carter or Bill Clinton, has
achieved.

The business community, polled by *Nation's Business*
magazine, was even more critical. In answer to the question
"Is Congress doing a good job?," 95 percent said "no." In a

multiple choice check-off, 91 percent said, "Members of Congress are mainly interested in: Protecting their jobs."

But when asked about their *own* Congressmen, 58 percent said he or she deserved to be reelected. Why the disparity? Because Congressmen are hometown people and geniuses at bringing home the bacon. With their enormous personal staffs, they do volumes of social casework—from chasing lost Social Security checks to helping someone get an appointment to West Point—for which voters are naively thankful.

This "constituent service," as it's lovingly called, builds voter loyalty. It's accomplished not only in Washington but in a string of some *1,000* district offices all over the country, a mainly postwar wrinkle that has hit up the taxpayers for multi-millions.

The important fact—how Congressmen actually vote on issues—is almost totally unknown back home. Not only is the public naive about this, but they don't seem to give a damn. The ignorance is echoed by most local newspapers, which generally avoid printing how their Representatives vote. "He's a nice guy," or "nice woman" is the usual comment in supermarkets and barbershops. God help us.

Meanwhile, these nice Congressmen and women have been pushing the nation down the slippery slope into the sink drain of disillusion and failure.

Just an Ordinary Man

In evaluating Congress, it's important to understand that our Representatives and Senators are not like many of our bureaucrats. They work *very hard*. They often put in long hours and operate under extreme pressures, both in their congressional jobs and in the anxiety and quest for reelection. They have demanding constituents, and must travel home constantly to hold their allegiance. They are pressured by lobbyists and have to raise money around-the-clock for their war

chests. They must continually fight with their own consciences and the demands of the Leadership and their party.
It is far from a bed of roses, although most would die at the
thought of being defeated and not reelected.

They are patriotic citizens who want to do the best for
their country. In the main, they are also reasonable, responsible, and moral people, like most of us. But if there is one
generalized personal fault, it is *hubris*. Too often they are
impressed by their own position, and pumped up with feel-
ings of importance that are not justified by their accomplish-
ments—a flaw that can distance them from the people from
whence they came.

Having said that about Congressmen *individually*, they
become different people when we speak of Congress *collectively*. They are then members of an organization that is ridiculously structured, and often operates against the best
interests of the American people, resulting in a pattern of failure.

What do they *collectively* do wrong? The answer, "everything," sounds flippant, but it is easily substantiated by the
facts:

1. They are generally ignorant of the details of the bills
they pass and often don't read them at all.

2. They spend too much time attending and publicizing
committee hearings.

3. They think they're social workers and devote most
of their staff time to helping constituents, a job that should be
done by a central "ombudsman" bureau.

4. They are part of a giant apparatus that has grown
five times faster than the population.

5. They have little independence and too often blindly
follow the party leadership, ignoring their constituents.

6. They obfuscate. One technique is to co-sponsor bills
for which they have no intention of voting.

7. Congress has too many committees and subcommittees. Every Congressman vies for the title of Mr. Chairman—and too many succeed.

8. They raise and spend too much money for their campaigns, from individuals and PACs, in their constant drive for reelection.

9. Their committees overlap. Several are often doing the very same job.

10. They personally serve on too many committees, spreading themselves thin.

11. They have enormous, excessive committee staffs.

12. They have enormous, excessive personal staffs.

13. They enjoy too many perks, from parking spots to worldwide junkets and lobbyist freebies, which makes them feel unrealistically important. This multiplies the problem of hubris, about which Cicero warned.

14. They exclude themselves from the laws they pass, a gesture of political insolence.

15. They talk about reform but refuse to truly change Congress. To retain power, for example, they've rejected the line-item veto for the President.

16. They have refused to adopt term limits for themselves.

17. They have repeatedly turned down a balanced budget amendment.

18. The Congress is overly permissive, and fails to exercise sufficient ethical discipline over its members.

19. They gorge themselves on pork, much of it valueless, helping to bankrupt the nation.

20. Despite the good work of their 5,000-member General Accounting Office, which oversees the Executive Branch, they seldom take its recommendations seriously.

21. Their bills keep getting longer and more complicated.

22. Congress's own budget is much too large.

23. They abuse their expensive franking privilege.

24. They pass laws without a "sunset provision," so the bills go on forever.

25. Their method of shaping a budget for the nation is convoluted, repetitive, archaic, and inefficient, at best.

To put it charitably, the U.S. Congress *as a body* can often be a narrow-minded, self-important, inefficient, philosophically corrupt, money-mad, insensitive, stubborn, self-serving, and rather pig-headed and pork-ridden institution. Otherwise, it's great.

And besides there's no alternative to the power of that mischievous body politic. God help us.

A Sample Bill

Can it really be that bad? Even worse. Let's take a look at one piece of giant legislation and how it was handled in the House.

The bill was called "Iced Tea." No relation to the rap singer, it's a euphemism for the Intermodal Surface Transportation Efficiency Act of 1991, a $151 *billion* highway bill for the interstate system. Not only was its cost monumental—$2,300 for each family of four in America—but the workings of the legislation booted up, like a home computer, several of the failures of the U.S. Congress.

The first problem was the physical size of the bill. The Federal Highway Aid Act of 1956, the granddaddy of the interstate system, was signed into law by President Dwight Eisenhower. That historic piece of legislation was only thirty-two pages long.

What about the new one? It was *484* pages in all, much of it small print text. (As Senator Boren of Oklahoma says, "Bills are five times longer on the average as they were just as recently as 1970.") The measure was so loaded with pork that grease leaked through the pages. It contained $6.8 *billion* in unneeded "Demonstration Projects," a gimmick invented by Congressmen to get their pet projects around the scrutiny of state highway people.

There was a $35 million monorail for downtown Altoona, Pennsylvania, population 57,000—a project greeted with such a negative howl that it was put up for national competition. Its sponsor, Congressman Bud Shuster of Pennsylvania took consolation in the extra $287 million in highway pork he grabbed for the folks back home. Three states got bike paths, one Senator got a boat ramp, which he named after his father. All told, there were 460 "demos" that the nation needed—like a hole in the head. (A simple piece of legislation would eliminate highway pork by leaving *all* road decisions to the states—Congressmen excluded!)

That's not the worst. The worst is that the Congressmen voted for the highway bill without ever reading it, or even having a chance to. It was congressional bullying from the leadership raised to an art form, all orchestrated in time to get home for Thanksgiving. When the chairman of the Public Works and Transportation Committee received the giant document, he forced his committee members to vote—and approve it—the same day.

Two different versions of the bill (as in the 1993 tax measure) were passed by the Senate and the House. In the joint conference committee, members haggled over their piece of pork, then returned the bill to the House for first action.

There was, however, one problem. There were no copies of the finished bill ready in time for the vote.

Two days before Thanksgiving, the conference committee handed out a sketchy two-page outline of the bill. The actual document was over *1,000* pages long, but no one had seen it. On Wednesday, November 27, in the wee hours of the morning the day before Thanksgiving, the House Rules Committee met. The normal House rule is that three full legislative

days must pass after the bill is printed in the Congressional
Record before it can be voted on. Rules hadn't read the bill either, but they waived the requirement and it went right to the
floor.

The debate began at 4:00 A.M., Wednesday. By 5:00 A.M.,
one copy of the bill was delivered to the floor of the House
and given to the Speaker. No one else had seen it. By 6:00
A.M., the vote was taken on the unread bill, and passed overwhelmingly—just in time to go home for Thanksgiving.

So much for studious, unhurried work on behalf of the
people.

(The House rule on waiting was also waived on President Clinton's Omnibus Budget Reconciliation Act of 1993.
Most members never read it, so the morning after it passed
many got a number of unwelcome surprises including
changes in moving costs, trusts for children, and a dozen
other last-minute items written in by the staff.)

This unholy practice of not reading the bill is tied to the
new tradition of giant bills, some over a *trillion* dollars, in
which Congressmen push the nation to the wall.

In the Reconciliation Bill of 1989, the text was brought
into the House at the last minute like a sacred icon. The over-
size cardboard carton filled with over 1,000 uncollated,
unindexed pages was gingerly placed down in front of the
House, all wrapped up with cord.

"We were permitted to walk down into the well and gaze
upon the bill from several angles, and even to touch it," re-
calls Congressman Chris Cox of California. But no one knew
exactly what the bill contained. There were no copies, and no
one could read it. They could only *look* at it in the box, then
vote up and down, yes or no.

Like the 1993 bill, it was full of surprises after the fact.
Rider after rider—pork, tax loopholes, et cetera—had been
added, but no one would know about them until the next
morning.

An Expensive Organization

In Washington, D.C., nothing succeeds like failure. The Congress of the United States is a growth industry breaking at the seams. It's also a very expensive operation. The cost is now up to $2.8 billion, or some *$5 million for each member of Congress*. Senate funding has gone up almost 40 percent in four recent years, three times faster than people's incomes.

Collectively, Congress is a group of mad spenders. If given its way in any one session, the combined outlay required by the new legislation would bankrupt the nation—on the spot.

The National Taxpayers Union "Congressional Budget Tracking System," for example, examined 427 bills originating in the House and 194 Senate bills in the 103rd Congress through April 5, 1993.

What did they find? That members had introduced bills that would raise spending $1.36 *trillion* dollars. However, spending cuts only totalled $95 billion, a ratio of spending over reductions of 14 to 1!

Reckless spending is a habit that grows on them. Freshmen were 23 percent more likely to cut than were their seniors.

Fortunately, there are sufficient bottlenecks to eliminate most of this manic behavior. But too much of it sneaks through and becomes law. A foreign observer would surely conclude that our Representatives and Senators have decided that spending money—not making sound legislation—is their major job.

How can we stop this? Obviously by electing only those Congressmen who *have a record of not spending*. The tracking report showed that only thirteen Senators had sponsored or cosponsored bills that, overall, would have saved the government money. The champion saver in the Senate was Phil Gramm of Texas (–$26 billion) and the champion spender was Daniel Inouye of Hawaii ($530 billion), followed by Paul Simon of Illinois ($511 billion).

In the House, the champion saver in that 103rd Congress was Dick Zimmer of New Jersey (-$55 billion), and the champion spender was Maxine Waters of California ($556 billion).

How can we stop this drain on the national treasure? One way is to limit the length of time that a bill can authorize spending. In many cases, they just go on and on.

But Senator Harry Reid of Nevada says that's not necessary. He has put in a "sunset law" called the "Spending Control and Programs Evaluation Act" (S. 186), which requires that each federally appropriated program would have to be reauthorized at least once every ten years. At that time, the program would be reevaluated and voted on again—either up or down.

(It would be much better to do this exercise every *three* years!)

The bill is still sitting in the Senate Governmental Affairs Committee. If and when it gets a hearing; if and when it gets out of committee; if and when it passes both houses of Congress, then we'll have a mechanism to stop such expensive long-term hangovers like Rural Electrification, helium stockpiling, wool subsidies, and many others.

But once again, don't hold your breath.

Thirty-Year Binge

To appease an angry public, Congress recently announced a 6.5 percent cut in their internal budget. It sounds good, but there was a hook. The reduction was in the "baseline," the fake dollar figure the budget *would have been* after inflation and built-in increases. The real reduction? A weak 1.5 percent, at best.

Congress has had an expensive thirty-year binge in staff and committees. In 1947, there were a mere 38 committees. In 1993, that number had risen to 251 committees and sub-

committees—a 600 percent increase, almost ten times the
population growth. In the Senate, with only a hundred members, there are 105 standing, select, special, and subcommittees, more than one committee per member.

Legislatively, the government is cut up into scores of little pieces, a patchwork that makes for multiple madness. In
the Senate and House combined there are *twelve* subcommittees just for Agriculture, *thirteen* for Judiciary, *thirteen* for
Commerce, and even *eleven* for Small Business, perhaps a
new governmental oxymoron.

The traffic jam is even worse in the Senate. There, only
fifty-six Democrats chair all the committees. Because they are in
the minority, Republicans are not allowed to head a single one.

Of the 314 Democrats in the House and Senate, the majority are committee chairmen. Seventeen in the House are chairmen twice over. (Just yell out "Mr. Chairman" in the House
mess and watch as most of the diners swivel about and smile.)

Not only are there too many chiefs, but the army of
Indians—federal employee staffers—has grown as rapidly. In
the past thirty years, the number of committee staffers in
Congress has increased from 700 to 3,700. While the population has gone up 40 percent since JFK's time, the number of
committee staffers rose well over 400 percent.

"We need to cut the number of Congressional committees in half and reduce the committee staff by 50 percent,"
says Congressman Christopher Shays of Fairfield County,
Connecticut. "It would make Congress more efficient and
save a small fortune."

There is accumulated danger in having too many congressional committees. Some of the repercussions are: (1)
time is wasted in hearings often held for publicity reasons; (2)
conflicting schedules force members to rush around the Capitol panting for breath; (3) there's overlap and duplication of
purpose to the tune of ten committees studying the same sub-

ject; and (4) it deprives Congressmen of time that should be spent talking to their colleagues and legislating.

Under the present system, Congressmen wear too many hats: perpetual candidate for reelection, fund-raiser, committee member, constituent worker, and, lastly, legislator.

"One of the most frustrating things for me as a freshman Senator was that I was supposed to be in forty different places at once," says Patty Murray of Washington, who calls the whole system "a haphazard mess."

The Senate claims that it knows the danger. Its rules restrict Senators from serving on more than two major committees and one minor one. Good idea. But congressional rules are often fakery, written to be broken. In reality, the average Senator now sits on *eleven* committees. In the House, the number is *seven*, too much for any civilized government.

America's Growth Industry

Ten-to-one is the general formula—congressional growth to population increase. Nowhere is it as true as in the burgeoning number of Congressmen's personal aides.

The typical House member under FDR had two or three personal assistants. Now, they are allowed *twenty-two*, eighteen full time and four part-time. The typical Senator had about four and now has *forty-two*. The population, we might point out, has only doubled since FDR's time, but the number of aides has zoomed to 12,500!

This is no ragtag, subsistence operation. The Congressional AA (Administrative Assistant—some of whom now prefer the pretentious title of Chief of Staff) draw up to $102,000 a year, while the aides to the leadership people are in the $120,000 range! In Congress more than 350 staffers make $100,000 or more. And many of these men and women are less then thirty-five years of age.

In all, Congress boasts a support army of 30,000 people

for 535 Representatives, a bloated system that is at the core
of the gridlock.

Much of this mayhem is the result of the so-called reforms of 1975, when a large crop of freshmen arrived in the
aftermath of Watergate. The "kids" quickly attacked the operation run by senior legislators and threw out a lot of the el-
ders. Greater fairness was the first result. But the second
result was anarchy. They multiplied the power positions so
everyone could reign, rule—and ruin.

The promise of freshmen new blood is often exagger-
ated in Congress, whose veterans are geniuses at co-opting
rebels and turning their enthusiasm into the pursuit of power,
which only the Establishment can hand out. After the 1992
election, for example, 110 new freshmen, including 63 Democrats, were elected. Many had advertised themselves as "reformers" who were going to "clean up" the Congress.

Before they arrived, the House bank scandal helped
stimulate some cutoff of House perks. The $5 House Barber-
shop haircut was raised to $10; parking ticket "fixes" were
made more difficult; members had to pay about $500 a year
for the previously free services of the Capitol doctor; free
pharmaceuticals were cut out; the gym club now required a
membership fee; and gifts were no longer sold at a discount.

But this wasn't the real reform to which the freshmen
had pledged themselves. The newcomers in both parties decided not to wait for the usual December orientation in Washington, where free-flying birds traditionally had their wings
clipped. Instead, they scheduled a bi-partisan meeting in far
away Omaha by their lonesomes.

"Lack of respect for the powers that be is a hallmark of
the incoming class of '92," trumpeted a newsmagazine. "They
are heading to Washington not only with an attitude but also
with an agenda for reform."

Really? No, not really. After dire warnings from the leadership that they could be ruining their Washington careers,

only the out-of-power Republicans showed. The leaders then flew out to three separate meetings with the incoming Democrats and told them to hold off reforms for the good of the administration. The economy, in the hands of the Democratic Congress, they were told, needed fixing first.

Guess what? It worked. The revolt was stifled.

The freshmen kept a few items in the agenda, including eliminating five select committees (out of 256), mild recommendations on campaign finance, and lobbyist expense deductions.

They quietly dropped the guts of their program: term limits for committee chairmen; restricting gifts to Congressmen to $50 a year; drastically cutting committees and staffs; challenging the seniority system; and even cutting out such perks as special parking spots at National Airport.

(One change involving Congress, which came from my prior book, pleased me. And the credit belongs to the freshmen. I uncovered the little-known Office of Former Speakers, a racket that provides departing Speakers with a hometown office costing $67,000 a year, plus salaries for three aides, one of whom can make $96,000. Their duties? None. Most shocking is that this package of perks goes on for *life*. The freshmen tried to eliminate it, but had to settle for closing them out after five years. Better than nothing, although the whole idea is still ridiculous.)

End of Rebellion

There was no revolution; most freshmen fell in line. "They're caught between their campaign pledges and their leadership," says Republican freshman James Talent of Missouri. Or as one newsmag so aptly put it: "Democratic Freshmen Demand Congressional Reform—Someday."

The *New York Times* summed it up: "Wooed by the old-guard leadership from the moment they arrived, some already have tempered their enthusiasm for change in the interests of getting along."

How did the leadership do it? The old-fashioned way: threats and seduction. If the freshmen didn't play along, they could forget about ever joining the leadership ranks, even as a minor Whip. The seduction came in the form of treasured seats in "pork heaven," the Public Works and Transportation Committee. Fifteen freshmen were given slots there and five were named to the Energy and Commerce Committee, the grab bag center for PAC contributions.

If seduction doesn't work, they can always push the rebels into congressional purgatory. Freshman Eric Fingerhut of Ohio proposed to cut off the automatic cost of living adjustment (COLA) on House pay raises. He soon learned that his first choice, Public Works, was out of the question.

The dictatorial leadership has won all down the line. But there's still a feeling among some Congressmen that things have to change—a kind of modern Puritanism trying to nibble away at the Establishment.

It takes many forms, some quite quixotic. Representative Roscoe Bartlett of Maryland wants to tie Congressmen's salaries to the reduction in the federal deficit. Representative Porter Goss of Florida wants to charge Congressmen $600 every time they put extraneous "propaganda" that doesn't involve legislation into the Congressional Record, which costs about $500 a page to print.

Another recommendation is to stop departing Congressmen from taking home, at deep discount prices, the furniture in their Washington and district offices. The bill is offered by Representative Bob Inglis of South Carolina, who says that his office in Greenville was stripped of everything except "a vinyl lime green swivel chair (picture available on request)."

What does it cost the government? A lot, because expensive furniture has to be purchased for the new Representative, another reason why federal decorating costs are now $2 billion a year, equal to the entire budget of North Dakota.

Occasionally, a fighting Congressman can take on the leadership and win. This took place in September 1993, when one Representative became angered by the House's excessive control over its members.

It happened this way:

Though the proceedings in the House chamber and its hearings are open, the leadership likes to keep things as secretive as they can. It helps to maintain their control over maverick Congressmen who don't want to follow the party line on a particular bill, especially when they want to kill it in committee.

One way they accomplished this was not to reveal the names of members who signed "discharge petitions." That petitition is a decent arm of democracy because it can foil the leadership when they want to bottle up a bill. Once the discharge petition gets a majority of signatures (218), it automatically forces the bill out of the Rules Committee for a floor vote.

But here's the kicker. Congressmen could sign the petition to please a colleague or a special interest group, then just walk away from the bill they were supposedly backing.

How could they get away with that? Wouldn't the press or their constituencies, or the special interest group, learn about it and get on their backs? No, because one gimmick rule of the House, which had been in place for fifty years, kept the names on the petition *secret* until the petition succeeded—if it ever did. In this way, Congressmen could safely play both sides of the street.

This was perfect for House leaders. As soon as a discharge petition reached close to the magic 218 number, they quickly put pressure on the Congressmen to take their names off, reminding them, with a wink, that no one would ever learn of their double-dealing.

The petition itself was guarded like gold. It was kept locked away in the clerk's desk, and the drawer could only be opened during a House session. Only members who had signed it could even see it again. They couldn't take notes and couldn't even bring a pen to the desk. They also had to read a statement acknowledging that disclosing any names on the petition was "strictly prohibited under the precedents of the House."

Punishment for violating it? Disciplinary action, including possible *expulsion* from the House.

This type of pressure from the leadership (who think they run America, and unfortunately, maybe they do) had been successful. Only forty-four of the 490 discharge petitions ever filed worked.

What kind of cockamamie childishness was this? It's all part of the adolescent nature of the body, a reflection of the games Congressmen falsely believe they must play to succeed. They can't get over the idea that they are not a club, but the legislature of the most powerful nation on earth.

Representative Jim Inhofe of Oklahoma, like most Americans, didn't like this kind of petty insincerity. He sponsored a bill that would force the Rules Committee to make all names on the discharge petition *public*, and to eliminate all the secrecy surrounding the document.

What has happened? The Rules Committee angrily bottled up his bill, determined it would never reach the floor. Inhofe then started a campaign to secure 218 signatures to get his antisecrecy bill out of committee for a floor vote. He had succeeded in getting 217 signatures, which is just one short of a majority.

But as soon as it reached that crucial point, the leadership applied the kind of pressure that they're famous for. They forced six House members to remove their names.

But that last feudal action by the leadership backfired. It brought on such a storm of national publicity, especially from the editorial pages of the *Wall Street Journal*, that angry mail and reverberations from radio talk shows flooded in. Anxious Congressmen quickly lined up to sign Inhofe's petition. He got his 218 signatures, and on September 27, 1993, by the overwhelming vote of 384–40, his bill was voted into law. Secrecy—at least on this bill—was left in the dustbin of history.

It proves that an awakened public can defeat even a recalcitrant Congress and an overbearing dictatorial leadership.

The leadership is still a little surprised by their defeat, but they aren't about to give up any power, nor even such perks as the Speaker's private dining room. After all, there aren't too many Inhofes in the halls of Congress.

A Peculiar System

So what's new?

Nothing much. The ridiculous way in which legislation is passed in the U.S. Congress rolls on. Invented by no one, the irrational system just evolved over the years. Every bill must go through at least three channels and several committees before it is funded and presented to the President.

Not only is there duplication, but there's built-in confusion. First, the House Budget Committee sets the *guidelines* for spending. What they produce is not law (which confuses everyone no end), and never gets to the President's desk. It's just an internal House document, created in the hope that appropriations will fall within its limits.

The other two streams (of consciousness?) are the scores of regular, or authorization committees, and appropriations committees, plus the Finance Committee in the Senate and the Ways and Means in the House. If it sounds obsolete and hopelessly entangled in bureaucracy, it's because it is. As one congressional aide commented, "When everyone is in charge, no one is in charge."

Let's say someone on a Public Works and Transportation

subcommittee (an authorization committee) has an idea for a
new highway project. His chairman will call a hearing, then
the staff will write a bill. Meanwhile, down the hall, another
subcommittee chairman has the same idea. He'll write a similar, but quite different, bill. This can go on in three or four
authorization subcommittees, each tailoring a somewhat different bill with a unifying idea.

The main committee—in this case Public Works—will
"mark up" the various bills and create a "Christmas Tree," a
compromise document ornamented with amendments and
pork that several Congressmen have demanded.

From there it goes to one of the appropriations subcommittees—thirteen in all—which divide up the government
and its goodies. This bill will go to the Transportation Subcommittee of Appropriations, where, now that it's been *authorized*, will be *appropriated*.

There are other caveats. The Rules Committee will have
placed restrictions on what the House can debate once it
reaches the floor, if it ever does. (Only in the Senate is debate
an honored idea.) And the Budget Committee will determine
whether it fits into the Budget Resolution they passed earlier
in the year.

Is that all? No way. We still haven't faced the Ways and
Means Committee in the House, which has been headed by
Dan Rostenkowski of Chicago for twelve years, and the Finance Committee in the Senate, now chaired by the scholarly
Daniel Patrick Moynihan of New York. Since these two pow-
erhouses hold enormous sway over taxation and entitlements,
any bill that involves either must also go through them.

This tortuous path has probably now altered the bill considerably from its original form, maybe even from its intent.

But surely we are now done. No way. Because the House
and Senate produce different versions, it must go to a Joint
Conference Committee. In 1990, the Clean Air Act went
through *seven* House committees, and no less than 140 House

members met to work out a compromise conference plan with the Senate.

After it's voted on, a piece of legislation is finally ready for the President's signature—if it's still recognizable by the title that's been put on it.

Failed Theory

Obviously, the present theory of government in Congress, if there is one, is not working. It is a self-destructive operation with no scheme, no rhythm, no philosophy. It's catch-as-catch-can with only one unifying principle: the bosses, in the form of the leadership, are in absolute charge. Let the Congressmen either eat cake or humble pie.

A smooth democratic operation would be simpler and cheaper. It would also put power into the hands of elected members. But the leadership and committee chairmen don't trust those chosen by the voters. They prefer the present convoluted system, which they can manipulate at any point in the operation.

And that's what they have created. God help us.

Is there a remedy? Yes. There are many, but the very first is to limit leadership posts, including the Speaker, the Majority and Minority Leaders, down to the Chief Deputy Whips, to four years. The same should be true of committee chairmen, to keep them from swelled egos and dictatorial nonsense.

Says Congressman David Obey of Wisconsin, "The way it now works, there's no accountability."

One reason it doesn't work is that the political parties, not the voters, run Congress. And they're not subtle about cracking the Whip. Patronage, which we thought went out with Tammany Hall, for instance, is alive and well in Congress, and a case in point.

The Democratic Personnel Committee, a euphemism for party backroomers, handles the hiring of some three hundred "grub jobs," as one spokesman put it. These positions, from make-believe running of the automatic elevators to the folding of papers, are pure patronage positions. The party, not the government, hands out these $16,000–22,000 jobs as a matter of unabashed, if unconstitutional, right.

What about the Republicans, who represent a large minority of Americans? (There's no sense even asking about the Independents, the largest group of American voters.)

"Well, the Democrats give us about twenty jobs to their three hundred—twelve of which are young pages. And we only have that out of the kindness of their hearts," a spokesman in the House Minority Leader's office says, sarcastically. "It's like we don't exist."

Line Item Veto

Just as the Democrats keep Republicans at bay, so Congress tries to ward off the White House. The less power a President has, the happier they are.

This "separation of powers" too often turns into a "confusion of powers," especially when Congress tries to stop the President from exercising his veto rights. As every schoolboy knows (or should know), the President's veto kills a piece of legislation unless Congress "overrides" it with a two-thirds vote. That's clearly spelled out in Article I, Section 7 of the Constitution.

The problem with the language of 1789 is its interpretation in 1994. The Constitution spoke of vetoing "a bill," which in its day was a single piece of clear legislation. Today, we have Omnibus Bills and Reconciliation measures that can total over a trillion dollars. To veto that "bill" would be to veto the government.

States get around this quite easily. They grant their governors in forty-three states the line-item veto, which enables them to approve a bill but still cut out any parts they don't want. (This has saved such states as New York from speedy fiscal demise.) But the President doesn't have, or doesn't think he has, this power.

Several constitutional experts believe the President already has this line-item veto power, implicitly. But no President has had the guts to exercise it or to challenge Congress in the Supreme Court.

All attempts in Congress to grant the President this antipork, antiexcess right have failed. The present practice of "presidential recession," as it's called, is a weak form of the line-item veto. It only gives the President the right to *try* to cancel monies already appropriated. The President sends his proposed cuts to Congress in the form of a "recession report," a kind of begging instrument.

If Congress agrees, they can pass a recession order confirming the President's request. But if they want to kill it, all they do is wait forty-five days, then do nothing. The President's desire to save money just dies, which is what usually happens. Of the cuts proposed by a President since 1974, only thirty cents on the dollar has been okayed by Congress.

The House passed a slightly stronger bill, the Stenholm-Craig Act, in March 1993, which at least forces the Congress to vote on a President's recession proposal, one way or another. But so far the bill has not been acted on in the Senate.

A stronger recession bill has been proposed by Senator John McCain of Arizona, which turns the tables. It requires that Congress vote against the recommendation if they want to stop the President from saving the money. If they do nothing, the President wins and the appropriation is killed. Several votes on the McCain bill have failed, but in a 1992 Senate floor fight, his amendment received a record forty-four votes.

A full line-item veto, granting the President the right to cut any bill down to size, is considered possible only with a constitutional amendment. Senator Strom Thurmond of South Carolina has drafted such a bill, but it's still languishing in committee. (The constitutional amendment on term limits is stuck in that same purgatory.)

Congress is now winning their battle with the White House. But there was a time when Presidents had a way around the legislature. They simply didn't spend all the money that was appropriated. This was called "impoundment."

When the government was smaller, Congress turned a blind eye to the savings schemes of chief executives. But when modern Presidents like Richard Nixon tried it, Congress decided to confront the White House. In 1974, it came to a head when Congress fumed against Nixon, then decided to permanently restrain, even punish, *any* President with an eye for billion-pinching.

They passed the Budget Control and Impoundment Act of 1974, which restrains Presidents with delusions of saving money. Every penny appropriated by Congress now has to be spent. In fact, it's an *impeachable* offense. If the President so much as "forgets" to spend money, say by not hiring a new secretary to replace one that's left, he could find himself looking for a new summer place to replace Camp David.

The 1974 act also set up dangerous precedents. One is that supposed budget cuts are more smokelike than before. The law set up the mammoth Omnibus Budget Reconciliation Act business, which now dominates, and ruins, politics. We saw it in the famed compromise tax increase of 1990 that sank President George Bush. President Clinton, master of the new Omnibus tax bill, may also find his political fate swinging in the same noxious winds.

Fake Savings

The biggest problem in these massive bills is that the tax increases are real but the cuts are often ephemeral. They generally await later action—if ever. The 1990 law put caps on discretionary spending, but they were not backed by the force of law. They could be waived by Congress, just as they were in 1993, for increased unemployed payment and Mississippi flood relief.

In the 1993 bill, many of the new spending cuts have yet to be appropriated. In fact, it might be a case of congressional (and White House) creative accounting. The supposed $250 billion 1994–98 "cuts" include $44 billion in reductions already provided in the 1990 bill. Twenty-five billion in increased taxes on Social Security beneficiaries are strangely thrown into the spending cuts column. Eighteen billion is actually new taxes in the form of user fees. Perhaps Congress should develop a new budget category called "Unreal."

The nation is lucky if it ever sees $125 billion in cuts over five years, or only $25 billion a year—less than 2 percent of the budget.

One supposed "saving" trick in the 1993 bill demands a standing ovation from veteran politicians. It's a $3 billion piece of sneakery involving COLAs (cost-of-living increases) for retired federal employees and nondisabled military retirees. It delays their expected January 1, 1994, COLA until April, then pushes back the January 1, 1995, COLA to October 1. It stays in October through 1998, when it's suddenly returned to January.

Is this really a budget cut or simply fiscal legerdemain?

It's mainly fake. In 1988–1998, the retirees get two COLAs in three months, putting them back where they started. What the U.S. government, in its infinite falseness, did was delay $3 billion dollars in outlay for five years to make the cooked books even more appetizing.

To quote the legislative aide of a House Budget Committee member, "It's a pure travesty."

That word should not be overused. Washington can top any stupidity or chicanery with the simple wave of a Congressional Record or White House executive order. According to the *New York Times*, for instance, Representative Norman Mineta of California, Chairman of the Public Works and

Transportation Committee, told President Clinton he couldn't vote for his 1993 tax bill.

Why? He wanted the additional 4.3-cent gas tax used for roads and highways, his bailiwick, and *not* for deficit reduction.

President Clinton, explained the *Times*, told Mineta not to worry. The money, some $21 billion, would simply sit in his promised, sacred, not-to-be touched deficit reduction "trust fund" until the five years were up. Then all the money would be handed back to Mineta for his highways! The Congressman voted for the President and the bill passed.

Some "deficit trust fund." Some government.

(Incidentally, the *Times* deserves a Pulitzer for that one revelation—if anyone except me read it.)

Much of the public sees Congress in a negative light and some Congressmen reinforce the negative image.

We went from the Senate PAC scandal, the Keating Five, to the congressional pay raise, to the House Bank fiasco, House Post Office matter, to an occasional criminal indictment of a Congressman, generally for election campaign hanky-panky. Before that we had the forced resignation of Speaker Jim Wright.

"What's next?" America asks, with trepidation. Citizens have even formed a skeptical group called "THRO" (Throw the Hypocritical Rascals Out!). Right now, ethics problems are handled by committees in both Houses, each made up of three Republicans and three Democrats, the only time the minority has had equal time.

Some think the system works; others say it's tough for one member to discipline another. The public fears that the most they'll get is a slap on the wrist, which is often true. James Hansen of Utah, on the House Ethics panel for twelve years, says that "members won't even talk to you for a while" after conducting an investigation.

On the Congressman's side, it's not easy for him to know

exactly what to do in certain circumstances. The Senate and House have different ethical rules, and only the House has a red-jacketed "House Ethics Manual." Still, some complain they often need a lawyer to get it all straight. Of course, if they would follow former Senator Proxmire's rule, they'd have no trouble. He sent back *all* campaign contributions and accepted no gifts.

The answer to the problem lies in total reform (read this *entire* book), but failing that, we should use retired federal judges instead of relying on self-discipline, which doesn't work. That will assure the public that buddy-buddy protection is over with in Congress.

"Include Me Out"

Congress lives in its own world. It even excludes itself from the legislation it passes to control us ordinary mortals—laws on civil rights, age and sex discrimination, disability laws, occupational safety acts, sexual harassment, ad infinitum.

They include: The Social Security Act of 1933; the National Labor Relations Act of 1935; the Minimum Wage Act of 1938; the Equal Pay Act of 1963; the Civil Rights Act of 1964; the Freedom of Information Act of 1966; the Occupational Safety and Health Act of 1970; the Equal Employment Opportunity Act of 1972; the Rehabilitation Act of 1973; the Privacy Act of 1974; the Age Discrimination Act Amendments of 1975; the Ethics in Government Act of 1978; and the Civil Rights Restoration Act of 1988.

For example, we all know that students are not allowed to pray in public schools because the schools are taxpayer supported. That's a Supreme Court decision, but Congress couldn't care less about the Supreme Court. They open all sessions with a prayer, which is fine with me. But they pay heavily for their claims of piety—with our money.

The House chaplain receives the phenomenal salary of $115,000 a year. The Senate chaplain has a $300,000 budget for himself and two secretaries. But as I previously pointed out, the money has thus far brought little divine intervention into the chambers of Congress.

Congress also likes to bend the law when there's no strict regulation. The case of Mrs. Heather Foley, wife of Speaker Tom Foley, is a political comedy/drama in point. She is the appointed *Chief of Staff* of the Speaker's office with a staff of twenty under her, two of whom make $118,000. She's not a government employee; she's been elected to no office, but she's possibly the most powerful person in America.

Chief of Staff Heather Foley is not even listed in the House Clerk's report, a quarterly that includes every employee and salary, plus a compilation of every penny spent. But anyone who deals with Congress will tell you that Heather is very much a part of the big-spending government equation.

Isn't there a nepotism law, you might ask? Yes, it's Title 5, Section 3110, and it was written in the 1960s after JFK named Bobby as Attorney General. But, in a circuitous twist, it seems to get Speaker Foley off the hook. The law lays out the prohibition against employing or appointing relatives, includes *wives*, then has the following tortuous legal paragraph: "An individual appointed, employed, promoted, or advanced *in violation* [italics mine] of this section is not entitled to pay, and may not be paid from the Treasury as pay to an individual so appointed, employed, promoted, or advanced."

This is the ultimate catch-22. Mrs. Foley, like Mrs. Clinton, works for nothing, even if Mr. Foley appears to be what might otherwise be "in violation," as the tangled law states. But the federal courts have recently held that Mrs. Clinton *is*, in effect, de facto, a federal employee. So, then isn't Mrs. Foley as well? And if so, doesn't the nepotism law apply to both of them?

In any case, Heather Foley indirectly runs much of the United States without any accountability to the people, the

Congress, or the President. Not by virtue of any election or true federal appointment, but by her marriage—not part of our political tradition.

She directly spends small amounts of the people's money on desks, telephones, secretaries, faxes, supplies, and so on, which seems strange for a private citizen. But indirectly she is involved in legislation that costs us trillions. She wields more power than any two-dozen Congressmen combined, yet she is not (or really is!) a government employee. Some Democracy. Some Republic.

Instead of obfuscation, how about a law, with teeth, that *truly* makes nepotism, paid or unpaid, involving the Speaker, the President, or anyone else working for the government, the law of the land? Is that too much to ask of a democracy, a government of laws, not individuals?

Another prime problem of philosophical corruption in Congress is the *franking* privilege, which gives Congressmen the right to mail whatever they want without stamps. A major abuse is the so-called Congressional Newsletter, which keeps constituents "informed" about what's happening to their Congressmen. Anyone who has received one (and that's all of us) knows that the franking is used here as a propaganda tool for reelection, a continuous process for House members.

Some Congressmen send out as many as three a year. Little wonder they have such an edge over challengers. The cost is not incidental. I have estimated it at $78 million a year. The laws should first be changed to cut down the mailings to one a year, and none in the last six months before Election Day for House members, and none in the entire year prior to elections for Senators. Having done that, we can move to the next step: cutting them out entirely.

Those Wonderful Junkets

As I have pointed out, Congressmen like to travel to the far corners of the world, generally accompanied by staff, guests, and spouses. Naturally, it's all done on the taxpayer's big nickel. We've already catalogued junkets to Paris, the Amazon, Hong Kong, etc, but new examples of this valued Congressional perk keep arising.

One magnificent journey was made by four Congressmen and *twenty-five* spouses and aides to China, Japan and Thailand to study—what else—the "infrastructure" of those nations. The study got so intense that they spent an entire day in the "Panda Preserve."

The cost? Some $550,000, which included $68,000 for meals and accommodations. (I wonder who books the travel arrangements?)

Reform is once again in the air in the halls of Congress. The perennial optimist, Senator David Boren of Oklahoma, is the chair of a new group of twenty-six Congressmen called "The Joint Committee on the Organization of Congress." Boren's goal is to streamline Congress, including changing and cutting the committee system, and eliminating such old, failed traditions as "proxy" voting, which allows Congressmen to serve on multiple committees without attending meetings.

The Joint Committee has held dozens of hearings, but attendance has been low, perhaps a reflection of Congressmen's fear of the leadership. Sometimes the meetings start off with a dozen or so members, but after a while they dwindle down to three or four. Reporters and staff end up listening to the testimony, virtually alone.

"I think they'll do a little cosmetic job on reform," says a congressional analyst at a Washington think tank. "But the leadership doesn't want real reform so I'll be very surprised if they do anything of substance."

The Way to Go
What then is the answer?

After a thorough study, I've compiled a list of *must* changes for Congress if we are ever to refute Will Rogers, raise the intellect and honor of Congress assembled, and in the process, maybe save the United States of America from itself.

Here they are:

1. Cut the number of congressional employees in half, from 30,000 to 15,000 employees.

2. Place a $85,000 limit on the salary of all aides, personal and committee staff.

3. Cut the number of personal aides for House members from twenty-two to twelve.

4. Cut the number of personal aides for Senators from forty-two to twenty-five.

5. Put all constituent work under a central ombudsmen organization in Congress, overseen by one staffer in each Congressman's office.

6. Cut the number of committees from 251 to 75 in both the House and Senate combined.

7. No Congressman shall serve on more than two committees.

8. There shall be no proxy votes on committees.

9. Committee staff, now 3,700 strong, should be cut to 1,500.

10. Committees should be reorganized so that House and Senate committees have the same names and same function, and relate to Executive Cabinet offices.

11. Committee chairmen shall be limited to four years in that post.

12. Term limits should be passed for all Congressmen: six years in the House and twelve years in the Senate.

13. Congress should adopt and operate under a balanced budget amendment.

14. Congress must grant the President an unfettered line-item veto.

15. Authorization and appropriations committees should be melded into one covering a single subject.

16. All leadership staff in Congress should be eliminated as party, not government, workers.

17. The rule that no vote shall be taken until three days after the bill is printed shall be made a permanent law, changed only by a two-thirds vote.

18. Congress should not be permitted to exempt itself from the laws of the land.

19. All perks, of whatever nature, including special parking privileges at National Airport, should be eliminated.

20. The Office of Former Speakers should be eliminated.

21. Ethical disputes should not be handled by Congressmen, but by retired federal judges.

22. Congressmen should be required to read a bill before voting on it.

23. Congressmen should be bound to vote for bills they co-sponsor.

24. Pork should be eliminated by making it illegal for committee members to vote extra funds for any district represented on the committee.

25. Mass mailings to constituents should be discontinued.

We can't afford to leave the reorganization of Congress entirely to its members.

Instead, the citizenry, the media, civic groups, the White House, and the cadre of concerned Congressmen must become involved in the great challenge of our day.

Otherwise, we'll be leaving Congress to its fate, which is still more public ridicule. And in the process, we'll fail to save representative government in the nation that invented it.

Chapter Nine

The Lobbyists

PERNICIOUS PERSUADERS

President-elect Clinton's voice was intense as he spoke about the evils of lobbying and lobbyists. With the tone of an impassioned TV evangelist, he decried the power of "influence peddlers," accusing them of "selling out for lucrative lobbying paychecks from foreign competitors."

His lilt was different from that of former President Bush, who had spoken of the evils of "special interests" in his clipped Connecticut voice and the determined stare of an Episcopal minister chiding his affluent, wayward flock.

But since both men are politicians, they had a great deal in common. In the *real* world, they've shown themselves highly tolerant, even privately enthusiastic, about their good friends, the lobbyists and special interests who mine the mother lode of Washington.

Early on, President Clinton claimed that he was determined to reduce the influence of lobbyists in the Beltway, where upwards of 50,000 people share in the enormous rewards granted for the manipulation, massaging, and mesmerizing of Congress and federal executives on behalf of *anybody* willing to pay the exorbitant price.

Not that these customers of the lawyers, lobbyists, public relations men, and combined lawyer-lobbyists are being cheated. So much of the nation's treasure is funneled into Washington every day from a large trough running from all corners of America down into the low-lying Beltway, that the smallest change in a tax code, a regulation, or a subsidy law can mean hundreds of millions, even billions, of dollars for the organization paying the lobbyist's bill.

No wonder the lobbying industry is sometimes called "The Fifth Branch of Government," the Fourth being the press.

Supposed Outrage

President Clinton was supposedly outraged by the present lobbying system, claiming he was determined to reduce its influence. Even before his inauguration, a transition chief, Warren Christopher, now Secretary of State, boasted that the President "intends to change the way business is done in Washington."

Really? The comment was greeted with huzzahs by public-interest groups, who've been waiting for just such a Messiah to clean up Washington. Even some wealthy gamesters in the Beltway revolving door, which moves players from lobby, law, and PR firms into government, then back again, were curious about what the President was going to do.

They didn't have to wait long. His first ruling involved his own transition team. That small army had screened and helped hire some 3,000 political appointees, everyone from

Cabinet officers to Deputy Assistant Secretaries, people who were going to run the country from 1993 to 1997. Who else could make such perfect lobbyists?

No, the President said. They wouldn't be permitted to cash in on their close relationship. There would be no payback from the people they helped select for high office. In fact, quite the opposite. They would be *prohibited* from lobbying the agency people they had worked with.

Great! How long would this ban be in effect? For life? Ten years? A minimum of five years before they could get into the lucrative multibillion-dollar lobbying industry?

Think again. This is Washington, the land of "entrepreneurial politics." President Clinton announced that his ban would last all of *six months*. After that, his transition team could go their merry lobbying way.

What? Did the President say only six months? Yes. The time is now up, and those who want to are poised to cash in.

As the 1992 campaign progressed, charges and countercharges of being lobby-lovers flashed across the television screen. Democrats accused some top Bush campaign aides of being beholden to foreign interests. And they may have hit paydirt. Unpaid Bush communications adviser James Lake is a member of the public relations–lobbying firm of Robinson, Lake, Washington insiders who represented Japan Auto Parts Industry Association, Mitsubishi, Suzuki, Minolta, and others.

Another top 1992 Bush campaign aide, Craig Fuller, had, until January 1992, been president of Hill and Knowlton, a public relations firm, where he represented the embassy of the People's Republic of China and reportedly was registered as a "foreign agent" with the Justice Department at the time. His firm had handled many Japanese accounts including Toyota, Mazda, and the Japanese Ministry of Foreign Affairs.

Democrats, Too

Democrats gloated—until they were quickly blindsided. It turns out that candidate Clinton had *eight* presidential advisers who personally, or whose firms, had worked for foreign governments or companies. Several were even registered "foreign agents," reveals the Center for Public Integrity. They include Thomas Hoog, a vice chairman of Hill and Knowlton, who like his Republican colleague, also handled the embassy of the People's Republic of China. His firm has had such clients as Fujisawa Pharmaceuticals and Hitachi.

Clinton adviser Paula Stern, who had chaired the International Trade Commission, had testified before her old agency for the Japanese Display Industry. Clintonite attorney Samuel Berger, a partner in the prestigious Washington law firm of Hogan and Hartson and a former Carter administration official, was also a registered foreign agent. His firm represented no one less than the embassy of Japan.

To stop this campaign hanky-panky, Senator Max Baucus, Democrat of Montana, put in a bill, S.3203, to prohibit senior presidential campaign officials from lobbying for foreign countries. Naturally, it quickly filled the committee's circular file.

Being named to the presidential campaign staff was only the beginning of honors for former lobbyists. For Secretary of Commerce, Clinton chose Ron Brown, head of the Democratic National Committee and partner on leave from the powerful Washington law firm of Patton, Boggs, and Blow— whose clients included such Japanese subsidiaries in the United States as Fuji Photo Film USA, Hitachi Sales Corp. of America, Mitsubishi Electric Sales America, Toshiba Corp. US, and others.

The trade representative chosen by the new President was Mickey Kantor, Clinton's national campaign chairman and partner in a law firm that has represented the Japanese electronics giant NEC.

Though friendly with lawyer-lobbyists, President Clinton has announced that he intends to curb the revolving door business of federal employees becoming lobbyists and vice versa. That's great news. But again, the outrage is mostly for appearance. There had been a one-year curb on lobbying after leaving the White House, a rule that got Michael Deaver and Lyn Nofzinger, former Republican White House aides, in some initial trouble.

Then, on January 20, 1993, President Clinton issued what *looked* like stern rules—Executive Order #112834. None of his political appointees and White House staff would be able to lobby for five years after leaving office.

It sounds impressive, but it isn't true. In the fine print, it says that the restriction applies only to *their own agency*, or, in the case of White House staffers, only those agencies for which they have had "substantial responsibility."

So, becoming a lobbyist the next day is a cinch. Once he leaves, a senior appointee to the *Department of Agriculture*, for example, can legally work for any lobby firm. All he has to do is snub his former Agriculture buddies at the Cosmos Club on Massachusetts Avenue, and instead focus his lobbying attentions on a friendly colleague from, say, Commerce, or even a senior congressional staffer he has once dealt with.

He can then ethically (if you want to call it that) make his lobbying pitch with impunity—as long as the Cosmos Club doesn't mind.

Try to Look Good

The *appearance* of integrity has become the key in newly frightened Washington, as long as there is no bite to it. Too much is at stake among the $250,000-plus-a-year crowd to jeopardize their industry because of any new morality, pretended or otherwise. Thus far, all attempts to clean up the influence-peddling world have failed, and Washington insiders are betting it will continue to be business as usual.

But since appearances do count, the Clinton administration has placed another *supposed* restriction on lobbying, this one addressed at the most lucrative and controversial of all, the "foreign agent" business.

A study conducted by author Pat Chaote listed over two hundred former top American officials—from the Chairman of the International Trade Commission to the National Security Adviser to a member of the House, to a Special Assistant to the President, to a Deputy Press Secretary, to a member of the U.S. Senate—who had gone into the foreign agent business, many for Japan.

The most startling fact about this informal "Friends of Japan for Cash" group is that 47 percent of former U.S. Trade Representatives had been lobbyists for the Japanese.

Japan's a logical customer for American politicians, since they ply the market with a seductive $100 million a year. In the opposite direction, recruiting Japanese government officials to lobby for American interests, there has been almost no business. So much for greed and patriotism in the good old U.S. of A.

President Clinton has ostensibly viewed all this with alarm. With great fanfare, he piously announced that no member of his administration will be allowed to work for foreigners once they leave office. For how long? For the *rest of their natural lives*!

Serious medicine, right? Wrong. Actually, it's quite amusing. It turns out that the restriction applies only to foreign *governments*. Once the glory days are over, former Clintonites can return to the real world where they can sign up all the Japanese and other foreign *corporations* they want. That's where the real money is anyway.

Not only is cashing in on public service legal in the ethical netherworld of Washington, but it seems to be de rigueur. There's a new theory (developed by this writer) that the normal emotions of shame and embarrassment are rapidly shed once one enters the fertile financial plain within the Beltway.

Says Charles Lewis of the Center for Public Integrity, a nonpartisan public interest group: "Lobbying in Washington is out of control. Not only is legal corruption rampant, but it has become a way of life—one in which the mercenary culture has overtaken the public interest. And it's worse than it's ever been."

The lobby industry can be quite partisan. Certain firms defend the lost honor of either the Democratic or Republican parties, and move personnel from their operation into national and state campaigns as needed. Though ideology counts in Washington, success, measured in bucks, is infinitely more important.

After the 1992 Republican presidential debacle, lobbyists loyal to Bush found themselves out in the cold. But they're not stupid. They began to regroup and join the enemy. Charles Black, a Bush man, hired away the top aide of Democratic Senator Joseph Lieberman of Connecticut. Cassidy and Associates, another Republican stronghold, signed on former Democratic Congressman Marty Russo of Illinois, who had lost his primary race.

One constant in this business is the revolving door. That enables any players—Congressmen, White House staff, Cabinet officers, campaign chiefs, public relations men, lawyer-lobbyists, Executive branch officials, heads of trade associations, congressional aides, congressional committee staffers—to move effortlessly from one job to another.

They glide in and out of the lucrative lobbying world where fees can run as high as $45,000 a month and salaries approach seven figures. In fact, many congressional staffers are learning to pick their own successors when they move off the Hill into lobbying. That way they'll have their own man in place.

It seems one can just as easily move in the other

direction—from lobbying into government. Howard Paster, a Hill and Knowlton executive and onetime union lobbyist, was recently picked by President Clinton to become the White House's own chief lobbyist with Congress.

Those Rich Former Congressmen

The most ubiquitous players are former Congressmen who have either retired or have been dethroned by the voters. Most chill at the thought of going home to Kansas or California. They rapidly submit to the affluent charms of Washington, and the chance to cash in on their years on the Hill—to the tune of $250,000–$350,000 a year to start.

About half the departing Congressmen become lobbyists. And they're among the best in the business. Why? Because not only do they know the routine, and have the most powerful of buddies, they're accorded a privilege *no other* lobbyist, or mortal, in Washington has.

When the crush of paid persuaders is held back from entering the House or Senate chamber by the doorkeepers, only one of them cannot be stopped. That's the former Congressman who has been transmogrified into a lobbyist.

With his arm around a powerful legislator, he merely flashes a pass and walks right onto the floor—even in the midst of a vote. What's more, he holds this ridiculous, philosophically corrupt privilege for life. It's probably worth all the money he's paid in the Beltway cash-for-influence trade.

Lobbying is Washington's second largest industry, topped only by government. But the junior partner fights every day for supremacy. The lobby industry is now larger, more complex, more powerful, and more financially rewarding than at any time in our history. But it's definitely not a new phenomenon. During the Jackson administration in the 1820s, one commentator wrote of lobbyists providing "lavish entertainment, hints of misappropriation and rumors of scandal and bribery."

In more modern times, there has been the Teapot Dome scandal during Harding's era, the "deep freeze" gifts and "five percenters" of the Truman administration, even the famed gift of a Vicuna coat that destroyed the career of Sherman Adams, Chief of Staff to Eisenhower.

Today, lobbyists are more subtle. There is no exchange of cash or ostentatious gifts (as far as we know), but there is still lavish entertainment and valuable favors offered on a broad scale—particularly for Congressmen. Unlike the Executive Branch, which has a ban on gifts, there are almost meaningless limits on how much legislators can be indulged by those richer than they.

Ten members of the House of Representatives and their spouses were recently treated to a four-day, all-expense-paid vacation by the Electronic Industries Association (EIA)— fellows just doing their job. The Representatives went to a posh resort on the west coast of Florida, where lobbyists from GE, Texas Instruments, and others wooed them with golf and talk. For the EIA, who will someday need these representatives of the people in a vote, entertainment seems less odious than a Vicuna coat, even if it costs more.

This vacation was topped by another lobbying group, which spent $250,000 on a weekend for 142 members of Congress at the posh Greenbrier resort in West Virginia.

Fake Restrictions

The ingenuity of lobbyists in courting Congress is amazing. So is the flexibility of Congress in encouraging it all. Members supposedly cannot take more than $250 in gifts *from any one source* in any one year.

Sounds a little strict, right? Baloney. House Rule 43, Clause 4 on gifts is really a gimmick that deserves mention as a historic violation of logic. First, $250 times, say, a hundred lobbyists, is $25,000. Second, and most important, *gifts of less than $100 do not even count toward the total*!

Lobbyists can—and do—buy Congressmen an unlimited number of meals and drinks, for example, as long as they are at restaurants within Washington, D.C. (Probably brilliant work by a lobbyist for the Washington restaurant industry.)

The no-limit-under-$100 rule makes life easy for everyone. Entertainment freebies become a natural ice-breaker. The Association of American Railroads spent $6,252 on Washington Redskin tickets for members and their staffs. One House member from Texas received two tickets to a Wayne Newton show in Las Vegas from the National Association of Broadcasters.

As we've seen, travel is a big lobbyist bonus. It's particularly popular with Congressmen and staffers, who love to get away from the fray. Again, Congress's rules make life easy for everyone—giver and givee alike. Lobbyists are allowed to pay for four days of domestic travel for Congressmen and staffs (the perfect long weekend) or seven days for foreign trips. There is no limit on food and lodging provided by friendly persuaders, and they may take along their spouses or other family members.

(This, of course, has nothing to do with official travel, or "junkets," which are open-ended, unlimited, and paid for by the taxpayers.)

The ingenuity of lobbyists and Congressmen are shown in these freebie marvels:

• Congressional staffers working on insurance legislation were flown down for a meeting in Key West, Florida, by insurance trade groups.

• House members took 4,000 privately subsidized trips during a recent two-year span. The Chicago Mercantile Exchange alone paid for 118 trips.

• A group of Senators got a free ski trip to Utah at which lobbyists who met them paid $2,500 each for charity.

• Seventeen staffers on a tax-writing congressional committee got an all-expense-paid weekend at the posh Kiawah Island Resort in South Carolina.

• Members of the House Energy and Commerce Committee and spouses received a freebie trip to New Orleans courtesy of the National Cable Television Association.

• One House chairman, obviously a golf enthusiast, went to nine tournaments. Most of the tab was picked up by unions and trade associations.

• In 1993, fifteen members of Congress were pampered at a Florida resort for a sports event headlined by tennis pros.

• Twenty-seven members received an all-expense-paid trip to a conference in Palm Springs sponsored by the Tobacco Institute.

Money also passes hands, but ostensibly for good causes. Lobbyists ingratiate themselves with Congressmen by donating thousands of dollars in a member's name to their favorite charities and foundations. (This is in lieu of $2,000 per appearance "honoraria," which were discontinued when Congress got its pay raise.)

One House chairman successfully diverted $100,000 of lobbyist money in his name to charities in just one year! A Senator, who had established his own foundation, happily received donations of up to $50,000 from corporations.

(By the esoteric rules of the House Ethics Committee, Congressmen cannot receive money for speeches or articles, but they can reap enormous rewards for *series*, meaning three or more articles, or a syndicated column, or even cartoons. Go figure.)

There are many congressional caucuses created for various functions, and they too can be on the legal take. One of them, the Congressional Sportsmen's Caucus, has its own foundation, which receives a good part of its income from corporations and lobbying groups.

Lobbyists as Santa Claus

Gratitude is the currency of successful lobbying. Perhaps no activity engenders as much gratitude from Congressmen as fund-raising that lobbyists do for their campaigns—a very active business in today's Washington. One prominent lobbyist, Tommy Boggs, wrote an op-ed piece in the *New York Times* in which he explained how that works for firms such as his.

"Lobbyists help by raising money (for Members) from clients, colleagues, and allies," Boggs wrote. "And the help brings influence, connections and returned phone calls."

The Washingtonian magazine commented: "Hardly a day goes by, for example, that Patton, Boggs, and Blow doesn't host a fund-raising breakfast."

Lobbyists can be real quick on their feet. Just twelve days after a freshman Congressman took his seat on the House Armed Services Committee, lobbyists for four defense contractors sponsored a fund-raiser to retire his campaign debt. What greater love hath any man!

Lobbyists salivate over any chance to socialize with members of Congress. They are inventive in arranging parties and events to do just that, using any pretext possible. National political conventions and inaugurations are excellent excuses. Says John Block, former Secretary of Agriculture and now president of a wholesale grocer's association: "They [the parties] give us a chance to rub elbows with and show support for the Members of Congress who are there. . . . We're not just throwing a party for anybody off the street."

At the 1993 Clinton inauguration, ten companies paid $3,000 each to sponsor a party honoring a prominent Senator. Several lobbyists actually paid good money to travel on the same train with congressional leaders going to the Democratic convention. A select few even had dinner with members of the Ways and Means Committee.

The Congressional Retreat is another favorite place for members and lobbyists to congregate. It's also a semicaptive arena, without escape. At one retreat for House Republicans, ostensibly organized to meditate about ideology and strategy, individual lobbyists spent $6,000 each to rub brains with the Representatives. (For an extra $15,000, a discounted bargain, the lobbyist could follow up with eight luncheons with the members throughout the year.)

Many in the lobbying business are dismayed by the low esteem the public holds them in. One discouraged lobbyist characterized it as "just a little above that of a pimp." They hate phrases like "Gucci Gulch," a Beltway name for the marble corridors outside the House Ways and Means hearing room. Lobbyists wearing their fashionable Italian loafers have paced up and down there over the years awaiting the verdict on their heavily pleaded tax interests.

But the modern variety of lobbyist fights back. He insists that not only is he quite respectable, but he's actually an "educator," bringing unknown facts and figures, and legitimate points of view, to busy, sometimes undereducated, Congressmen.

When the information is offered in a dignified way without the razzmatazz of junkets and not-so-subtle bribes, there's some merit in the argument. But others counter that intelligent Congressmen don't need lobbyists to do their work for them, which can include the actual writing of parts of legislation.

Instead, Congressmen can, and should, call on the able work of the Congressional Research Service, the General Accounting Office, and the Congressional Budget Office, which together spend upwards of a billion dollars of taxpayer money gathering material.

The world of Washington lobbying (and its counterparts in the states, where 42,000 lobbyists are busy) is diverse and creative. In a strange way, its aggressively winning ways are somewhat protected. Not as much as the press's First Amendment, but the Constitution does provide "the right of the peo-

ple to petition Congress for a redress of grievances." That's
the lobbyists' claim to legitimacy.

That right can best operate through citizen petitions,
marches on Washington, and the work of a host of nonprofit
public interest groups, from the Citizens Against Government
Waste to Common Cause and the National Taxpayers Union.

But on the other side of the "petitioning" coin are the
more mercenary operators who work for corporations, domestic and foreign, trade organizations, foreign governments,
and every special interest group one could name. That Fifth
Branch of government does over a billion-dollar business a
year.

Lack of Regulation

Is the industry controlled, and how seriously?

The answer is somewhat, but not very seriously. Those
people and organizations that lobby Congress are required to
register with the Clerk of the House, where a total of 11,298
are on the roster. At the Department of Justice, those who
represent interests outside the country must register as "foreign agents." (The law was passed in 1938 to control Nazis
operating in the United States.)

There are 3,500 of these registrants, but the exemptions
in the law make it impossible to know how many unregis-
tered lobbyists are actually working for foreign interests.
Lawyers, for example, are generally exempt as are persons
"engaging only in private and nonpolitical activities in further-
ance of the bona fide trade or commerce of such foreign
principal"—whatever that means.

There are about 13,000 lobbyists and clients listed in *The
Washington Representative*. But many in the great army of
persuaders are not registered or listed with anyone. They're
the ones hired to persuade the White House and the executive
branch of government, including all fourteen Cabinet agencies.

No present law requires them to register or disclose anything. But a new, controversial piece of legislation is about to change that. But again, only *somewhat*.

Senator Carl Levin of Michigan is the author of the Lobbying Disclosure Act of 1993 (S.349), which the Senate overwhelmingly passed on May 6, 1993. (A counterpart has not yet passed in the House.)

Everyone—domestic and foreign lobbyists, those working on Congress or the Executive Branch, lawyer or not—will register in the new Office of Lobbying Registration and Public Disclosure set up in the Department of Justice.

Each lobbyist, whose official ranks will probably now double or quadruple, will be required to disclose the income from each client and the amount of money spent on lobbying.

But a strong hooker in the bill was quickly noticed by Fred Wertheimer, president of the watchdog Common Cause. Wertheimer saw that real teeth were missing from the law. Lobbyists only have to disclose the total amount of their spending. There is no requirement that they tell anyone what they spent on a member-by-member, staffer-by-staffer, name-by-name basis.

Without that, those subsidized trips to Las Vegas and London are not only still possible, they are just as likely and just as hidden.

Senator Paul Wellstone, Democrat of Minnesota, quickly offered an amendment that, after futile attempts by the Democratic leadership to talk him out of it, passed the Senate. Under this amendment, any gift of $20 or more, or a yearly total of $50, would have to be disclosed by the lobbyist, with the member's name attached. (It's nice, but the bill won't be law until the House passes it too, which is as likely as Wellstone playing center for the Knicks.)

In the House, a reform bill similar to Senator Levin's has been offered by John Bryant of Texas, and is being considered. Without House approval, which is less likely, lobbying will change little in the Beltway.

The President has also added his fillip of reform. The 1993 tax bill cuts out corporate deductions for lobbyists, which makes companies wince but will hardly stop the drive to control America's laws with cash.

What Can We Do?

Still, all of this falls far short of what's required if lobbying is to become a respectable activity that educates and informs Congress instead of seducing it.

To truly change the business of pernicious persuasion and save the honor of government (if there's any left), we need a whole set of tight new laws.

What kind? I suggest the following program, which I call: THE GROSS PLAN TO KEEP CONGRESS UNTRAVELED, UNDERFED, AND UNDERENTERTAINED, AND KEEP THE WHITE HOUSE AND PRESIDENTIAL POLITICAL APPOINTEES IN A PERMANENT NON-CASHED-IN STATUS.

The plan is simple and comes in eight parts:

1. Former Congressmen who are lobbyists will no longer be permitted "floor privileges," eliminating their edge.

2. After leaving office, Congressmen will not be permitted to become lobbyists at all for a period of ten years. (By going home, they will be providing a national service.)

3. No "foreign agent" shall be permitted to serve in an advisory capacity during presidential campaigns.

4. No federal political appointee shall afterward be permitted to lobby for a foreign government or *corporation* for the rest of his or her life.

5. No presidential transition official shall be permitted to lobby anyone in either Congress or the Executive Branch for a period of ten years.

6. No registered "foreign agent" shall *ever* be eligible for appointment to a senior position in the federal government.

7. No member of Congress, or staff member in the House or Senate, will be allowed to accept even one dollar in entertainment, meals, travel, junkets and vacations, parties, retreats, meetings and seminars, gifts, charity donations, or any new gimmick we haven't thought of that will be invented by the inventive Fifth Branch in the future.

8. Repeat No. 7.

If a Congressman is in desperate need of information from a lobbyist, he will be permitted a friendly meeting at which the *member* can buy the persuader a cup of coffee, or a McDonald's Big Mac. But only on his, and not the taxpayers', nickel.

Using the basic laws of human nature, *access*, as it is known in the trade, will automatically drop off by 99 percent.

More important, the citizens' voice may once again be heard in the land.

Chapter Ten

The Immigration Racket

OPEN BORDERS, OPEN CHECKBOOK

The scene is not an uncommon one at 911 emergency headquarters in San Diego County, California, square on the border with Mexico.

The phone rings with a call from one of the several Spanish-speaking barrios in the area, home to thousands of legal and illegal immigrants to the United States. This time it's from an illegal, a woman who has just crossed the border two nights before, a common occurrence in the target San Diego area, which directly abuts Tijuana, Mexico.

This illegal immigrant is an unmarried seventeen-year-old who arrived in the last days of her pregnancy and requires immediate help. The midwife is frightened by the signs of a difficult birth and prefers the help of a professional doctor. She fears that a cesarean section, complex abdominal surgery, is necessary to deliver the child.

Within minutes, the balmy October air is split by the wail of an ambulance carrying two paramedics from the county hospital. They arrive at a house crowded with relatives and friends, some of whom, like the prospective mother, have recently arrived from over the porous border between the two countries.

The pregnant young woman is speeded through city traffic. Moments after arrival, moving aside patients waiting hours for emergency treatment, she is examined and rushed to the operating room. There, the obstetrical surgeon, an assistant, the nurse-anesthesiologist, and two operating nurses perform the surgery. An hour later, the patient is in a hospital bed in a semiprivate room.

Hours after that, when the general anesthetic has worn off, she is presented with a healthy seven-pound *Mexican* baby boy.

Right? Wrong. The mother knows better.

"*Mi Americano!*" she cried out in joy. "*Mi chiquito Americano!*"

"My American! My little American!"

According to an irrational law of the United States (so what's new?), the child, the product of a sexual encounter in Tijuana nine months before, is now an American citizen, a privilege others invest years to achieve. By an interpretation—and as we shall see, probably a misinterpretation—of the Fourteenth Amendment to the Constitution, a child born within our borders, regardless of the citizenship or status of the parents, is automatically an American citizen.

The fact that the mother arrived here illegally is of no consequence. His parents quickly learn how to take advantage of this eccentric American law, one which exists only in the United States, and recently in Canada (which wants immigration), and nowhere else in the Western world. Unfortunately, these biologically naturalized tykes will become *very expensive* new citizens of the Republic.

The mother stayed in the hospital for a week, then returned to the crowded barrio. Though she was known to be illegal, she was not reported by the hospital to the Immigration Service or to the Border Patrol she had evaded just a few days before.

She never saw the hospital bill. It was overwhelming— more than $7,000! But it was rapidly paid, without any question, by Medi-Cal, California's version of Medicaid. The teenager, who had come over with her boyfriend, the eighteen-year-old father of the new American, had no assets whatsoever.

So what? you might ask. If the state of California is foolish enough to tolerate, even encourage, such behavior and pay the hospital bill, that's their problem. Right?

Wrong, on two counts.

First, California is helpless in the face of federal law and court rulings, both of which work against the taxpayer. In the Omnibus Budget Reconciliation Act of 1986 was a provision that "undocumented" (illegal) aliens must be given free emergency medical services, including maternity care, as part of the federal Medicaid program.

When California realized the law was going through, it quickly worked up an application to question illegals as to their status, and possible assets, or income. Medi-Cal, the state Medicaid service, was supposedly reserved for indigent legal residents.

"Very quickly, the immigration special interest groups took local authorities to court, claiming that even the application form violated the rights of the illegals," explains the assistant to a local California state senator. "The Alemeda County Superior Court agreed and issued an injunction prohibiting Medi-Cal authorities from asking *any* questions as soon as the immigrant said he was illegal. Just by saying that they were 'undocumented,' they received care and that was it. The application forms were discarded."

(Even the U.S. Supreme Court has defended rights of the illegals. In 1983, in a case from the Texas border town of Brownsville, the court ruled that the state must provide the children of illegal aliens with an education.)

The second point is that the cash doesn't only come out of the pocket of Californians. By law, Medi-Cal pays only 50 percent of the illegal immigrants' medical bill. Where does the rest come from? Me and you, naturally. Federal matching funds, $3,500 of that bill for the cesarean, is picked up by all American taxpayers, from Bangor, Maine, to Seattle, Washington.

Just the Beginning

Is that the end of the story, and the cost, of this one illegal immigrant?

Hardly. Actually, it's only the beginning. Before it's over, the pregnancy that started in Mexico, probably with this scenario in mind, will cost taxpayers upwards of more than a half million dollars. By manipulating the irrational American law, the young couple had, in effect, won the lottery.

The first step in cashing in came the morning after the birth. Accompanied by the smiling mother, the nurse carried the baby down to the Spanish-speaking social worker. Not only didn't the nurse report her to the Border Patrol, but she calmly assured the social worker that the baby was "an American." The child was entitled to immediately sign up for the welfare program Aid to Families With Dependent Children (AFDC). Courtesy of California and Uncle Sam, the mother would be given a monthly cash allowance plus food stamps for her new "American" family.

The mother can also use the baby to tap into a half

dozen other welfare programs, including low-cost housing or rent paid in a private building with a rent voucher. She will also receive a WIC (Women, Infants, Children) allowance, which will give her extra food as the mother of an "American" infant, with special food vouchers, or even a basket of food delivered right to the barrio house.

Her boyfriend, who has also evaded authorities, though he was standing alongside her hospital bed for a week, will go to work in the underground economy for $4 an hour. But he will not openly live with the mother of his child, or marry her, or openly support her. That would break the welfare chain.

As time goes on, the birth certificate will turn out to be an even more valuable piece of paper. First, the mother, as the begettor of an American citizen, will probably have little difficulty with the Immigration authorities. If they try to deport her, she will point to her "American" baby and the need to take care of him. Usually, she will be allowed to stay here and on the dole until her *Americano* is eighteen. The welfare chain will last longer, and get larger, if she produces another "American" out of wedlock.

Is our little *Americano* an exception, one of an elite group of alien-citizens?

Far from it. Of all the children born in the county hospitals of Los Angeles, *70 percent* are the offspring of illegal alien mothers, and thus instant American citizens. In Los Angeles County alone there are now *250,000* such newly anointed citizens! Since they're all eligible for AFDC welfare, and already represent 25 percent of the welfare cases in California, county officials fear the cost of that one benefit alone to illegals will reach $1 *billion* a year locally by the end of the decade.

If the taxpayer feels wounded, he will really experience pain at the next blow—the extraordinary power of the new *Americano*, who is totally unaware of what is going on around him. When the child reaches twenty-one, he will be able to orchestrate the destiny of his extended family still in Mexico. By simple application, he will be able to get permanent resident status for his parents, then "reunite" the rest of his immediate family, including brothers and sisters. They will now come into the United States legally, thus converting the geography of birth into a national transplantation.

The new citizen can also sponsor all members of his immediate family, who *must* be legally admitted into the United States even though their original entry was illegal. Once the members of the nuclear family (spouses, parents, siblings) become citizens, they can also sponsor other relatives for immigration, extending the roots of the entire family tree from Mexico, or wherever, into the American backyard.

To the Immigration and Naturalization Service (INS) this is ominously known as "Chain Immigration," a system that has all the power of mathematics behind it. For how long? In perpetuity.

Not bad for a surreptitious dash across the Tijuana–San Diego border by a pregnant, unmarried seventeen-year-old.

How It Started

This part of the scenario was made possible by the Immigration Law of 1965, passed under the Lyndon Johnson administration. Though few Americans know it, the law dramatically changed the face of America, setting up a fertile environment for many of the present immigration abuses. And there are many.

The 1965 "reform" eliminated the old national quota system, which had mirrored America's ethnic makeup. Instead, it put the emphasis on bringing families together, the theory of "reuniting." Since immigration after 1965 has been mostly from the Third World—Mexico, Cuba, Philippines, Vietnam, and Korea—the nature of the whole system shifted. From then on, fewer than 10 percent of legal immigrants were European.

The result is an ominous pressure on welfare and medical services throughout the country, but especially in five key states that handle the bulk of immigration: California, Texas, Florida, New York, and Illinois.

The cry against excessive immigration is now reaching its pinnacle. Sixty-one percent of Americans, a nation of immigrants, think it's time to cut it way down, an abrupt rise from 1986 when only 40 percent thought so. In fact, even the majority of American Hispanics think that too many Latin immigrants are entering the country.

This fear by a nation made up of people from other nations is a new emotion. Immigration has always been celebrated as the strength of America, and Ellis Island, which saw 12 million come through its gates, was the symbol of that system.

But today, the fear is real, and it's both financial and cultural. It's also symbolic. Many Americans are afraid we're losing our sovereignty as we lose control of our borders. There's also fear that with a lingering slow economy, foreign workers willing to take low-paying jobs are injuring the pay scale of Americans, and forcing others into unemployment.

The figures support the fears. First, there is the sheer number of immigrants. How many immigrants actually come in each year? How many are illegal? What does it cost us? Are the fears justified by the numbers, or is it just a case of resurgent national jingoism?

The numbers are instructive. There are approximately 900,000 legal immigrants taken in each year, a figure that will soon reach 1 million. The number of "illegals" is less well known, with estimates varying from 500,000 to 3 million annually, with about 1.5 million a year being a conservative guess. The total number of immigrants, say 2 to 3 million annually, doesn't seem so overwhelming in a nation of 265 million. Does it?

Yet the numbers are deceptively innocent.

The Census Bureau, looking at the demographics of immigration, has drastically altered its estimate of U.S. population for the year 2050. Just a half dozen years ago, they predicted a topping out of population at 300 million, a near-permanent plateau. But now, by projecting the implications of the new wave of immigrants, they've changed their mind, with a vengeance.

By 2050, the Census Bureau now says, there will be 383 million people living here, 83 million more than they first thought. There has been some increase in the birthrate of native-born Americans, but the real effect comes from the immigrants. Not only do they have a higher birthrate, but the "reuniting" law brings in their extended families, with their own higher birthrate.

A Different America

The result, projects the Census Bureau, is an America of a different cultural and demographic profile. By ethnic composition, America is now 75 percent of European descent. But by 2050, with the continuation of Third World immigration from Mexico, Latin America, Philippines, Korea, China, Vietnam, and so on, it will change drastically to a nation with only 53 percent Europeans and 47 percent minorities. Not long after that, those of European ancestry will become a minority.

In the last decade, for example, the only appreciable European immigration was from Ireland, and most of that was illegal.

By 2020, only twenty-seven years down the line, the Hispanic population, which was 9 percent in the 1990 census, will grow to 15 percent. The Asians will increase from 4 to 7 percent, and the European population will drop to 64 percent of America.

So? What's the difference? Legal or illegal, they're all Americans—or will become Americans. No? Doesn't Emma

Lazarus's epic poem on the Statue of Liberty—"give me your huddled masses"—still have meaning?

Not the way it used to. The difference is that the original wave of immigrants, which was heaviest from the Civil War to World War I, were no drain on the taxpayers. Although they were equally poor, they worked hard for low wages. They took virtually nothing from the government social services, which were almost nonexistent, and actually pumped *up* the economy.

Today, in contrast, the illegal immigrants, like the mother of our instant American, are walking into one of the most expensive and elaborate, if crackpot, welfare systems in the world. And they're drawing on it heavily. In addition, the first wave of immigrants arrived when there was a surplus of work and a shortage of labor, and they helped to fill it. Today, there is a surplus of workers, and a shortage of work.

State Senator William Craven of California has issued a report on the problem, one that threatens the stability of the once–Golden State.

To give away the punch line, illegal immigration now costs deficit-and-recession-ridden California over $3 billion a year, a figure expected to rise to over $10 billion by the turn of the century.

The report, "A Fiscal Impact Analysis of Undocumented Immigrants Residing in San Diego County," details the medical, welfare, and education price of caring for "undocumented" aliens, as illegals are euphemistically called.

The report estimates that there are 200,000 illegals living in San Diego County, or one in ten people. In Los Angeles, that figure jumps to 700,000. The illegal population of California is conservatively estimated at 1.3 million, but could be as high as 2 million.

In just one county, San Diego, the cost to prosecute criminals among the illegals, which accounts for one in eight arrests, runs over $100 million a year. Known medical costs are $27 million; the price of their education is $61 million; and welfare takes another $13 million. The total is $206 million for that county alone. The state estimates that San Diego holds 5 percent of California's illegals, so the full impact is twenty times as high—the $3 billion-plus figure.

The Overwhelming Price

If California is so hard hit, what is the whole tab, nationally?

The cost is enormous. FAIR (Federation for American Immigration Reform) estimates it to be $6 billion a year, and growing.

In 1991, the nonpartisan Center for Immigration Studies in Washington estimated the *direct* cost of illegal aliens at $5.4 billion. A June 1993 report from Rice University in Houston, Texas, raises that to $7.75 billion for 1992, which includes education, medical care, housing assistance, criminal justice, and welfare.

But do the costs stop there?

Not really. There are two other factors. One is the loss of jobs by low-skilled American workers who can't compete with off-the-book illegals. The study shows that 900,000 unskilled American workers, most of whom are Afro-Americans and Hispanics, had their jobs taken by illegal immigrants. That cost in unemployment insurance, job retraining, and welfare was another $6.9 billion. The total taxpayer tab for illegals alone was $14.7 billion in 1992.

No one knows for sure what the future holds, but the author of the study, economist Donald Huddle, gives it a try. He guesses that by the end of the decade, illegals will have cost us a frightening $180 billion.

This does not include illegal immigrants who have tapped into social welfare programs by posing as "legals" with fake Social Security and Green Cards, a thriving business in high immigrant areas. That group adds several billions more to the bill. Neither does it anticipate what will happen down the line, when our instant citizens come of age and bring the whole family to America!

"For a long time you couldn't talk about the problem," says a spokesman for the Immigration and Naturalization Service. "In a nation of immigrants, it was politically incorrect to talk against immigration, even if there were abuses. But that's changing now as we lose control of our borders. Today, the outrage is coming from both parties. Democrats and Republicans in Congress are falling over each other to sponsor all kinds of legislation to stop what's happening."

The spokesman points out that the crisis has been building by stages, as the borders became more porous.

"We have only about 800 border patrolmen on duty at any one time—to handle almost 2,000 miles of our border with Mexico. They apprehend 1.2 million people a year, but many more than that get through—if not the first time, then on the second, third, or fourth try.

"We now have less than 4,000 border patrolmen in all and we probably need 6,600 just to slow down the flood. But that still wouldn't seal the border. For that, you'd need the army. And besides, there's the enormous business of false documents—Social Security cards, driver's licenses, even birth certificates. If we're going to make a dent in this, we need to produce tamper-proof documents."

Since these illegals make such use of our social welfare system, why aren't they immediately reported to the INS by authorities? I asked, innocently.

"The medical and social work people have no interest in enforcing our laws. They just don't report illegals to us. They don't think that's their job."

Not just the social work system, but Congress itself has been counterproductive in the attempt to control immigration. Frustrated by the number of illegals in America in 1986, Congress passed the Immigration Reform and Control Act. In effect, it granted all illegals, then estimated at 3 million, amnesty and permanent residency in America. Within five years, a time that has now arrived, they would be eligible for citizenship and welfare services.

Naturally, this generosity was rewarded with a still greater avalanche of illegal immigration. By 1990, Americans were reacting, and a poll showed that 77 percent of the public wanted *fewer*, not more, immigrants.

How did Congress respond? Naturally, by *increasing* the number of immigrants by 30–40 percent.

"That bill, the Immigration Act of 1990, was the result of congressional horse trading," says an INS spokesman. "Everybody on the Hill was making a deal so they could get immigrants in for their special interests. Senator Kennedy managed that for 16,000 Irish; one Congressman was able to bring in 1,000 Tibetans; DeConcini wanted El Salvador refugees to get protection from deportation for eighteen months; others wanted immigration status for Chinese students, and so on."

The result is that the modern record for immigration is expected to be broken in this decade. There will be over 10 million new *legal* immigrants, and an untold number of illegals, almost all from the Third World. An educated guess is a total of 20 million new people, plus their offspring, and, later, their relatives.

"We have distorted the meaning of the Statue of Liberty," says the INS man. "In those days, almost all immigrants were legal. Still, when they arrived at Ellis Island, we turned them down for any number of reasons, including health. Today, things are out of control."

One reason for the recent immigration avalanche may not be obvious, except to those on the Hill. For years, Democrats wanted more and more immigrants, for every new resident was considered another vote for that party. Republicans secretly pushed for increased immigration because they felt it was good for business, especially in the agriculture and construction fields, where immigrants provided cheap labor. So there was an unspoken agreement from both parties, in some ways against the interests of the native-born working man.

A Newly Concerned Washington

Attitudes are now beginning to change in Washington—or they seem to be. The Hill is abuzz with pressure from constituents. New legislation is being proposed on both sides of the aisle, and from veteran and freshman legislators alike.

Representative Anthony Beilenson, Democrat from the Los Angeles area, has introduced several bills. They include plans to increase the size of the border patrol from 4,000 to 6,600, create a tamper-proof Social Security card (holograms) to cut down on fake documents, and reimburse states for incarcerating criminal illegals.

Despite her reputation as a liberal, Senator Dianne Feinstein, also of California, is so troubled by the Mexican assault on her state's borders, that she has outlined a plan to "protect the American dream" against illegals.

It includes: (1) increasing the Border Patrol; (2) more four-wheel drive vehicles for patrolmen; (3) stiffer penalties for conviction of alien smugglers; (4) quicker deportation of aliens convicted of crimes; (5) forcing alien criminals to serve their prison sentences in their own country; (alien prisoners are now given a choice!); (6) amending the Medicaid laws so that maternity costs of illegal aliens are not paid by the government.

To cover the cost of a beefed up Border Patrol, Senator Feinstein has a unique plan: a $1 fee on all border crossing points into the United States, paid by tourists, citizens, and legal immigrants, which is estimated to raise $400 million. The illegals will not, of course, be expected to ante up.

On the Republican side, Senator Alan Simpson of Wyoming is facing up to another aspect of the immigration problem—the racket of illegals seeking "political asylum" because of oppression in their home country, a formula that would apply to more than half the world. Most are really economic refugees without papers, but the technique is used by thousands every day at the major airports of entry.

Political asylum requests have increased 300 percent in the last three years. Some 260,000 such illegals are now living in the United States awaiting hearings, which take well over a year and can go as high as the U.S. Supreme Court. But half of them will never show up for the hearing, disappearing into the world of friends, relatives, and forged documents.

"I've introduced a bill to eliminate most of these frivolous claims," says Senator Simpson. His bill would give specially trained INS agents the job of determining the "credibility" of asylum cases at the moment the claim is made, and deport those not considered true political victims. He believes his bill will eliminate most of the 90 percent who are now turned down after a tedious, expensive process.

Misreading the Constitution

Another gnawing problem in the immigration racket is also being looked at—finally. It's the nonsensical idea that the child born here of an illegal alien has automatic American citizenship, like the baby born in San Diego.

This is a false interpretation of the Constitution, one bandied about as fact and acted upon. These "baby citizens" are an enormous burden on the taxpayers, now and tomorrow.

Where did this strange idea come from? A study of the Constitution makes no mention of it whatsoever. Then how did it spring into our culture and become a very expensive, irrational law of the land?

It started in 1868, three years after the Civil War, when the Fourteenth Amendment to the Constitution was passed to confer citizenship on former slaves. Section I of the Amendment conferred citizenship by birth in America, then added the supposedly clarifying statement that this involved people "subject to the jurisdiction thereof of the United States," referring to former slaves.

Meant for one thing, that clause has falsely been interpreted for another, costing America billions in cash and uninvited citizenry. No mention was made in the Fourteenth Amendment about illegal immigrants because at the time there were none. America had no laws restricting immigration. You just boarded a boat and landed here, joining the others on a virtually equal basis. As a matter of fact, the Fourteenth Amendment, instead of being inclusionary, was quite exclusionary. It specifically excluded American Indians from citizenship if they paid no taxes. (American Indians did not receive full American citizenship until 1924.)

Professor Peter Schuck of Yale Law School is one of those who have pointed out this error of interpretation. In his book, *Citizenship Without Consent: Illegal Aliens in American Polity*, he states that the Constitution does *not* confer the right of citizenship on offspring born here of those who've entered the country illegally.

Not surprisingly, America has long been the only nation in the Western world with this irrational law. Citizenship in England, France, Germany, Japan, and Russia depends on the citizenship of the parents. Australia grants citizenship to the child of an immigrant, but only if the parent has entered legally. Canada, which had the same law, has now adopted the American system.

Two legislators have taken up the gauntlet and hope to make the American law more rational. Representative Elton Gallegly, Republican of California, is trying a two-pronged approach. He is proposing a constitutional amendment to change the Fourteenth Amendment and specifically exclude any person born of parents not legally on our soil. He is also proposing simple legislation to amend the Immigration code in case a constitutional amendment is not necessary, as this author believes.

What Can We Do?

So what's the real solution for America's massive immigration problem, one that threatens to overwhelm the country?

President Clinton has announced his reform plan. It's of help in some areas, but as a real solution it's hopelessly inadequate. His best move is in the cases of "political asylum," where he is advocating a system of speedier dispatch of claims right at their airport origin. It's similar to Senator Simpson's plan and is a valuable suggestion.

The other reforms are too little, too late. He is asking for six hundred new Border Patrol people when we need at least five times that number just to slow the tide. He is also seeking a crackdown on the smugglers of Chinese, but the numbers are relatively small. Overall, some help, but not enough.

What then is needed?

The answer is once again quite simple: THE GROSS PLAN TO MAKE IMMIGRATION WORK FOR AMERICA, INSTEAD OF THE OTHER WAY AROUND:

1. Triple the size of the Border Patrol on the Mexican border.

2. This will *not* fully seal the border. Therefore, whenever necessary, make use of the state militia in the affected states.

3. If this is not sufficient, bring in the U.S. Army to the border area.

4. Pass legislation amending the Immigration and Nationality Act to eliminate the concept that children born of illegal aliens are citizens. Reserve that privilege for offspring of legal immigrants.

5. Make illegal entry into the United States a criminal

offense, thereby forcing administrators, doctors, nurses, social workers to report such an individual to the border patrol.

6. Eliminate all social benefits, including medical care, education, and welfare for illegal immigrants. The only exception should be medical care at the first point of contact, followed by deportation.

7. Make all government documents—Social Security cards, driver's licenses, birth certificates—tamper proof with the use of holograms, plastic covers, and photos.

8. Create a single, all-purpose tamper-proof, with photo, document for all legal immigrants.

9. Immediately deport all illegals convicted of a crime to jails in their own country. Do not offer them a choice.

10. Weed out 90 percent of political asylum claims at the port of entry and immediately deport them.

11. Provide the Border Patrol, and/or state militias with sufficient four-wheel-drive cars, helicopters, night-vision capability, and modern communications.

12. Erect more substantial physical barriers at accessible border crossing points with Mexico.

13. Immediately deport undocumented aliens applying for asylum who have arrived from a country not their own.

14. Streamline the hearing procedure for that small percentage of asylum applicants who are credible.

15. Adopt Senator Feinstein's idea of $1 for each legal border crossing, money to be used to beef up the border patrol.

16. Start criminal proceedings against employers who help smuggle in illegals.

17. Crack down on below minimum-wage businesses.

18. Change the family reunification system back to one of national origin, reflecting the present makeup of the United States.

19. Consider a moratorium on *all* new immigration for three years.

20. Set up communication between Social Security and INS to check out authenticity of documents.

In this land of immigrants, it's hard to bite the philosophical bullet and realize that the newest group seeking the American dream must be people of our choosing—not theirs.

A nation without borders is not a nation. In this era of complex problems, this is a hard but necessary lesson for us all.

Chapter Eleven

Reshaping the Cabinet

THE SUPER-CONFUSED AGENCIES

America has fourteen Cabinet departments, headed by all those people recently attacked or blessed but finally confirmed by the U.S. Senate. As the President says, they look like America.

They may, in racial, religious, and ethnic compositions. But the Cabinet departments they head look nothing like America as it really is. If they did, we wouldn't have as much of the confusion, chaos, and debt that we now enjoy.

Probably at no time in the history of the United States—or for that matter in the history of the Western democratic world—has such a morass of overlap, duplication, false definitions, bad historical accidents, and simple ignorance come together in what we call the Executive Branch of government, of which the Cabinet system is a major player.

Vice President Al Gore's report on "reinventing" government had a small oversight. He forgot to reinvent the Cabinet. Here, then, is an attempt to redesign that historic body so that it better suits logic and twenty-first-century America.

First, let's look at the origin of the Cabinet system as we know it. In 1789, after the inauguration of President Washington, three Cabinet-level agencies were formed: the Department of Foreign Affairs, which became the State Department; the War Department; and the Treasury Department. A Postmaster General and an Attorney General were also named, but they did not run Cabinet-level agencies.

A Department of the Navy was established in 1798. Fortunately for America, a half-century passed before the Cabinet bureaucracy was expanded, giving the country a chance to grow. In 1849, as we gained more land out West from the Mexicans and the Indians, a Home Department was created, later renamed the Department of Interior—the present behemoth.

In 1870, the Attorney General's operation became the Department of Justice, and two years later, the Postmaster General's jurisdiction was elevated to the Post Office Department.

In 1889, after the establishment of millions of farms, the Department of Agriculture was created. Then in 1903, the Cabinet grew again as the Department of Commerce and Labor, a combined operation. In 1913, the government changed its mind and the two were split into separate agencies—the Department of Commerce and the Department of Labor.

For thirty-four years, despite the radical governmental changes of the New Deal, the Cabinet ranks didn't grow. But we've made up for it since.

In 1947, the separate service branches were consolidated into the Department of Defense. In 1953, the mammoth grab bag called the Department of Health, Education and Welfare (HEW) was formed.

Expansion was now fully in gear. In 1965, the Department of Housing and Urban Development (HUD) was created, followed in 1966 by the Department of Transportation. In 1977, following the energy crisis, we got the Department of Energy. In 1979, HEW took on the new euphemism of Department of Health and Human Services (HHS), shedding the Office of Education, which was raised to Cabinet level as the Department of Education.

The last addition was the Department of Veterans Affairs, which was formed in 1989 from the lower-echelon Veterans Administration.

Is that all? Hardly. There is increasing talk of still new Cabinet bureaucracies. Rumors of elevation circulate around the Trade Representative's office and especially the Environmental Protection Agency (EPA), which may soon become the Department of Environment.

Thus, after numerous "reinventions" by various administrations, we now have fifteen Cabinet slots (with Environment), almost twice as many as Harry Truman's eight.

It took almost 160 years to do the first half of the job, but only 46 years to reach what we now have. Think of what awaits us in the next half-century.

This chapter will not be a catalog of all the sins of all Cabinet-level agencies, which would be impossible to detail. Instead, it will be a guide to updating, reforming, eliminating, and consolidating several of the group, ending up with fewer agencies, and a format that makes more sense in terms of duties and accountability.

Along the way, we'll try to clean up the bureaucratic swamp of everybody trying to do everybody else's business.

DEPARTMENT OF AGRICULTURE. Surely, America's best-known Cabinet-level agency is the Department of Agriculture, which at one time was a helpful part of the American scene. In those days, in fact through the 1930s, America was a heavily agricultural nation. The thousands of small towns that backed up the farms were a vital part of Americana, the stuff of Norman Rockwell and Booth Tarkington.

And today? While we have very few farms, by some strange twist of bureaucratic logic we support an enormous Department of Agriculture. The department is no longer famous for what it does but is known for the irrationality of its size—and how much money and manpower it wastes on its ever-decreasing mission.

It's a massive organization with 124,000 employees and an extravagant $62 billion annual budget (just its rent is $80 million a year) to pay for a cornucopia of 43 subagencies, 250 programs, a collection of unrelated objectives, and a penchant for waste and overreaching.

Let's say you were in the lumber business and wanted to buy trees from the government, wholesale. Call up the D of A. Let's say you're looking for funding for a community center in an inner city, light years away from any farm. Call up the D of A. How about welfare, and with it food stamps and school lunches for your kids? That's right. Contact the D of A.

And let's say you lived in a rural area and wanted a telephone installed. Call the D of A? Absolutely. And, to top it off, let's say you lived nowhere near a farm and wanted cheap rent in a new housing project in a small town. You know who to call.

What if you're a suburbanite and feel left out? Don't panic if your lawn is turning brown before the frost. You guessed it! Call up the D of A. And what if you're a woman who has just given birth and you want a food basket of goodies delivered right to your house? You guessed it. Call up your friendly Department of Agriculture.

All of this, and more—in addition to the myriad programs for the few farmers we have left—is handled by the glorious and ridiculous Department of Agriculture.

Without fear of exaggeration, we can say that the D of A is so mired in bureaucratic morass and skewed goals that nothing will improve the reputation of the federal government until most of this department is eliminated. On a score of one to ten for waste and irrationality, the D of A registers a resounding twelve.

And for all this, its employees got not only a half-million-dollar celebration at a posh Washington hotel last year, but bonuses and awards that cost the taxpayers $35 million!

The extraordinary story is that the department kept growing *larger* as its mission got *smaller*. At the turn of the century, there were five million farms. Some 20 million people were directly involved, plus millions of others dependent on farmers. We're talking about a third of the nation.

How large was the D of A then? All of 3,000 people, one lonely bureaucrat for every 1,800 farms.

Farming continued apace, and by the time of FDR, there were 6.3 million farms. What about the D of A? It had now grown to 20,000. There was one bureaucrat for every 300 farmers.

Today? You won't believe it. There are about 60,000 D of A employees (of the 124,000) involved in farming. But as people leave the farm, the number of farms is down to 2.1 million—half of which are part-time operations run by people with outside jobs.

That creates a stomach-curdling ratio. There is one bureaucrat for *every sixteen* full-time farmers. If we continue the graph, by the year 2040, the number of full-time farmers will be down to 150,000, while the number of farm bureaucrats will reach the same level. One for one. The graph lines will cross.

The peculiar nature of this racket is shown by the overwhelming number of offices maintained by this out-of-touch organization.

Guess how many? You'll never come close. *There are*

12,000 field offices of the Department of Agriculture, *40* percent of all 30,000 government outposts in the nation. In that
ludicrous operation, there's one D of A office for every 160
farmers, and one for every *80* full-timers. In Gregg County,
Texas, there's a conservation office that serves only 15 farmers!

Mr. Gore plans to reinvent the department by cutting out
ten percent of these offices over the next five years. A rather
modest proposal I would say. More than this could be accomplished just by eliminating offices in nonfarming rural and
suburban areas. Five out of six of their Stabilization and Conservation offices are not even in farm counties.

What's the real medicine for the ailing agency? We
should cut out 50 percent—6,000 of the 12,000 offices—for
now, and probably more later. No one, including the farmers,
will notice the difference.

The current plan, highlighted by Gore and Agriculture
Secretary Mike Espy, is to reduce the featherbedded manpower
ranks from 124,000 to 116,500! (I'm trembling at their radical intentions.) The reality is that within five years, the number of
personnel should be cut in half—to 62,000, again with the guar-
antee that no one will ever know that they're gone.

This should be done by attrition and by not hiring re-
placements for most of those who retire, die, or leave the
government. Using the federal attrition rate of 7 percent a
year, plus personnel transfer to agencies with fewer reductions, it will take about eight years.

Three years later, as the number of farmers continues to
decline, we should consider cutting it again by another 25 per
cent. In the first years of the twenty-first century, the D of A
can enter the civilized world with a total of 48,000 workers.
Now, *that's* reinvention. (By removing two of its major functions, as we shall see, it will become even smaller.)

Let's look at some its operations:

THE U.S. FOREST SERVICE. By some stretch of the
imagination, the government-owned forests are part of the

Department of Agriculture. This started in 1891, when President Benjamin Harrison created the first preserve, the Shoshone National Forest. Where did the land come from? It isn't hard to tell: from the Indians.

Then in 1905, Gifford Pinchot, a friend of Teddy Roosevelt, was angered that the Land Office of the Interior Department, which had been administering the forests, was riddled with graft. He renamed the operation the U.S. Forest Service and transferred it to the Department of Agriculture, where it still is.

According to a D of A historian, the Forest Service had fewer than 5,000 employees in the early years of FDR. Today, though the acreage has increased only 10 percent, it's now run by 34,000 people! The service controls 191 million acres, 9 percent of the entire country, and operates everything from ski resorts to grasslands for cattle.

Its cutable forests make up only 25 percent of the vast acreage, and the Forest Service invites wood products companies to come in and take the trees. Unfortunately, sixty-eight of its forests, or more than one-fourth its volume, are big money losers. So Uncle Sam takes a beating every time one of those trees is taken out. The loss runs up to a half billion a year on the sale of below-cost timber. Instead of a money-maker, the rich-in-natural-resources Forest Service costs the U.S. taxpayers $2.4 billion a year.

What to do? Quite simple: (1) the number of personnel should be cut by more than half, down to 15,000; (2) nonforest lands should be given over to the Bureau of Land Management; (3) recreation activities should go to the National Park Service; (4) the lumber subsidy and free roads should be eliminated—Uncle Sam has got to become businesslike; (5) the whole operation, which has nothing to do with agriculture, should be transferred to the Interior Department—another inefficient agency.

FARM SUBSIDIES. This government program has cost Americans $190 billion since 1980, and has raised the price of

food at least 10 percent. The Congressional Budget Office estimates that for 1993, farm subsidies will cost the taxpayers
some *$15 billion!*

The two famous subsidies that I have already exposed—
wool and honey—have gone through many phases. First, the
President was going to knock them out, then they were put
back in. Now, Al Gore wants to take them out again. Together,
they cost taxpayers $200 million a year.

They should be discontinued, of course. But there are
several other farm subsidies with much larger price tags that
no one is planning to do away with.

The 1993 budget bill did reduce some subsidies, but the
programs—everything from dairy products to sugar to basic
grains—are mainly intact. The enormous grain subsidies are
based on so-called deficiency payments, the difference between what the farmer actually gets and the government's
"target price."

The D of A claims that it subsidizes farmers so that they
can produce more food. But that's not really true, because at
the same time they're subsidizing other farmers to produce
less. What is called "conservation" generally involves marginal
land, and now takes up an area equal to the state of Indiana.

In fact, farmers can make almost as much money for
not-planting as for planting, with less energy and aggravation.
This D of A scheme is called the "0–92" program, which
means that participating farmers get a check for 92 percent of
what they would have gotten had they planted. (Now, that's a
welfare program!)

Even Congress is getting sensitive about this boondoggle. In the 1994 budget, they've cut some of the "0–92" back.
By how much? Less than 10 percent. Henceforth, it will be
mainly a "0–85" program, which still beats the hell out of having children out of wedlock.

As you may have guessed, some of the same people—
those who plant and those who don't—get paid twice. Many

farmers receive checks for conservation, then get irrigation subsidies for the crops that never were. These farmers of corn, barley, rice, and cotton received $379 million to limit their production while they received $66 million in irrigation subsidies to produce more crops.

Then how has this distorted operation been able to stay around all these years? Surely there aren't enough votes in the farm states for a majority in Congress.

A top staffer in the House Agriculture Committee gives away the secret. "It's a simple political deal," he says. "There's a swap. The farm Congressmen back all that money that goes to the cities and welfare, and city people back our farm subsidies. That's how the country is run."

Naturally, the middle-class urban and suburban population, the great majority of Americans, are caught smack in the middle and end up paying for both of them.

Is there an answer?

Yes. End *all* farm subsidies by phasing out the program over a five-year period. The savings will be enormous and the farming community will continue to operate, and well.

FOOD STAMPS. The Department of Agriculture, as we've seen, is big in the welfare business, through food stamps, school lunches, WIC, and so on. Studies have shown that at least $2 billion a year is wasted through clients selling their food stamps for cash (thirty or forty cents on the dollar) to buy liquor, cigarettes, and drugs. In Baltimore, a program to use D of A credit cards instead has been successful, and should have been adopted nationwide years ago.

Another fraudulent operation may cost taxpayers even more. Income eligibility claims for food stamps are *not* checked with the IRS, and even more foolishly, eligibility is based on monthly, not annual, income.

Says a limo driver in Puerto Rico: "I make about $30,000 in the winter tourist season, then I go on food stamps for the other six months."

OTHER D OF A BOONDOGGLES. We have already discussed closing the REA and the Rural Telephone Bank in the D of A. We also need to eliminate all the so-called rural activities, which have nothing to do with farming. That includes the Rural Development Administration, Rural Rental Assistance, and programs that provide mortgages for rural residents at as low as 1 percent interest. (Why not do the same for hard-working suburbanites?)

The Farmers Home Administration, which has over $50 billion out in loans, has an atrociously high delinquency rate. It has already lost $21 billion and is expected to lose another $18 billion.

The Extension Service, which began before World War I as the aggie school for those farmers who couldn't get to school, has an honored history but has mainly outlived its usefulness and should be cut back drastically. Its present budget of $448,264,000 could be cut in half, or more.

The new D of A should concentrate *only* on farming. It shouldn't be a rural aid agency or mortgage organization, or a forest products outfit, or a welfare conglomerate. The welfare roles of the D of A should be shifted out (we'll see where shortly), and that includes Food Stamps and school lunches and WIC, community centers, and whatever.

Overall, the D of A should be pared down to half its size, and after transferring out portions, considerably smaller.

Before these cuts are made, what is the D of A expected to cost us over the next five years? The "current services budget" indicates that it will run some $325 billion.

With all their talk of reform, what is Washington doing? The House Committee on Agriculture bragged that the August 1993 budget will reduce the new D of A budget by $3 billion over five years—out of $300 billion plus.

And what about the "reinvention"? The report by Gore lists his savings in an addenda to the report, agency by agency.

What's the cut in the Department of Agriculture? *All of $2.9 billion over five years.*

What? That's less than *1 percent* of the Agriculture budget. Some reinvention!

DEPARTMENT OF INTERIOR. This giant grab bag has gotten so large because we defeated Mexico and the Indians. Instead of giving the land to the states as they were formed, Washington decided to keep it for itself. They had no constitutional authority, but they took it anyway, thank you.

It's now in the care of the Department of Interior, which oversees so much federal land that it's a virtual government within a government.

Washington owns approximately 30 percent of all the land in the United States, but has almost nothing in Connecticut, which was here before the U.S. So why penalize the Western states that came later? Since the winning of the West, enormous tracts have been taken by Washington, which the states could use for profitable mining, timber, towns, residences, farming, recreation, or whatever.

It's as if the federal government doesn't trust the states and the people, the true sovereigns of the nation, to utilize the land well. Washington owns more than half the west, whose states could use, conserve, and exploit that land much better than faraway Washington.

The relatively new state of Alaska is already screaming, and rightly so, about federal restraints on the use of its land, most of which is claimed by Washington. In fact, when it comes to land grabbing, Alaska is a favorite victim of Uncle Sam. The original statehood pact granted Alaska 90 percent of the oil and mineral royalties on federal lands, which represents about two-thirds of the state. But in 1980, Washington placed 165 million acres of that land (almost half the state) in "conservation units," robbing Alaska of a chance to mine it and collect royalties.

"Just this July 1993, we sued the federal government because they are, in effect, violating the statehood pact," an Alaska spokesman states. "We're asking for just compensation of $29 billion."

How do we try to make Interior a better Cabinet agency? We need to do several things immediately:

1. Take the Forest Service out of the Department of Agriculture and incorporate it into Interior. We should add all other similar activities, then rename the agency the Department of Natural Resources. Stop such silliness as one agency creating electricity at federal dams (Interior) and another (Energy) selling it through power authorities.

2. Change the regulations on mining and timber exploitation so that the government makes a profit. Naturally, close down the helium operation.

3. Declare a moratorium on all land purchases for five years, and stop the building of new national parks for the same period.

4. Most important, start a national debate on reducing the power of Interior by transferring huge tracts of federal land controlled by it *back to the states*, which can then use the land according to the wishes of the people.

One thing I've learned: It's never too late to start to practice democracy.

Or is it?

DEPARTMENT OF ENERGY. This department, developed almost out of thin air, should be eliminated and most of it fused into the new Department of Natural Resources.

The nuclear and atom bomb activities of the department, however, should be separated out and given to an Office of Nuclear Affairs, an independent agency whose costs can be watched. As part of Energy, nuclear expenditures became bloated and impossible to track.

As it's presently constituted, Energy is involved in every-

thing from atomic bombs to electricity welfare and has no co-
hesive mission. Its contracting work has been assailed by the
General Accounting Office and the Inspector General as everything short of fraud.

As part of the new Department of Natural Resources,
the production and selling of electricity through the five
power marketing agencies should become self-sufficient and
not rely on tax money. Right now, the dams are supported by
the government through interest subsidies. The electricity is
sold to customers at bargain basement prices, or about one-
sixth what most consumers have to pay. Overall, this is a welfare program that costs taxpayers upwards of $1.5 billion a
year.

The same is true of the water from the dams, which is
virtually given away to rich farmers in California and others,
another welfare program that sets us back about $1 billion a
year.

The answer is to turn the new Department of Natural
Resources, through market prices on electricity, water, lumber, mining, and other items, into a *profit*-making, not
taxpayer-money-wasting, operation.

Meanwhile, a good goodbye to Energy, a department we
never needed in the first place.

DEPARTMENT OF INDUSTRY AND LABOR. In the
twenty-first century, American labor and business had better
hang together, or as our Founding Fathers reminded us,
they'll hang separately, especially in today's world of global
competition.

The days of adversarial relations between the two are
antiquated as labor takes on corporate ownership (as in the
case of airlines and Avis) and starts to worry about keeping
businesses afloat so that they can have good-paying jobs.

A way to help achieve this is to eliminate the separate
Department of Commerce and the Department of Labor and
fuse them into one: the Department of Industry and Labor.

By placing both under the same roof, we'd not only promote jobs more efficiently but improve the development of technology, management-labor relations, and job training. Here's a chance to integrate business and labor, something we surely don't do now.

Job training is a perfect example of American failure. Handled in fourteen agencies, and directed mainly out of Labor, it provides few good jobs for workers at an enormous cost.

But a coordinated effort out of the new Department of Industry and Labor would be able to create an apprentice program like that run by the German Chamber of Industry in concert with the German government. Before they finish high school, youngsters in Germany can "drop into" (not drop out of) an apprentice program in which they split their time between high school and productive work in a company.

It's generally a three-year program, during which the apprentices get paid between $5,000 and $8,000 a year. At the end of their training *in the company*, they get their high school diploma, their journeyman status—whether in electronics, construction, draftsmanship, or whatever—and the job they were training for. Their salary then jumps to over $20,000. The head of the Hanover Chamber of Industry credits this program for the success of postwar Germany.

Can we copy it? We couldn't under the old Cabinet system. But, with an integrated Department of Industry and Labor, we can call in the Germans, who can pay us back (remember the Marshall Plan) by showing slow-witted Washington how to do it.

ENVIRONMENTAL PROTECTION AGENCY. There is no doubt that this is among the most incompetent agencies of the government. President Clinton has promised it Cabinet status as the Department of Environment, which is a grave error at this stage. We should wait for it to get its house in order, if that's possible.

Its largest task has been the Superfund, the work of cleaning up toxic sites. The words *failure* and *sloth* are too mild to describe the results to date. The program is now thirteen years old and has identified 1,270 toxic sites, and completed only fifty-two of them. The agency has only enough Superfund money until next year, and has asked for more.

But even our spendthrift Congress wants to know what's happened to the old money, and is demanding accountability and reform. But, naturally, they'll give them more—and more—when the furor settles down.

As far as its work with states and cities goes, the agency has a reputation for arrogance and lack of common sense. It requires strict adherence to its regulations, but fails to remember that Washington usually isn't paying for it. As we've seen, the burden is put entirely on the local citizens through the unfunded mandates (taxation without representation?), which no one can afford.

Mayors and governors everywhere know the importance of cleaning up the environment, but few are fans of the EPA.

So, President Clinton, before you award it with cabinethood, let the EPA first learn how to think, add, and behave.

DEPARTMENT OF WELFARE. As we've shown, the welfare work of the nation is handled by at least six different Cabinet agencies, and several sub-Cabinet ones. It's an organizational maze we can no longer afford. All the welfare—money and benefits to people of limited or no income that comes to them through seventy-eight programs—should be transferred out of HHS, Agriculture, HUD, Labor, Energy, and so on, and placed in one new Cabinet agency, the Department of Welfare.

In the new Department of Welfare, a central computer will tell us at a touch how much a particular individual is receiving, and from which sources. It will also be able to add up the real cost of the programs, making alternatives thinkable, even possible.

If the Congressional Research Service can bring all seventy-eight programs into one book, with a price tag of over $300 billion a year, then we can surely put all welfare into one agency, where it can be watched and evaluated. Just the elimination of several levels of administration will save billions.

Prior to establishing the full work program (see Chapter 5), we can easily eliminate half the seventy-eight welfare programs and save $100 billion annually. A reduced $218 billion budget, when coordinated and handled out of the new department, would still raise *every* poor family and person in America over the poverty level.

Remember the formula for real "reinvention": one mission, one agency! That's the story of good, smaller, government.

SOCIAL SECURITY. The federal government's behavior toward the aged has been nothing short of criminal. In Fiscal Year 1994, which began on October 1, 1993, the government will collect $346 billion in FICA taxes and interest.

That massive amount is called the Social Security Trust Fund, even though there is no fund, and surely no trust.

According to the budget, the outlay will be $283 billion. That leaves a *surplus* of $63 billion.

Good. That's means there's lots of money in the till for the upcoming aged—like the baby boomers of 1947 who are already forty-six, and will start on the roles in as few as sixteen years. Right?

No, it doesn't mean that at all. *There's not a nickel in the till,* as I have lamented before. All $63 billion will be taken out this year by Uncle Sam and used to pay the bills of the general fund.

It works this way, almost literally. The FICA money comes in Monday. The government steals approximately 20 percent on Tuesday and sends the rest back to the aged on Wednesday. So if they hadn't taken the money, there would be an enormous surplus waiting for the boomers, or the FICA taxes could be cut 20 percent right now, or the benefit checks could be increased by 20 percent.

But the government has a vested interest in chicanery.

In this case, it's using the money to pay other bills and to make the deficit seem smaller. If it hadn't stolen money, and had to borrow it outside, the deficit would be $63 billion higher. And with the theft of other funds, like airport and highway "trust" funds, we're talking about $100 billion taken each year to pay the government's bloated bills.

Calling on arithmetic, an outmoded discipline in Washington, the real deficit this year, which is estimated at $275 billion, will actually be closer to $375 billion.

To get back to the aged, how much does the government owe them at this point? And when can they pay it back?

The answer to the first question is $418 billion, according to the 1994 budget, appendix, page 635. The answer to the second question is "NEVER!"

The Social Security fund, if we want to fantasize that there is one, does not get a negotiable Treasury bond in exchange for the "borrowed" money, as would a Japanese investor, who could sell it in Tokyo or New York the next day. The "fund" receives an IOU bookkeeping entry, on the back of which is surely emblazoned the legend, "Lots of Luck." It's all part of the $4.3 trillion debt, which we *never* expect to pay back.

Then how will the baby boomers get their Social Security benefits?

Easy. The government will just raise the FICA taxes again, from 15.3 percent to 20 percent, or 25, or even *double* them to 30 percent.

Or, they will go *outside* to borrow the *trillions* of dollars they have sneakily been taking from Social Security on the *inside*. Then the deficit will show its true numbers by zooming up to historic highs as the game they have been playing with our Social Security money comes back to haunt them.

Sorry, I mean *us*!

The deficiencies of the Social Security scheme, and the extent to which the aged are cheated, are legion. They say the money is "invested" in government certificates, but that's just fiction. Had the money, both the employee's and the employer's total of 15.3 percent as of now, been truly *invested* in government-guaranteed securities or in accounts in a person's own bank, earning just bank interest on long-term CDs, the aged reaching sixty-five after forty-seven years of work would today be retiring as millionaires, and not be forced to live on the piddling $653 a month present average pension.

What to do?

Simple. Get the government's hands off our cash.

There's only one way to do that: remove Social Security, which is now part of HHS, out of the Cabinet system. Social Security should be separated out, along with its funds, which must be made untouchable. A new nonpartisan *Social Security Board* made up of nine Governors, each a prominent American citizen, should be named by the President and confirmed by the Congress for a period of ten years, so that their terms overlap administrations.

Under this plan, the board, and no one else, shall control the monies and invest them as they see prudent, except for common stocks. It can invest in *negotiable* government bonds, high-rated municipals, Ginny Mac and other secondary government markets, even top-rated industrial bonds. *None of the money can be ever be borrowed by Uncle Sam or any one else.*

The fund will be actuarially sound, and the baby boomers and everyone else can rest peacefully knowing that Washington can't get its hands on it. Neither the Congress nor the President shall have any control over the money.

Just watch as the fund grows, FICA taxes go down (instead of up yearly as they do now), and benefits increase.

All it takes is a vote from an intelligent Congress. Best of British luck to us.

The Social Security system has been changing over the years, moving from the concept of a "pension" into a welfare scheme where everyone pays in, but the poorest (and as we'll see, the richest) take out much more. This was not the original intention, but politicians have cleverly moved Social Security from a "right" into a "privilege," without ever alerting most citizens.

Under this peculiar system, a person of sixty-five who cannot afford to retire and live on the $653-a-month pension—or even the $1,128 maximum—must keep working. But as he earns money, his pension is reduced. At the point that the average recipient earns more than about $33,500, he gets nothing at all.

So a decently employed senior citizen of sixty-five receives none of his promised "pension" even though he has been paying in for forty-seven years! In fact, if he's sixty-nine years old, self-employed, and earning the $59,000 FICA ceiling, his Social Security payment going *into* the government will be $7,500, and his benefits *coming out* will be ZERO.

Now who thought up that scheme?

There's one other concept that not even I can handle—philosophically, emotionally, intellectually, or actuarily. It's that mad.

Keep in mind our last example of the hard-working, tired senior citizen who is receiving no Social Security check and who's still paying into FICA. Then switch quickly to someone who's *not* a struggling aged worker. Instead, you're looking at a rich retired man aged sixty-five worth $40 mil. All he need do is clip tax-free bond coupons and go on cruises, play golf, and visit his two nieces in Sydney, Australia, and Helsinki, Finland.

What about his Social Security check? Does he get it? Well, of course he does. Isn't that obvious? Since he's not *earning* any money, just pulling it in, *he gets every nickel of the $1,128-a-month maximum from Uncle Sam* like clockwork on the first of the month!

Does he continue to pay into the fund like our poor working slob? No way. Millionaires pay nothing in when they reach sixty-five because they're not *earning* anything! Dividends, interest, annuities, munis don't count with Social Security. What do you take them for?

Now, how's that for logic and fairness? The working aged pay in and get nothing out, while the idle rich stop paying in and get their full check out! Who thought that one up? And more important, is he still institutionalized?

Of course, at age seventy the working slob will get the same check as our millionaire did five years before at age sixty-five. *But*, during the past decade, our politicians have devised ways to take it back. After the FICA taxes were raised in 1983, they collected income tax on 50 percent of the benefits from people who still had a reasonable income. Now they'll be taxing 85 percent of that benefit for couples with a *combined* income of $44,000.

How could our Presidents, present and past, sign such laws into being?

Ask them—but don't press. After all, their pensions are for *$146,000* a year.

There are even madder scenarios in this, the worst pension system in the Western world. There's the "notch babies" born in several of the years following the end of World War I who get *less* benefits than others just because of their birthdate.

Now, that's an idea that *nobody* understands.

The answer to all this is that once Social Security is separated out as the *Social Security Board*, we can work toward truly investing the money, then eliminating the means test, the earnings penalty, and the taxes on benefits, and make it into a true pension in which all the aged, rich and poor, get their checks, free and clear, when they reach one determined age.

DEPARTMENT OF HEALTH. Without welfare and Social Security, both since separated out, what's left for the mammoth-dinosaur agency Health and Human Services to do?

Health, naturally, which should be its *sole* mission. This will require some restructuring, slimming down, and a name change to the Department of Health.

There, the hundreds of programs extant, like Medicare, plus many more sure to arrive, will keep everyone plenty busy.

DEPARTMENT OF EDUCATION. This agency is not a tragedy waiting to happen. It has already happened. Despite the fact that it will spend $31 billion this year, it has the honor of not educating one single American child.

Some social scientists (not me) like to correlate factors even if they are not exactly related. But if we toy with that, we'll see that the *decline* in American education exactly parallels the phenomenal *growth* of the Department of Education.

In his "reinventing," Vice President Gore has recommended that the department's 230 different programs be cut back to 183. His cut looks good in those numbers—as if it's 20 percent. But he's actually cutting *less than $1 billion* from the department's bloated budget, or only 3 percent.

What should we really do with this impotent bureaucracy?

Now, fifteen years after it was elevated to Cabinet status, the department should be "de-elevated" back to sub-Cabinet level. As the Education Commission, its personnel should be reduced from 5,000 to 500. Its 230 programs should be cut back to the most promising dozen, and its budget slashed to $10 billion. Its main function should be the administering of college student loans—always with an IRS-controlled payback so as not to repeat the present default debacle. The D of E lost $14.7 billion from 1981 to 1991, and expects $7.6 billion more in defaults.

Education is historically a revered local function. Washington's attempts to help it, or capture it, depending on your viewpoint, have all been failures. We all want more money for our troubled education system, but Washington is the *worst* place to put those dollars. Their financial contribution to elementary and secondary education is only 6 percent of the total, and it has proven not to provide a whit of benefit. There's no sage reason why the federal government need any longer be involved.

Incidentally, my suggested cut of $21 billion a year in the present Department of Education budget is equal to *all* of Al Gore's reinvention.

DEPARTMENT OF HOUSING AND URBAN DEVELOPMENT. This agency has been bedeviled with incompetence, favoritism, and fraud for decades. Despite the sincere attempts of former HUD Secretary Jack Kemp to straighten it out, with some success, the agency still has a weak theoretical basis.

It tries to house poor working people, welfare clients, the homeless, and the aged; make the cities work; save the rural areas; provide home ownership at low cost; and clean up the minority ghettoes all at once. But that's too much for any agency, particularly if it comes out of Washington.

There are more than seventy-five active programs in HUD and they overlap. The agency is the result of scores of unrelated pieces of congressional legislation that have set up separate bureaucracies under this one roof.

We've already suggested eliminating one of its large programs, the Community Development Block Grant, a $4 billion boondoggle that has accomplished little over the decades.

What's left is mainly housing of every variety, which is a conundrum of the highest order and has yet to be attacked satisfactorily. The cost is enormous. The agency's total budget is $29 billion, and $21 billion goes to public housing of some variety, which accounts for 4.8 million housing units, generally apartments of one and two bedrooms.

The Federal Housing Administration, which has provided mortgage insurance for 21 million low- and moderately priced homes, is a sound idea, mainly because the mortgagee is buying the property and is paying a user fee—two reasons to expect stability.

The low-income housing concept, however, has been a disaster, both socially and fiscally. Socially, the large urban housing "projects" have become centers of crime, drugs, and conflict. They were popular in the era of architectural bigness in the 1950s, and they have failed. Each of these apartments costs the government an average of $3,000 annually.

A solution to the problem, and one that will stimulate independence, is to give (read "sell for $1") the apartments to the project tenants, making them owners. This concept made Maggie Thatcher popular in England when she turned the Council Houses over to tenant ownership for a small fee.

Jack Kemp has suggested this, but thus far nothing has happened. By giving title to the tenants for a token, they will be forced to set up a management organization. HUD can help in providing expertise and some seed money. Otherwise, the deteriorating condition of public housing will soon reach the disaster level.

Some groups have not backed the idea, fearful that tenants cannot handle ownership. The cost is no problem, for the maintenance should be less than the rent, which is now paid either by welfare or the tenant, or both. Cities should cooperate by making the buildings tax free.

The opposition is short-sighted. How else can the poor become prideful, property-owning citizens?

Because of the social disaster of the "projects," the government started to rely on other programs as well. One is the

Section 8 subsidized housing, which investors built mainly for tax breaks. The tenants, who can earn up to 50 percent of the median income of their area, pay a rent equal to 30 percent of their adjusted gross income, while the government picks up the rest. In the case of welfare clients, the government pays all.

Unfortunately, the tax breaks for investors were taken away in the 1986 tax "reform," and in the present real estate recession, a number of these apartment houses are going bankrupt.

A newer method is the "voucher," an expensive program that costs taxpayers about $5,000 a year per family. The government voucher is as good as money and pays the "fair market" rent in a private facility for low-income families, who contribute a portion of the rent. In the case of welfare clients, it can run Uncle Sam up to $1,200 a month, and perhaps more.

None of this is a solution. But HUD's failure is part of the whole government attitude toward poverty and minorities, one tied to dependence rather than real help to advance them to become members of the working, then middle, classes. (They did this to American Indians, if you remember.)

The Thatcher plan, adapted to the United States, would be one method of creating ownership, the backbone of democratic capitalism and the route to dignity.

Jack Kemp has suggested "enterprise zones" for the inner cities, where businesses will get large tax breaks by coming in to provide jobs. That's a good idea that should be made into law. But the decline of the cities is the *symptom* of false sociological and governmental theories involving minorities. Until they change, nothing HUD can do will make much difference.

The best program for HUD today is to concentrate on ownership. They can also clean up confusion and overlap in many of its projects, consolidating them into only a dozen or so programs.

Once again, one mission, one agency.

Now, for the score card on our Cabinet reorganizations:

We have merged Commerce and Labor into the Department of Industry and Labor.

We have reduced the Department of Education to sub-Cabinet status.

We have delayed the Cabinet elevation of EPA until it gets its house in order.

We have redesigned and downsized the Department of Agriculture.

We have taken the U.S. Forest Service out of Agriculture and put it into the new Department of Natural Resources, which used to be Interior.

We've closed the Department of Energy and put many of its functions into the Department of Natural Resources, moving its nuclear activities into a sub-Cabinet agency.

We have taken Social Security out of HHS, and set it up as a separate, solvent, untouchable Social Security Board.

We have placed all health services, and nothing else, into HHS, and renamed it the Department of Health.

We've taken all the welfare services out of several agencies and put them, and nothing else, into the new Department of Welfare.

We've suggested consolidating the numerous HUD programs and pushed for sale of public housing to its tenants.

We have suggested changes in the Department of Interior, including returning large tracts of federal lands back to the states.

Instead of fourteen (going on fifteen) Cabinet agencies, we now have only twelve, and the Cabinet *really* looks more like America.

As we reorganize the Cabinet, we must keep alive the

theme of one agency, one mission. That requires curbing the mad overlap and duplication that now strangles the Cabinet. More than ever, every agency wants to do everything, and all at the same time, costing us billions in waste.

We saw that graphically in welfare, but there are hundreds of other examples. The federal government is the Tower of Program Babel. Environmental affairs are handled in ten separate programs; American Indians, as we've seen, are provided for by twelve agencies. Infant immunization comes from four sources; infant mortality from three.

Five groups handle diet and physical fitness, from School Health Activities to National Institutes of Health Exercise and Fitness Research. Education stems from fourteen agencies, as does job training. Coastal America is the province of four; wetlands is handled by five.

This mismanagement, which has the touch of mania about it, costs us billions and contributes to the accurate view of Washington as a disturbed operation.

How to cure it? Try this:

Memo to Vice President Gore
Dear Veep:
If you sincerely want to redo the government, please follow this nine-part GROSS PLAN TO WIPE OUT OVERLAP AND DUPLICATION IN OUR CABINET SYSTEM AND SUBSTITUTE RATIONAL ORGANIZATION OF ONE MISSION, ONE AGENCY.

1. Get yourself a good computer. (If you go to a discount store, you'll pay only half what it will cost the government.)

2. Call in the General Accounting Office, the Congressional Research Service and the Congressional Budget Office for help.

3. Define every single mission (job training, Indian sup-

port, child care, environment, etc.) of our confused government and give each one a number.

4. Enter each mission into the computer.

5. Give each Cabinet agency, sub-agency and independent agency a code *letter*, and use the *number* code to label each of their missions. Enter all this info into the computer.

6. Collate the two—agencies and missions—then print out every mission along with all the agencies handling it.

7. Choose only one agency to handle each mission.

8. Put all the similar missions under one appropriate agency.

9. Shift all the extraneous and random missions out of the inappropriate agencies, and put them in the best possible place.

If you've done this right, there will be no overlap and duplication—although the line up may not look much like your present Cabinet structure.

But Al, I promise you this. It will be an eye-opener, and you'll see what reinventing government is all about!

Yours in democracy,
Marty

Chapter Twelve

The Great
Budget Game

HOW TO BALANCE IT—
WITH NO NEW TAXES

The federal deficit and debt are sustained by many things. One, of course, is Washington's mad propensity—even compulsion—to spend as much as possible. Another is its apparent need to confuse the American people by playing with the numbers. Through obfuscation and other forms of statistical hanky-panky, the government has effectively kept the nation near bankruptcy for years—without telling the voters the truth.

The nation has been catching on. But the full story has yet to be revealed.

Washington has established several myths that it wants the people to believe. One of them is the bugaboo word *enti-*

tlements. With a threatening stare, politicians warn that we can't get the deficit under control unless we cut these supposed vehicles for the general public good. Too much money is being spent, they imply, on the average American.

Really?

What do we understand when we hear "entitlement"? We think of a smiling Uncle Sam handing out checks to all Americans, providing holiday cheer around the calendar. As if without his avuncular blessings we'd all starve.

What are these entitlements they're always talking about, anyway?

Actually, an entitlement is just a government payment that does not need an annual appropriation. Once set in motion by Congress, it just goes on and on, spirited upwards every year by inflation.

One of these entitlements is Social Security, the punching bag of spenders who hint that unless we cut back on the aged we cannot survive. Another is Medicare, health care for seniors. What's another entitlement? There, we've stumped most voters, who, if pressed, might add "welfare."

What is the truth?

The truth is that entitlements are not what anyone thinks they are. What first comes to mind are Social Security and Medicare, but these are paid for separately by our FICA taxes. As we've already seen, these programs for the aged *maintain the government,* not vice versa. The Medicare hospital plan, Part A, has a $130 billion surplus despite its support of medical education, unneeded hospital expansion (35 percent of the beds are empty), and its financial backing of such exotic technologies as MRI and CAT scans.

So where's that giant surplus of the Medicare entitlement now? In the pocket of the aged? No way. Just like Social Security, it's buried in the swamp of the Federal Treasury, in an area marked "No Return."

So tell us: What then are those entitlements that come

out of Uncle Sam's generosity and are supposedly so popular with the average American, as the press constantly tells us, that they cannot be cut without "angering" the bulk of the people?

As a chart from the Congressional Budget Office indicates, there are sixteen major entitlements, plus several merely categorized as "Others." But they seem to have almost nothing to do with the average citizen—as Washington would like us to believe. What they really are is a bag full of giveaways for special interests, just like most everything that emanates from Washington.

For example?

Did you know that the taxpayer-paid health insurance for government retirees, some of whom are getting pensions of $75,000 a year, is a $4 billion entitlement? Isn't that very popular with the American people? Doesn't that make you happy?

Did you know that the practice of giving angora goat farmers a taxpayer-paid subsidy check is an entitlement? In fact, all *$15 billion* in farmers' subsidies in 1993 were entitlements. Doesn't that thrill you nonfarm people who make up 98 percent of the population?

Did you know that the *wonderful* entitlement program includes another $15 billion a year for "Other" and "credit reform liquidating accounts"?

("Other" is a favorite, rather expensive, term for "miscellaneous" in the Washington lexicon.)

Did you know that those supposed entitlements for the middle class include $35 billion each year for federal civilian employee pensions? Were you aware of another "popular" entitlement in which we taxpayers make contributions of up to 5 percent of federal employee salaries so that they can buy stocks and bonds for themselves?

Doesn't that captivate you?

The poor get a lot of entitlements—Medicaid, food stamps, SSI, Earned Income Tax Credit, family support, child nutrition, social services. That totaled $150 billion in 1993, says the CBO, plus billions more from the states, plus billions more as a result of the 1993 budget-tax bill. That might, or might not, be money well spent. But it's surely not an entitlement for the working middle class.

The only entitlements for the middle class, who pay the taxes to support all of this, are a small amount of student loan money and most of Part B, the doctor plan of Medicare. But they're more than made up for by surplus FICA taxes taken by the government.

So on net, how much of the entitlements do non-special-interest, ordinary, sweating, working, middle-class Americans get from Washington?

The answer is *Nada*, Nothing, *Rien*, Zippo, Zero. The sucking sound you hear is the money being vacuumed out of your pockets to pay for the entitlements of others.

So the next time a statistically weak politician threatens to cut off your entitlements to help balance the budget, tell him to be your guest. But remind him (1) that you get none of it to begin with and (2) to keep his hands off Social Security, which we pay for several times over, somewhat like the cost of the George Washington Bridge.

The answer to Social Security, as I've indicated, is to give it a separate, independent, solvent governmental life. After that it will no longer be listed as one of those entitlements that go to the rich, the federally comfortable, and the poor—to everyone except the typical working American man and woman.

End of that myth, thanks be to God.

Another myth is that the budget system used by Washington makes sense. Actually, it makes no sense at all. All it does is take the accumulated waste, mismanagement, and inefficiency of the past fifty years and add more of it each year. If the government would use ZBB (zero-based budgeting), in which it would start from scratch and analyze the true needs of the organization, it would realize that what we have now is not even related to good government. It would probably also learn that the federal establishment could be cut as deeply as half and still function as well, or probably better.

But that's not going to happen as long as we have the present group of politicians. The best we can hope for is just to cut, cut, cut away at the amount of the deficit until we reach a desired point. The government will make as little sense then as it does now, but at least it will be smaller and more manageable.

In trying to make order out of the budgetary chaos of Washington, we should outline what we're going to do in this chapter. We're going to list the cuts we've made in this volume, plus some others. We'll not provide a lengthy compendium of cuts, which would number in the hundreds, perhaps thousands, but we'll group them in general categories. Then we'll simply add them up, being careful not to double count. That's sometimes inevitable, so we'll cut at least 10 percent more than our $325 billion per year, for good measure.

We will not include the President's 1993 supposed $250 billion in cuts, most of which are ephemeral. We'll do that to keep the reductions clean.

Now, to return to our budgetary myths. Another one that sustains the deficit and people's view of it are those pie charts in the front of the budget document, which are often used by politicians to explain why they can't really cut deeply.

Part of this myth is that federal employees don't cost the taxpayers much, and cutting them back saves little. In fact, on the elusive pie charts in the front of the 1994 budget, federal employees don't even exist. They're lumped in with "direct benefit payments to individuals," which ostensibly takes 46 percent of all government expenditures. This sounds like working for Uncle Sam is either a welfare program or a volunteer operation like one of those Thousand Points of Light.

What's the true cost of the federal staff? It's actually

quite a lot—$182 billion per year in salaries, benefits, and pensions, not counting the office overhead, which is abnormally high.

That pie chart in the 1994 budget is a masterpiece of obfuscation. It shows slices of defense, payments to individuals, interest on the debt, grants to states, then leaves only *6 percent* for "other federal operations," which is supposed to be everything else.

Really? Only 6 percent, or $90 billion, to pay for all the rest of the government? Apparently, the subliminal message is that there's nothing left to cut.

Is it true? No, not at all. When the fake numbers are cut away, there's enough fat in that budget to fry a whale.

Fortunately, there are other documents floating around Washington that are more accurate. One of them, from the OMB, is "Gross Obligations by Object Class." This calculates how much Uncle Sam actually spends, or contracts to spend, each year on every item. It covers salaries and telephones and consultant fees, even boxes of paper clips.

Every penny spent by government has an "Object Class" number, which is repeated over and over in the budget document for each agency and subagency. But the elusive budget gives out no totals. The travel item, "Travel and Transportation of Persons," Object Class No. 21.0, for example, appears hundreds of times in the 1994 budget. But nowhere is it added up. It would be too easy for journalists and citizens to ask questions.

But the Gross Obligations (not my name this time) sheet has it all nicely tallied. There is travel, bright as an airliner over the clouds—$7.362 billion in 1993. That's followed by "Transportation of Things," $11.7 billion; then by rental payments, a total of $10.8 billion; then communications and utilities, $12.3 billion; then printing, $2 billion; then consulting, $3.2 billion.

The total so far is $52 billion. That's still less than the

$90 billion the budget indicated was all that was used to run the rest of government. Maybe they were right?

Hardly. Just wait. The next item is the magical "Other Services," No. 25.2. That's *$246.432 billion*—the over $246 billion we've already mentioned. Followed by "Supplies and Equipment" for another $62 billion.

So, the total overhead of the U.S. government—no salaries, no benefits, no pensions, no entitlements, no programs, no welfare, no nothing except computers to paper clips—is $356 billion. And it doesn't include $135 billion more that the government "obligated" itself for in 1993 for "Acquisition of Capital Assets."

The reality is that the looseness and shiftiness of the federal budget makes it as easily cutable today as it was expandable over the last thirty years. With little effort, and much determination, we can reduce the non–Social Security portion of $1.2 billion by 20 percent, 25 percent, even 30 percent, with only positive results for the nation as a whole.

Let's try to prove that with arithmetic. Not the federal type, just the old-fashioned form I learned in P.S. 77 in New York City.

The Fiscal Year 1994 has already begun (October 1, 1993). That budget figure of $1.515 billion, which is larger than 1993's, was passed by the slimmest of margins—218–216 in the House and 51–50 in the U.S. Senate. The administration's prognostication is that even with the new taxes in place ($250 billion's worth), there will still be a $200 billion deficit by 1998.

THE GROSS PLAN TO ELIMINATE THE DEFICIT WITHOUT TAXES OR ANGST will have to begin with Fiscal Year 1995 and go for five years like the Clinton plan. It's just that I'm starting a year later.

To reach my balanced budget, we will start with the assumption that the deficit for Fiscal Year 1994 will be in the neighborhood of $275 billion, which should be on target. It will be my goal to eliminate *all* of that.

In addition, I will add a substantial kicker for the middle class with a tax cut of 10 percent across the board ($52 billion). New taxes? *NEVER!*

If everything is put in practice, that will be followed by a 3 percent tax cut each year for the next four years, adding up to a 22 percent overall tax cut.

Of course, if the voters prefer, we can delay eliminating the total budget deficit in just five years and split the money saved, in any proportion, between deficit reduction and tax cuts.

In order to keep things decipherable, we will use 1993 dollars for everything. And unlike Washington, I'll try to keep it all simple and clear.

Here goes:

FEDERAL EMPLOYEES. As of 1993, we had 2.2 million federal employees. The President had said he would cut 100,000 by attrition, and Al Gore's new plan, reacting to public furor over waste, has said the government would increase that cut to 252,000.

How much can we really reduce the federal staff? Well, we've seen that the Department of Agriculture could easily be cut in half. The Department of Defense is also stuffed—not with servicemen, but with civilian paper shufflers.

In World War II, there was one civilian for every seven servicemen, and I believe we won the war. Today, there are almost a million civilians (950,000) for only 1.7 million servicemen, or one for fewer than two. The Pentagon is cutting 300,000 more servicemen, but only one-fourth as many civilians. So down the line, the ratio will be one civilian for every one and a half servicemen. Maybe the civilian employees can carry the soldiers' dufflebags into war.

Half the civilian employees in the Department of Defense could be spared, but we'll settle for one-third, the ratio for all our personnel cuts.

So how many civilian government employees can we do without? Easily 725,000, or one-third the present number.

Because we can't afford any more unemployment, we can only do this by attrition. Since 7 percent leave, die, or retire each year, it will take about seven years in all. We will rehire 20 percent of those slots deemed essential and do some shuffling between agencies so as not to disturb law enforcement and other vital activities.

How many does that eliminate from the government roster in five years? Almost 550,000—from 124,000 the first year to 97,000 the last year. To get the full 725,000 reduction in staff, we'll need another two years. We'll use that for later tax cuts, but we won't count these savings now.

Each federal employee costs $83,000 a year in salary, benefits, and currently paid-out pensions. (The future unfunded pension amount is so large we won't even talk about it.) So the fifth year savings here is $46 billion, and the total for five years is $140 billion.

The pensions of federal employees, beginning with the FERS plan, which came on line in 1984, is a threefold program; (1) Social Security; (2) defined benefit in which Uncle Sam adds about $20 for each $1 employees put in and (3) federal matching of up to 5 percent of their salary for their private investments.

In addition, when they retire at fifty-five, the government provides them with a Social Security Supplement until age sixty-two. This does not come from the regular Social Security fund but directly out of the U.S. Treasury.

In all, most of these people will retire with some 70 percent of their best three-year salary, then get COLAs after their retirement at fifty-five. We should cut back the federal pensions about 20 percent, and eliminate all COLAs from age fifty-five to sixty-five.

We should also cut out the ridiculous Social Security Supplement, which no other American gets. This overall savings should be about $12 billion a year.

Whatever the changes, federal work, with its extraordinary benefits (including riding the Metro for free for up to $240 a year) will still attract all the government employees we want.

OVERHEAD. We've already seen that amount—$356 billion. This is one of the great scams of the government, which spends a horribly excessive amount on travel (that $7 billion could handily be cut to $3 billion), rent, computers, telephone, furniture ($2 billion a year, which should be on a five-year hold), supplies, planes, cars, limousines, and so on, and so on, without consideration of usual business controls.

This item, which includes "Other Services," can be easily cut by one-third overall. Except in abusive cases like travel, buildings, and decorating—which should be curtailed immediately—this should not be done by selective cutting, which will alienate special interests. It must be done across the board by formula.

A simple plan would be to cut 8 percent a year for five years, which will give us a net reduction of some 33 percent. In the fifth target year, then, we'll have a savings of $119 billion. The total savings would be in the neighborhood of $380 billion.

AGENCY CLOSINGS. We've already outlined a number of agencies to be closed or cut back (Chapter 2) with a savings of about $7 billion.

PORK. A conservative estimate is a savings of about $8 billion a year if we follow the plan of making it impossible for members of Congress to make special allotments for their districts.

GRANTS TO STATES AND CITIES. This item, which has now reached $225 billion a year, covers the 606 "categorical grants" that states and cities receive if they match the government money with a certain percentage of their own. A reading of the grants, which ranges from such well-known items as Medicaid to such esoterica as money for the Dance, makes it clear that one-quarter of this can easily be eliminated—with a gain for the states as well. Savings? $56 billion a year.

DEPARTMENT OF AGRICULTURE. Just by eliminating all subsidies, we save up to $15 billion a year. The closing of 6,000 offices plus the needed reduction in the Extension Service and other subagencies yields $2–3 billion more, while reforms in the Farmer's Home Administration adds several billion more in savings. The Forest Service can provide still another billion. The total savings here are at least $20 billion.

DEPARTMENT OF EDUCATION. Because this Cabinet agency has not improved education in America, and because it has no jurisdiction over the schools, we have saved $21 billion a year by reducing it to a subagency.

DEPARTMENT OF INTERIOR. By eliminating land purchases and subsidies for electricity and water alone, we save $2.5 billion, plus at least another $2.5 billion income from royalties and land sales under the proposed new system. Savings plus income equals $5 billion.

WELFARE. Part of these cuts have already come out of the "Grants to States." But as we have seen, there's easily another $75 billion a year in reductions from the giant $318 billion, and growing, cost.

OVERLAP AND DUPLICATION. The reshaping of the agencies to handle the concept of "one agency, one mission," will easily save us $10 billion a year. In fact, we can save that much alone in consolidating the 150 job-training and employment programs.

CONGRESS. A serious effort by our Senators and Representatives could easily cut $1 billion off the $2.8 billion budget.

MISCELLANEOUS. Even this has an "Other." Here we can include purchasing savings, inventory control, and dozens of small projects that have no value, some of which we've already discussed. Another $5 billion.

What have we done so far? We were aiming for $325 billion to handle the deficit and tax cuts, but we've tallied $385 billion, with more to go if we continue to pursue it.

For now, however, we'll settle. After all, for the two years following this five-year plan, we have those 200,000 fewer federal employees—up to our 725,000 attrition goal. That's another $17 billion a year. We've now reached a $402 billion total, and we've saved enough to ensure tax cuts.

The five year total in savings is $1.25 *trillion*, or five times the administration's claimed spending cuts and ten times the actual reductions.

Not bad. But *is* it doable? Yes. But not if strangling political considerations and the selfish White House and congressional wish lists throw us off the needed focus. Like any successful venture, it's a matter of resolve—perhaps even obsession. If we *must* do it, we will.

There are those who are skeptical, saying that the present crew in Washington is incapable of such dramatic action. This may be true. But when frightened by the prospect of a citizen revolt, they can change. And if they don't, we might be dealing with another group of politicians beginning after the 1994 elections.

The need is so overwhelming that history tells us that nothing can stop what has to be done. Those who stand in the way will do so at their own political peril.

How to Make a Citizen's Revolution

A PEACEFUL CALL TO ARMS

All I hear, from too many citizens, is: "The whole thing is hopeless and out of our hands. There's no way to get those politicians to do what's needed to save the country."

The despair now cuts two ways. It pushes some voters into an apolitical lethargy, in which they turn their backs on national concerns. Instead of protesting, they plunge even deeper into their work to make enough money to pay the excessive taxes, turning their minds away from the fact that most of it is wasted.

But for every one of them, there's a member of a new breed arising in the land. That's the modern day Minuteman

and Minutewoman, patriots who love their country too much
to see it continue its present decline.

They read, talk, listen, argue, join. In the process they
are becoming formidable opponents of those politicians who
have an agenda—open or secret—of destructive spending,
taxing, building debt, and increasing the power and size of
wayward government at all levels.

How large are the ranks of these active people?

Ten years ago, you could count them in six numerals,
less than one million. But the potential revolutionaries of
today—those who know that tinkering with the broken en-
gine of Washington is not going to do the trick—are gaining
exponentially in number every day.

Organizationally, their ranks are still small, probably less
than five million in a dozen assorted groups. But if we look
into the minds of the American people, I would guess that
there are now some thirty million who have become aware of
the seriousness of the political and economic crisis dogging
our nation, and who want to work to rectify it.

Who Are They?

They are the impetus for any seismic change for the better.
Who are these people? They are Democrats. They are Republicans. They are Perot people. And there are those who are
absolutely unaffiliated and undefined—except in the certainty
that we need a radical change in Washington, in the state-
houses, and the cities, if the nation is to survive and return to
the healthy state we once enjoyed.

"Everything is wrong," they lament, and they are right.

I receive an enormous number of letters from these dis-
affected citizens, asking what they can do to help their
country.

I can't answer them all personally, but I can lay out here
a method of joining the revolution, of coming together in

spirit and person with others who understand the urgency of this cause.

Occasionally on talk radio, someone will call in and while agreeing with my diagnosis, will complain about my naivete. "You'll never get real change the way you want to do it," they bellow in frustration. "We need to take up guns and go down to Washington."

Of course that's ridiculous, and frightening. But it does express the depth of feeling of the alienated, who see Washington as a cleverly organized conspiracy against the common man—and especially themselves.

What can we do? Is there hope?

Absolutely. An infinite amount of hope. Just this past October 16th, there was a Taxpayer's Action Day rally near the Washington Monument organized by the Citizens Against Government Waste as part of a coalition of eighteen citizen groups. This was not the typical march by minorities or abortion activists on either side. These people, joined by a half million in 160 cities around the country, were working middle class Americans of all races and religions who want their country back.

What is it that unites them? Is "The Movement," as I call it, dedicated to just cutting taxes and leaving the government striped and ineffectual—a kind of ritual return to know-nothingness?

Absolutely not. There are very few mean-spirited people here. No, what unites them is a patriotism that has both a pragmatic American streak, and an idealistic one that wants the nation prosperous and free. As the old colonial banner stated: "Don't tread on me."

They want the government to work, to be efficient, to do those things that the private sector cannot do, as with Social Security or some form of a national health plan. But they want to undertake only those projects that make eminent sense and which can be accomplished within our budget.

As responsible people, they do not want the federal or state governments to use the banner of good intentions to do bad. They want a tax structure they can afford; they want to eliminate the deficit; they want to cut extravagant, wasteful government; they want a Congress and a Presidency free of pettiness and self-serving attitudes; they want a *direction* that will lead to prosperity and freedom.

On one point they all agree: we do not have such a government today, and have not had it for years.

They are not theorists, and have few Utopian visions *except* for what we call the "American Dream."

Strangely enough, without a computer print out, we all seem to know what that is: opportunity, merit, freedom and a dividing line between a government that cares and one that oppresses.

Who could possibly divine where such a vague line lies?

We can. It's as if by growing up in America, we are imprinted with a national genetic code that gives us that knowledge as finitely as we know our own backyard boundaries. Whenever the government, whether from the town hall or Washington, oversteps that line, we feel it—and we're learning how to holler.

What Can We Do?

And now that we sense this oppression from all quarters of government, what can we do about it?

First, we must become amateur scholars.

The government and the politicians are equipped with staffs paid to accumulate research and devise arguments to advance their continued spending. To counter them, the voter *must* become sophisticated. There are resources. He can read my two books, others, and immerse himself in coverage of the issues.

Radio talk shows have become invaluable. Without the restraint of conventional opinion, many of their hosts have

MARTIN L. GROSS   271

become as knowledgeable as politicians, if not more so. Television, which was once a laggard in the debate of our time, is now marching to catch up. Such programs as "20/20" and "Prime Time," plus a host of others, are giving real exposure to the issues of government spending and taxing, and the efficiency of those who represent us.

Who would have ever thought that C-Span television would attract an enormous audience of people who insist on knowing what is happening in Congress, and in every aspect of our political life?

But has any of this new education been of value? Has the Movement accomplished anything?

Yes, very much so. I can go back as recently as June, 1992, when *The Government Racket* was first published, to see the difference. My first appearance on television was the day of publication, on "Good Morning America." The staff went carefully through the book and prepared charts on "pork" and the now well-understood excessive growth of government.

The people were shocked. But now, less than two years later, we *know* and accept the fact that government propaganda had lulled our usual American skepticism.

We have seen how this knowledge of waste and incompetence has helped shape the public protest against more taxes. In August 1993, it forced the Omnibus budget bill of 1993 into a tie in the Senate that the Vice President had to break. We see it in the new hesitancy of politicians to promise to spend more, and in their understanding that frugality, not debt, is today's hallmark of the better public servant. We see it in Vice President Gore's attempt to mollify citizen anger with his National Performance Review—albeit a half-hearted plan.

In just a short time, the tenor of the entire public debate has changed. There is the sense of a new determination—with or without our professional politicians—to get the job of improving government done.

We might go as far as to say that the "revolution," started by many in 1992, entered Year II in 1993. With 1994 as Year III, we can look forward to greater expectations as the Movement accelerates.

What can the voter do right now?

The first thing I could recommend would be to join one of the citizen's groups involved in smaller, better, more ethical government. I have selected a dozen or so such groups, covering everything from cutting waste to term limits to higher standards of integrity for public servants. (See the Appendix for list.) Membership is inexpensive, usually only $15 to $25 a year in dues.

Several of these groups have excellent newsletters that carefully probe the governmental scene. For anyone intent on educating themselves on the debate, they are invaluable.

Soldier of Democracy

In addition to joining one or more of these national organizations, the soldier of democracy should become active locally—in the political parties (even running for office), in anti-tax groups, on the school board. Many of the national groups I have listed have local chapters, which need volunteer help.

And, of course, there are standard, effective ways of being heard, including letters to your local papers, commenting on local issues and the votes of your representatives. Naturally, we should continue our campaigns of writing (and faxing) to our Congressmen and to the President. Such efforts have always had an impact on those who want to stay in office.

One of the most important jobs to be done on behalf of *direct democracy* is gaining the Initiative and Referendum for your home state so that all citizens can participate in, even start, the legislative process. It was the existence of the state Initiative that made the fourteen victories for term limits possible at the polls in November 1992.

Contacting the U.S. Term Limits in Washington (see Appendix) is a way to begin this fight, one which can eventually lead to great democratic rewards. If your state already has the Initiative, it can be used for many purposes, including citizen-created laws to block tax increases, or to get term limits—if you do not already have them.

But most states (twenty-seven) do not have the Initiative, which makes that a primary job for a citizen revolutionary. Speak with your local state legislator, or neighboring one, and find out whether (1) you have the right of Initiative; (2) whether there is a citizen's taxpayer group in your area. Get them interested in lobbying for the Initiative, which is to their benefit. If not, start a group yourself.

In most states, there is a nucleus of legislators who wants the Initiative for the people, but hasn't had the power to get it past the state political leadership. A well organized citizen's group is vital in creating the demand for such a move.

Once the Initiative becomes part of the citizen's revolutionary armament, virtually any reform, from campaign financing to limiting taxes, to pressuring your state legislature to apply for a constitutional amendment, is within your grasp.

There are several Constitutional amendments which the nation desperately needs and which can begin either in the Congress or through a constitutional convention called by the states, either through their legislatures or by the Initiative. Those amendments are: (1) balanced budget amendment; (2) term limits; (3) line item veto; (4) majority elections through run-offs; (5) popular election of the President and elimination of the Electoral College; (6) national referendum; (7) Initiatives for the people in *every* state; (8) elimination of privately funded political campaigns.

But aside from this direct action, there is still the question of becoming a scholar, which in the final analysis will determine the success of the peaceful revolution. Jefferson perhaps did more with his pen than Washington with the sword.

If the voter wants to become a scholar, what should he learn first?

There's a vast repository of knowledge necessary to become a true agent of change, and all of us should begin that long-time journey of education in democracy. But there is one simple piece of information that we all need *immediately*. That is the voting record of our Representatives and Senators.

Not their claims or their speeches. That's all nonsense.

Both the Citizens Against Government Waste and the National Taxpayers Union, the two largest groups in the Movement, closely follow all members of Congress and evaluate them each year by their *performance*. Every member of the House and the Senate gets a score on how much he spends, saves, or tries to spend and save. It is an accurate insight into how to evaluate our representatives.

The reports are non-partisan and not weighted against any party. Only the member's own voting record counts. In this era of deficit and debt, these are invaluable tools for concerned Americans who need this knowledge to cast an enlightened ballot.

Socrates once commented that the true evil is ignorance. We are suffering as Americans today because of that ignorance. We can hold those who have been in charge of our nation for a generation responsible for their intellectual failings. But we must also allot part of the blame to ourselves, for countenancing it, for *not knowing* what was going on and how to correct it.

Fortunately, those days seem to be coming to an end. The nation is awakening from its costly slumber and is marching to a better drum, one of concern and intelligence.

There will be a peaceful revolution. Of that I am sure. And as it moves forward each day, we can feel confident that it will be the American citizen, as it was in 1776, who will save our blessed land.

APPENDIX
List of Public Service Organizations

Citizens Against Government Waste
1301 Connecticut Avenue, N.W.
Suite 400
Washington, D.C. 20036
202-467-5300 or 1-800-BE-ANGRY

The leading citizen's group in Washington, D.C. with 600,000 members and 320 chapters nationwide, works for waste-cutting legislation, and other reforms to make government more accountable to taxpayers.

National Taxpayers Union
P.O. Box 96549
Washington, D.C. 20090
202-543-1300 or 1-800-TAX-HALT

The nation's leading taxpayer's watch-dog group with more than 200,000 members nationwide promotes key tax and budget reforms to make elected officials at all levels accountable to taxpayers.

United We Stand America
P.O. Box 516987
Dallas, Texas 75251
214-960-9100 or 1-800-925-4000

The nationwide movement started by Ross Perot that has all politicians running for cover. United We Stand focuses on reforming government and empowering citizens to change the status quo.

U.S. Term Limits
1511 K Street, N.W.

Suite 540
Washington, D.C. 20005
202-393-6440

The leading term-limits group in the nation spearheading the
movement to limit the number of terms elected officials can
serve at the national, state, and local level of government.

Americans for Tax Reform
1301 Connecticut Avenue, N.W.
Suite 401
Washington, D.C. 20036
202-785-0202

Americans for Tax Reform (ATR) is a coalition of individuals
and hundreds of state and local taxpayer groups working to
oppose increases in taxation at the state, federal, and local
level. ATR runs the TAXPAYER PROTECTION PLEDGE which
candidates are asked to sign to commit themselves to oppose
higher taxes.

Citizens for A Sound Economy
1250 H Street, N.W.
Suite 700
Washington, D.C. 20005
202-783-3870

A 250,000 member free-market organization that focuses on
policy changes in the areas of tax and budget policy, trade,
regulation, and legal reform.

Concord Coalition
1025 Vermont Avenue, N.W.
Suite 810
Washington, D.C. 20005
202-737-1077

The Concord Coalition founded by former Senators Paul Tsongas and Warren Rudman is a grassroots organization working to implement reforms to bring fiscal sanity back to government.

Congressional Accountability Project
P.O. Box 19446
Washington, D.C. 20036
202-296-2787

One of Ralph Nader's groups focusing on the Congress and how it spends tax dollars. The Congressional Accountability Project (CAP) advocates cutting congressional pay and eliminating perks and privileges that waste taxpayer dollars.

National Empowerment Television
717 Second Street, N.E.
Washington, D.C. 20002
202-546-3000

A national grassroots satellite television network linking thousands of activists nationwide to discuss public policy issues from a limited government perspective.

Tax Foundation
1258 H Street, NW Suite 750
Washington, D.C. 20005
202-783-2760

Nonpartisan, half-century-old organization that makes Americans aware of the cost of government.

Public Citizen
2000 P Street, NW
Washington, D.C. 20036
202-833-3000

Founded by Ralph Nader, Public Citizen represents citizen interests in open and ethical government, campaign financing, and lobbying reform.

The National Center on Public Policy Research
300 I Street, N.E.
Suite 3
Washington, D.C. 20002
202-543-1286

The National Center on Public Policy Research (NCPPR) educates grassroots activists on current political issues facing Congress. They issue a series of "Talking Points" for use during radio talk shows, letters to the editor, etc.

Common Cause
2030 M Street, N.W.
Washington, D.C. 20036
202-833-1200

The major organization in the fight for cleaner campaign financing for all elections.

The Center for Public Integrity
1910 K St., N.W., Suite 802
Washington, D.C. 20006
202-223-0299

A leading activist organization for better ethical behavior by members of the legislative and the executive branches.

Voter Research Hotline (VOTE SMART)
1-800-622-SMART

This organization offers a toll-free service to all citizens. It provides, without charge, information on your representatives, including their issue positions, voting records, and evaluations by over seventy groups.

ABOUT THE AUTHOR

A Call for Revolution is the fifth nonfiction work of author, editor, and educator Martin L. Gross.

It follows directly after the publication of his phenomenal bestseller, *The Government Racket: Washington Waste from A to Z*, which triggered a national debate on the subject of government spending and inefficiency.

The book was a *New York Times* bestseller for more than twenty weeks and reached the No. 1 position on the *Washington Post* list.

Mr. Gross has appeared on a host of national television shows including "Larry King Live," "Good Morning America," "20-20," "CBS This Morning," "Prime Time Live," "The Tom Snyder Show," CNN, and C-Span to share his investigative research.

The author testified before the Senate Governmental Affairs Committee on the subject of Washington waste and inefficiency, spoke to the staff of the House Budget Committee, and received thanks from the Vice President's office for his revelations, several of which were used in the *National Performance Review*.

Ross Perot has called the book a "handbook for cleaning out the stables" of the federal government. The book has also been praised by former Senator William Proxmire and other public figures.

The former editor of *Book Digest* magazine, Mr. Gross is an experienced reporter who covered Washington for many years for national publications. His syndicated column, "The Social Critic," appeared in newspapers throughout the country, including the *Los Angeles Times*, *Newsday*, and the *Chicago Sun-Times*. His articles have been published in a variety of magazines, from *Life* to *The New Republic*.

The author's prior nonfiction works were selections of major book clubs and aroused significant controversy.

His first, *The Brain Watchers*, was a critique of psychological testing. Called the "bunkraker" by *Time* magazine, Mr. Gross was a leading witness at Congressional hearings, resulting in legislation curtailing their use in federal employment.

His second work, *The Doctors*, an indictment of poor medical care, received strong support from academic physicians, including the director of the prestigious Massachusetts General Hospital. The author was attacked by the AMA, whose organization has since followed most of his recommendations to improve the quality of medicine in America.

The author's third work, *The Psychological Society*, was a critique of American psychiatry. Mr. Gross was the leading witness at a U.S. Senate hearing, which resulted in legislation that followed his recommendations for increased research into mental illness.

His current work, *A Call for Revolution*, is a penetrating study of the underlying weaknesses and errors of the American government, with a plan to correct them.

Mr. Gross served on the faculty of the New School for Social Research for many years and has been Adjunct Associate Professor of Social Science at New York University.